vienna philharmonic
and vienna state opera orchestras

volume one
discography 1905-1954
compiled by john hunt

Contents

5	Acknowledgement
6	Introduction
13	Index of works
21	Discography 1905-1954
257	Index of conductors
275	Index of operas
283	Credits

Wiener Philharmoniker 1
Published by John Hunt.
© 2000 John Hunt
reprinted 2009
ISBN 978-1-901395-05-1

Sole distributors:
Travis & Emery,
17 Cecil Court,
London, WC2N 4EZ,
United Kingdom.
(+44) 20 7 459 2129.
sales@travis-and-emery.com

Acknowledgement
These publications have been made possible by contributions or by advance 3-volume subscriptions from

Masakasu Abe	Richard Ames
Stefano Angeloni	Stathis Arfanis
Yoshihiro Asada	Jack Atkinson
Charles Brooke	Stewart Brown
Peter Buescher	Edward Chibas
Siam Chowkwanyun	Robert Christoforides
Robert Dandois	Dennis Davis
F. De Vilder	Richard Dennis
John Derry	Hans-Peter Ebner
Henry Fogel	Peter Fu
Nobuo Fukumoto	Peter Fulop
James Giles	Jens Golumbus
Jean-Pierre Goossens	Johann Gratz
A.G. Greenburgh	Michael Harris
Tadashi Hasegawa	Naoya Hirabayashi
Martin Holland	Bodo Igesz
Richard Igler	T.M. Jensen
Andrew Keener	Rodney Kempster
Koji Kinoshita	Detlef Kissmann
Bent Klovborg	John Larsen
E. Legge-Schwarzkopf DBE	Lanny Lewis
Tony Locantro	Douglas MacIntosh
Norman MacDougall	John Mallinson
Carlo Marinelli	Finn Moeller Larsen
Philip Moores	Bruce Morrison
W. Moyle	Alan Newcombe
Richard Osborne	Hugh Palmer
Jim Parsons	Laurence Pateman
James Pearson	Johann Christian Petersen
Tully Potter	Patrick Russell
Yves Saillard	Robin Scott
Neville Sumpter	Yoshihiko Suzuki
H.A. Van Dijk	Mario Vicentini
Urs Weber	Nigel Wood
G. Wright	

Vienna Philharmonic Orchestra discography

To chronicle the activities of any significant artistic institution is to hold a mirror up to the achievements of an entire cultural movement. And whilst the Austro-Hungarian Empire can boast of its highest lasting achievement in the 18th and 19th centuries being the production of the composers Mozart, Schubert and Bruckner, as well as the hosting of those other giants Beethoven and Brahms, so its flagship in the 20th might be said to be the recorded work of its finest orchestra, the Vienna Philharmonic.

Founded comparatively late in the day in the Austrian capital's period of glory (it is amazing to think that before 1842 there was no permanent group of professionals responsible for playing the compositions of the classical masters), the orchestra's dual function has remained unchanged to this day: to give concerts of that musical heritage and to provide orchestral players for the Vienna Opera. It is said that a successful apprenticeship as rank-and-file player in the Staatsoper is in fact a pre-requisite for entering what we might describe as the first team, that is playing for the subscription concerts.

The title *Wiener Philharmoniker*, which has become a byword for musical execution at the highest level, has always been reserved for the orchestra in its concert capacity in Vienna, its concert and opera work at the Salzburg Festival, and when giving concerts abroad. The same prestigious title has been retained for the major recording programmes which the orchestra has carried out for HMV, Columbia, Decca and Deutsche Grammophon. Elsewhere the orchestra goes by its name of *Orchester der Wiener Staatsoper*. Confusion has arisen when the orchestra has occasionally made recordings for other (usually) minor recording companies or when recordings of live opera performances have been published officially (and indeed unofficially on the pirate market).

It might be said that the gramophone was invented primarily to preserve the sound of the human voice, and in the years of the medium's infancy it was the operatic aria (or other vocal item) which was the record industry's bread and butter. As soon as it became feasible to assemble a group of instrumentalists around the primitive recording horn, they replaced the original pianoforte. In Vienna, as in the other musical centres where recordings took place, it was natural that these orchestral players should be drawn from the city's opera orchestra. They were described variously as *Hofopernorchester* or *Philharmonisches Orchester*. 1924-1925 saw some purely orchestral items being recorded - the odd symphonic movement or orchestra showpiece - but primarily popular works by Johann Strauss under the baton of a certain Josef Klein. As Klein cannot be identified from any reference work or musical encyclopoedia, one can only assume that this was a pseudonym for a house conductor, a common practice in the gramophone's early history. What is more strange is that these earliest Strauss recordings are overlooked both in the orchestra's official histories and in the

mammoth CD compendium which Deutsche Grammophon recently produced to mark the Strauss family's various centenaries.
In addition to Klein, a number of other shadowy figures feature in the orchestra's early catalogue. The first recording of a complete symphonic movement (Schubert) was directed by the Dutchman Dirk Foch (1886-1973), who was already active in Scandinavia and the United States when he made the recording.

The advent in 1925-1926 of the electrical recording process was of course a signal for the start of serious orchestral recording, and this means in Vienna's case that we have early sets of classical symphonies from leading musicians of the period like Franz Schalk, Clemens Krauss and Erich Kleiber. They were later joined on HMV's and Columbia's roster by Felix Weingartner and Bruno Walter, although the latter provides us with an early example of a star conductor endangering an artistic project by means of unreasonable demands: Walter was due to conduct HMV's 1933 set of selections from *Rosenkavalier* (with the singers Lehmann, Schumann and Mayr), but The Gramophone Company refused to pay his exorbitant fee and engaged a less exalted conductor, Robert Heger, to replace him.

Also in this period came the first primitive recordings of the Opera orchestra in live performance, thanks to the initiative of *Operndirektor* Krauss: he personally authorised the technician Hermann May to preserve initially fragments – and later more extended extracts – from the stage of the *Staatsoper*. These were cut into wax discs with a very limited playing time, which miraculously survived wartime destruction but which have officially only seen the light of day after loving restoration and publication on CD by the enterprising Koch company. The series covers the period 1933-1944 and even includes items in which the *Staatsoper* company and orchestra were performing outside Vienna.

Although the Vienna Philharmonic Orchestra's golden period of association with HMV and Columbia was temporarily halted by the Second World War (when the field lay open to HMV's German branch Electrola and other German companies like Odeon and Telefunken to step in with an albeit more fragmented recording programme), it would resume in 1946 through the offices of EMI's Walter Legge, who brought both Wilhelm Furtwängler (HMV) and Herbert von Karajan (Columbia) for intensive recording programmes with the Orchestra. These late examples from the 78rpm era, just before the advent of the long playing record, have over the past decade been re-issued on Compact Disc, and reveal a truly glorious era in the Orchestra's recording history.

In 1950 the Orchestra entered into a recording association with the Decca company, which was much vaunted - probably for commercial reasons as much as for anything else - as an exclusive contract. However, the only two periods when the Orchestra was not working for any other company were the comparatively short ones of 1955-1957 and 1967-1969. From this early Decca period - and one must admit that the LP format brought a new fidelity to orchestral sound *per se* - one can admire the craft of such masterly interpreters as Clemens Krauss, Erich Kleiber, Hans Knappertsbusch and Carl Schuricht. Decca's sound quality is, however, not to my taste, with its somewhat glassy treble, and the records from this period which do the orchestra most justice are the HMV LPs from the late 50s and early 60s: again with Schuricht (Bruckner Symphonies 3, 8 and 9), with Rudolf Kempe and with a group of "non-Viennese" conductors, Constantin Silvestri, André Cluytens, Paul Kletzki and Sir Malcolm Sargent.

Staying for a moment with the 1950s, the problem of the designation *Vienna State Opera Orchestra* again rears its head. Having stated at the beginning of this introduction that these would be included in the catalogue of the Philharmonic's own recordings, I must now explain why a considerable quantity of recordings described as being played by the *Vienna State Opera Orchestra* in the early days of LP do not qualify for inclusion. I refer to the performances captured in Vienna by the American companies Vanguard, Westminster, Nixa and other associates. I have it on the authority of both H.C. Robbins Landon (the Haydn Society edition which he master-minded was promoted by Vanguard) and Decca recording producer Christopher Raeburn that although some State Opera members may have been involved, the bulk of this *ad hoc* orchestra was comprised of players from the *Volksoper* supplemented with many freelance players who were eager for work in that economically austere post-war period. One could easily be misled in this matter by the fact that the *Staatsoper*, until the re-opening of its own war-damaged house in 1955, was performing in the *Volksoper* building, among other locations. Christopher Raeburn has also explained to me that groups which Decca later billed as *Vienna Opera Orchestra* and *Vienna Haydn Orchestra* on several opera sets and on many operatic recitals was drawn entirely from members of the *Volksoper* orchestra. And thanks to research by Michael Gray I have now been able to establish that a group of LP recordings undertaken for the Concert Hall label and using the name *Vienna Festival Orchestra* (under conductors Krips, Schuricht, Otterloo and others) – recordings incidentally which I for a long time thought displayed certain *Philharmoniker* qualities – are in fact performances

by the *Wiener Symphoniker*. Collectors may recall that this was the
orchestra exclusively contracted to the Philips label during the
1950s (for which reason they simultaneously appeared on the Vox
label as *Pro Musica Symphony Orchestra*!)

Once into the late sixties competition on a big scale became
the order of the day, and by 1970 Deutsche Grammophon added
the Vienna orchestra to its roster, alongside the already
established Berliners. The next 20 years, with the eventual
transition from LP to CD, saw this company boasting not
only two complete Beethoven and Brahms Symphony cycles from
Karajan in Berlin but in addition precisely the same repertoire
from Vienna with Böhm, Bernstein and (in the case of
Beethoven) Abbado. All these artists had originally recorded
with the Vienna orchestra for Decca, but were soon lured by Deutsche
Grammophon as the prestige of the British company lessened in this
area and it became obliged to turn more to the USA, or less
expensive European locations, for its star recordings.

The recording association between Herbert von Karajan and the
Wiener Philharmoniker constitutes rather a special case.
As is by now well known, Karajan stayed firmly in control of both
artistic and commercial aspects of his own work. Eventually
lured away from an exclusive agreement with Columbia by
the burgeoning Deutsche Grammophon (but on the way
working with the Vienna orchestra for Decca, where he was
the only musician to outwit the wily executive Maurice
Rosengarten on the question of artist royalties), Karajan
returned for serious work in Vienna as his relations with the
Berliner Philharmoniker worsened in the 1980s. The *Wiener
Philharmoniker* were more than happy to step into the
breach, resulting in a late Indian summer of recordings
which, for my ears and feelings, represent the final real peak
in this orchestra's work as recording artists. No doubt the
84 years which I have chronicled will soon become a full century,
but I shall leave it to another to document that most recent
past with its falling standards and lack of individuality among
the modern *maestri* who lead the *Wiener Philharmoniker*.
Of course there are "hopefuls" already in the wings or at work,
and I shall endeavour not to be too pessimistic !

The changes which have affected the *Wiener Philharmoniker*,
on the evidence of a rich legacy of gramophone recordings,
are probably the same for all great symphony orchestras.
It is just that when the organisation has in the past scaled
such remarkable heights, the descent to respectable mediocrity
seems all the more disappointing. How can the changes be
rationally explained ?

What really concerns us is the levelling out, the honing away, of an orchestra's individual qualities, which usually seems to start with brass and woodwind sections. And one has to admit that the process stems from increased exposure of an orchestra at an international level, where a largely indiscriminating public expects a foreign orchestra to sound as similar - usually meaning as technically competent - as the other orchestras which they can hear at home from their record collections. Whilst becoming more sophisticated in our listening habits both in concert hall and our music room at home, we are actually contributing to increased commercialism and trend towards uniformity, whether the orchestra be from Vienna, Leningrad or Amsterdam. The praise heaped on Decca's stereophonic LPs in the 1960s meant that we expected the *Wiener Philharmoniker* to sound as excessively exotic and glaring in colour as they did on the records, even when we were actually hearing them in one of London's concert halls, for example. My impression was that they sounded nothing like the orchestra playing for Georg Solti's much lauded *Ring des Nibelungen,* but much more like the finely blended and rounded group heard on the contemporaneous HMV recordings under Rudolf Kempe and the like, which I mentioned above.

I think that my first experience of hearing a visiting foreign orchestra when I was a student in London was a concert by the Amsterdam Concertgebouw Orchestra under Eduard van Beinum. Here was a wonderfully saturated density of tone, the colour of dark mahogany, with woodwind rising imperceptibly from the string mass. Vienna's sound, when they eventually appeared with Karajan in London in the 1960's, was certainly less glutinous but still obviously weighted in favour of low and high strings, out of which their deliciously piquant - almost acid - woodwind again emerged. I had not then begun to listen to recordings so closely, or I would have noticed that this was precisely the model sound which Herbert von Karajan had been endeavouring to imbue into the Philharmonia Orchestra during his long association with them in the recording studios.

Now take, for example, a recent CD reissue from Decca (actually Belart) in which the *Wiener Philharmoniker* play Mozart symphonies under the Hungarian conductor Istvan Kertesz. Symphony 29 is a recording which dates from about 1963, and the orchestra still shows its strong individual flavour, a blend and buoyancy inherited from years of experience of working with conductors of the older generation. Turning to Symphony 39 from 6 years later, one hears that those old virtues are gradually receding in favour of a more efficient sameness in the orchestral picture - this could be the London Symphony Orchestra, or one of the American orchestras, on a good day !

The discography is arranged chronologically by sessions or groups
of sessions. In recording sessions which were spread over a period
of several days or even weeks, it should not be assumed that recording
work necessarily took place on every date within the period.
Similarly in sessions containing more than one work it should not
be assumed that work on an individual piece took place on every day
of the session period. A heading to each session gives a session
number, date and venue (within Vienna unless otherwise stated).
Following this the first column contains title(s) of work(s), the second
one names conductor, chorus and main soloists. When that second column
is blank, it can be assumed that the artists remain precisely the same as
for the previous entry. The main (third) column contains the
catalogue numbers in the main formats of 78, 45 (EP), LP,
CD, VHS, Laserdisc and DVD in the main European and
US territories (cassette tapes are not included). In the case of European
Decca and RCA, when at times during the LP era these companies
used local numbering systems but at other times reverted to the British
or American numberings, those European numbers are omitted, as
are most Japanese domestic catalogue numbers. Japanese numbers are
only included in cases where they constitute the only available edition
of a recording: otherwise it can be assumed that the major companies
within Japan have published their material in a constant sequence of
changing numbers and repackagings.

In the case of video material on videocassette, only the European VHS
numbering is given, and it should be remembered that other (non-VHS)
numbers would have applied for other territories. Furthermore the
recording dates shown for video performances are the dates for the
sound recording (in the case of opera recorded by the playback method,
the filming sessions may well have taken place at a later date and in
another place using the pre-recorded soundtrack).

For the comparatively few number of recordings in which legitimate
Philharmoniker described themselves as *Orchester der Wiener Staatsoper*,
these are marked with an asterisk on the session heading (these recordings
are not to be confused with the large number of records which actually
feature the *Volksoper* musicians – see above).

The recordings of Mozart Dance Music, Serenades and Divertimenti
made by Willi Boskovsky, deemed by those of us from the older
generation as fundamentally *orchestral* pieces, are included, whereas
the records of chamber music made by splinter groups such as the
Vienna Octet, Schneiderhan and Barylli String Quartets and many others,
are not included as part of the orchestra's discography.

In order to maintain managability of the data the discography is divided
into two volumes. The first of these covers the first half-century of
recording which ended in 1954 with the death of Wilhelm Furtwängler,
the second the later decades ending in 1989 with the death of Herbert

von Karajan. These can be regarded as two symbolic watersheds as far as tradition and quality are concerned, for reasons explained earlier in this introduction. For ease of reference, introductory material and the index of conductors are given in full in both of the volumes.

Lower case typeface is used throughout the main discography. Once accustomed, the eye should find this a positive aid in areas of tightly-packed text.

At the end of the volume you will find a list of the collectors and correspondents who have assisted me in this garagantuan task with data and other helpful suggestions. But I must single out for special mention the input of both Michael Gray and Malcolm Walker: it could well be that this particular discography might not have materialised without their generous encouragement.

John Hunt 2000

Postscript
World Encyclopaedia of Recorded Music (2 nd supplement 1953) listed a recording of Mahler Symphony No 8 on the label Classic Editions, in which Karl Alwin conducted the *Wiener Philharmoniker*. This was apparently also announced in a Schwann catalogue of the time, but the recording never appeared. As Alwin emigrated from Austria in 1938, the chance of such a recording having existed seems remote.

At the time of going to press, the independent British label Symposium announces a CD including part of the Adagio movement from Beethoven's Ninth in a 1942 performance by Furtwängler and *Wiener Philharmoniker*. If this proves to be genuine, it will probably have been taken from the public concerts on 21-24 April 1942 and will be an important addition to the discographies of both conductor and orchestra.

index of concert works closely associated with and recorded by the orchestra, including the works premiered in the city of vienna; light music featured in the traditional new year concerts is not included; numbers are session numbers, not page numbers

bayer die puppenfee
0724

beethoven symphony no 1
0161	0461	0470	0471	0670	0846
0888	0975	1137	1343	

symphony no 2
0025	0312	0349	0461	0747	0888
0975	1115	1173	1179	1184	1325

symphony no 3 "eroica"
0099	0117	0310	0332	0408	0470
0471	0535	0600	0642	0734	0820
0975	0999	1023	1115	1288

symphony no 4
0391	0472	0492	0849	0906a	0975
0999	1039	1137	1232	1349

symphony no 5
0029	0352	0415	0416	0503	0623
0877	0888	0907	0921	1014	1088
1104	1185	1186	1340	

symphony no 6 "pastoral"
0011	0469	0130	0280	0454	0470
0628	0855	0948	1088	1137	1232
1314				

symphony no 7
0111	0390	0500	0527	0578	0625
0635	0836	0903	0975	1022	1039
1137	1173	1179	1184	1211	1327

symphony no 8
0011	0039	0111	0317	0477	0527
0640	0759	0888	0892	0975	1137
1325				

symphony no 9 "choral"
0091	0331	0423	0440	0451	0463
0478	0548	0765	0813	0824	0872
0917	0921	1132	1154	1189	1303

piano concerto no 1
0433	0436	0610	0922	1229	1248

piano concerto no 2
0429	0645	0922	1289	1248

piano concerto no 3
0286	0400	0627	0834	0907	0922
1109	1248			

beethoven piano concerto no 4
0435	0500	0509	0610	0734	0826
0922	1067	1248		

piano concerto no 5 "emperor"
0085	0312	0479	0586	0594	0645
0922	1038	1122	1123	1248	1312

violin concerto
0080	0342	0665	1157

triple concerto
0161

choral fantasy
1314

meeresstille glückliche fahrt
1314

grosse fuge
0527

string quartet no 14 arranged by bernstein
1104

coriolan overture
0336	0381	0445	0500	0609	0921
1194	1288			

egmont incidental music
0915

egmont overture
0161	0454	0492	0578	0609	0855
0907	0912	0921	1194		

fidelio overture
0244	0507	0609

die geschöpfe des prometheus overture
0111	0836	0921	1137	1362

könig stephan overture
0014	0023	1137	1362

leonore no 1 overture
0453 0507

leonore no 2 overture
0507

leonore no 3 overture
0011	0116	0177	0289	0345	0507
0508	0609	0734	0903	1040	1042
1088	1366			

die ruinen von athen overture
0118 1362

beethoven die weihe des hauses overture
0849

missa solemnis
0198 0651 0652 0841 0924 1028

berg lulu suite
1034

wozzeck fragments
1211

berger rondino giocoso
0630

brahms symphony no 1
0142 0305 0325 0449 0469 0575
0596 0636 0657 0869 0958 0989
1040 1042 1044 1060 1190 1207
1271

symphony no 2
0250 0314 0384 0482 0580 0640
0713 0740 0784 0858 0869 0931
1044 1089 1222 1347 1366

symphony no 3
0032 0116 0341 0483 0596 0691
0869 0989 1044 1047 1194

symphony no 4
0405 0443 0556 0658 0869 0885
0980 1162 1166 1207 1374

piano concerto no 1
0483 0986 1143 1249

piano concerto no 2
0461 0473 0541 0598 0853 0885
1062 1228 1278

violin concerto
0325 0512 1032 1206 1222

double concerto
0449 0567 1222

haydn variations
0280 0373 0381 0449 0586 0869
0989 1047 1087 1207

academic festival overture
0160 0586 0869 1207

tragic overture
0493 0541 0586 0714 0869 1044
1060 1207 1374

hungarian dances
0020 0373 0675 1213 1273

brahms ein deutsches requiem
0331 0427 0493 0514 0592 0612a
1168 1238 1287 1330

alto rhapsody
0586 1067 1153

schicksalslied
1168

bruckner symphony no 1
0897 0914

symphony no 2
1005

symphony no 3
0509 0823 0932 1364

symphony no 4 "romantic"
0444 0445 0534 0781 1004 1285

symphony no 5
0439 0558 0751 0878 0908 1012
1200 1348

symphony no 6
0979

symphony no 7
0186 0273 0380 0790 0818 0846
0886 0996 1020 1023 1035 1038
1075 1178 1212 1306 1307 1372
1373

symphony no 8
0300 0510 0581 0719 0774 0804
0851 0949 1059 1130 1148 1265
1266 1311 1360

symphony no 9
0490 0722 0733 0805 1034 1068
1121 1350 1351

mass no 2
1083

te deum
0152 0303 0548 0686 0733 0966
1064 1121 1275

von einem philadelphia symphony
0882

furtwängler symphony no 2
0474

gluck alceste overture
0505

gluck iphigenie in aulis overture
0474   0505

ballet suite arranged by mottl
0724

goldmark rustic wedding symphony
0014

overtures
0028

haydn symphony no 83 "la poule"
0704

symphony no 88
0020   0444   0469   0531   0630   0747
0973   1249

symphony no 89
0973

symphony no 90
0992

symphony no 91
1001

symphony no 92 "oxford"
1001

symphony no 93
0468

symphony no 94 "surprise"
0415   0424   0595   0640   1211   1296

symphony no 96 "miracle"
0142   0582

symphony no 99
0595

symphony no 100 "military"
0167   0467   0704

symphony no 101 "clock"
0531   0640

symphony no 102
0939   0940

symphony no 103 "drum roll"
0754

symphony no 104 "london"
0244   0436   0582   0636   1152

sinfonia concertante
0992   1296

haydn piano concerto in d
0261

overture in d
0014

mass no 5
1029

mass no 12
1147

die schöpfung
0270   0814   0858   1102   1220

die jahreszeiten
0243

hindemith die harmonie der welt
0491

symphonic metamorphoses on weber
0822

liszt hungarian rhapsody no 4
0633

mazeppa
0839

mephisto waltz
0839

les préludes
0244   0504   0839

mahler symphony no 1
0518   0720   1026

symphony no 2 "resurrection"
0343   0760   0812   1037   1235

symphony no 3
0961   1182   1286

symphony no 4
0407   0673   0962   1097   1247   1281

symphony no 5
0960   1225   1334   1336   1337

symphony no 6
1077   1225   1357

symphony no 7
1026   1276

symphony no 8 "symphony of a thousand"
0687   1051   1052

mahler symphony no 9
0168   0879   0942   1262   1328

adagio/symphony no 10
1026   1221   1262   1289

das lied von der erde
0119   0327   0458   0833

kindertotenlieder
0382   0584   1286   1359

lieder eines fahrenden gesellen
0439   0471   0584   0906a

mendelssohn symphony no 1
1065

symphony no 2 "lobgesang"
1079

symphony no 3 "scotch"
1072   1074

symphony no 4 "italian"
1103   1139

symphony no 5 "reformation"
1065

violin concerto
0990

a midsummer night's dream
578   0600

hebrides overture
0359   0370   0439   0514   0632   1139

other overtures
0514   0852   1074   1139

die erste walpurgisnacht
1117

mozart symphony no 1
1124

symphony no 8
0259

symphony no 13
1375

symphony no 14
1375

symphony no 15
1375

mozart symphony no 18
1375

symphony no 21
1322

symphony no 22
1322

symphony no 23
0553   1322

symphony no 24
1322

symphony no 25
0215   0335   0564   0980   1124   1290
1359

symphony no 26
0337   1290

symphony no 27
1290

symphony no 28
0931   1267

symphony no 29
0804   0980   0994   1089   1175   1180
1267   1336

symphony no 30
1267

symphony no 31 "paris"
1124   1290

symphony no 33
0318   0533   0741   0906   1162   1212
1315

symphony no 34
0530   1031   1290

symphony no 35 "haffner"
0261   0553   0562   0567   0577   0578
0700   0751   0980   1031   1036   1143
1180   1277   1341

symphony no 36 "linz"
0411   0700   0770   0831   1031   1277
1341   1347

symphony no 38 "prague"
0016   0130   0530   0685   0700   1124
1143   1296   1321

symphony no 39
0384   0741   1149   1207   1322

mozart symphony no 40
0457 0216 0222 0258 0289 0359
0533 0635 0980 0994 1023 1061
1255 1257 1332a 1375

symphony no 41 "jupiter"
0167 0222 0227 0285 0372 0685
0700 0745a 0876 0994 1043 1061
1213 1255 1281 1327a 1375

piano concerto no 12
1188

piano concerto no 14
1188

piano concerto no 15
0831

piano concerto no 17
1261

piano concerto no 18
1020

piano concerto no 19
1061 1180

piano concerto no 20
0144 1024 1188

piano concerto no 21
0759 1024

piano concerto no 22
0316 0450 0553

piano concerto no 23
0798 1061

piano concerto no 24
0436 0569 1261

piano concerto no 25
0316 1045

piano concerto no 27
0538 0554 0682 0798 0928 1000
1045

concerto for 2 pianos
0369 0972 1000

violin concerto no 1
1245 1290

violin concerto no 2
1280 1290

mozart violin concerto no 3
0079 0285 0685 1216 1280

violin concerto no 4
0469 0971 1290 1324

violin concerto no 5
0970 0997 1216 1324

other works for violin and orchestra
0997 1290

sinfonia concertante for violin and orchestra
0906 1245

concertone for 2 violins and orchestra
0215

sinfonia concertante for wind
0258 1046

bassoon concerto
0974

clarinet concerto
0231 0386 0743 0974 1334 1335

flute concerto
1015

flute and harp concerto
0743 0930 1046

horn concerti
1138 1143 1161

oboe concerto
1015

cassations
0916

3 salzburg divertimenti for strings
0997 1141

divertimento no 1
0894

divertimento no 2
0894

divertimento no 7
1008

divertimento no 10
1141

divertimento no 11
1008

mozart divertimento no 15
1141

divertimento no 17
1008

serenade in d k100
0916

serenade no 3
0894

serenade no 4
0871

serenade no 5
1141

serenade no 6 "serenata notturna"
0337   0906   1141

serenade no 7 "haffner"
0693   0985

serenade no 9 "posthorn"
1008   1216

serenade no 10 for 13 wind
0333

serenade no 12
0876

serenade no 13 "eine kleine nachtmusik"
0130   0195   0285   0318   0373   0694
0770   0894   0971   0997   1056   1216

ein musikalischer spass
0916

notturno k286
1141

adagio and fugue in c minor
0338

maurerische trauermusik
0340   0879   1143   1206

dances and marches
0142   0184   0231   0800   0827   0851a

les petits riens ballet music
0231

trinitas mass
1029

coronation mass
0966   1292

mozart waisenhausmesse
1055

requiem
0152   0561   0564   0686   0736   0816
0817   0944   0984   1006   1036   1305

exsultate jubilate
0322   0459

overtures
0014   0023   0036   0037   0167   0258
0318   0372   0469   0569   1045

nicolai die lustigen weiber von windsor overture
0173   0425   0632   0666   0890

pfitzner symphony in c
0376   0900

von deutscher seele
0313

das käthchen von heilbronn overture
0309

reger mozart variations
0312

reznicek donna diana overture
0469   0606   0890

schmidt symphony no 2
0619

symphony no 4
0950

variations on a hussar's song
0599

notre dame intermezzo
0181   0724

das buch mit 7 siegeln
0653

schoenberg pelleas und melisande
0902

verklärte nacht
0619

schubert symphony no 1
0952

symphony no 2
0639   0952

schubert symphony no 3
0663   0802   0952   1133   1361

symphony no 4 "tragic"
0663   0769   0920   1324a

symphony no 5
0769   0920   1161   1274   1361

symphony no 6
0802   0952   1324a

symphony no 8 "unfinished"
0116   0193   0312   0381   0390   0416
0517   0519   0562   0593   0639   0673
0694   0768   0880   0887   0895   1041
1113   1187   1274

symphony no 9 "great"
0271   0317   0491   0599   0770   0912
0994   1041   1111   1123   1202   1301a

rosamunde
0038   0231   0289   0327   0393   0424
0600   0724   0768   0852   1029

marche militaire
0666

mass in e flat
0308   1319

schumann symphony no 1 "spring"
0445   0909   1063   1277

symphony no 2
0909   1174   1239   1297

symphony no 3 "rhenish"
0868   1195   1277

symphony no 4
0747   0868   0906a   0940   0941   1063
1138   1256   1327a   1356

piano concerto
0572   0661   0969   1018   1256   1271
1272

cello concerto
1256

introduction and allegro appassionato
1320

overture scherzo and finale
0909

manfred overture
0425   1195   1239   1297

schumann other overtures
0852   0909   1174

3 scenes from goethe's faust
0709

j.strauss graduation ball
0674   1081

strauss alpensinfonie
0569   0573

also sprach zarathustra
0291   0396   0637   0788   0795   1236

aus dem werkstatt eines invaliden
1316

aus italien
0497

der bürger als edelmann suite
0030   0291   0466   0848

couperin divertimento
0291

don juan
0291   0396   0415   0464   0467   0504
0605   0662   0783   0931   1089   1169

don quixote
0481   0788   0795   0873

duett-concertino
0501

feuersnot love scene
0605

festliches präludium
0291

ein heldenleben
0291   0466   1061   1091

horn concerto no 2
0275

josephslegende
1099

4 letzte lieder
0483

die liebe der danae symphonic fragments
0501

macbeth
1236

strauss metamorphosen
0331   1302

rosenkavalier suites/waltzes
0040   0848

sinfonia domestica
0283   0456   0501   0515   1244

tanz der 7 schleier/salome
0006   0204   0691

till eulenspiegels lustige streiche
0291   0396   0469   0475   0484   0504
0571   0677   1169

tod und verklärung
0291   0390   0446   0487   0571   0677
0747   0756   0783   1169

wagner der fliegende holländer overture
0373   0476   0717   0993   1167

funeral march/götterdämmerung
0083   0232   0370   0392   0504   0558
1227

lohengrin prelude
0504   0604   0840   0993   1167

lohengrin act 3 prelude
0385   0840   0993   1047   1167

meistersinger von nürnberg overture
0092   0283   0373   0469   0840   0880
0993   1041   1042   1043   1138

meistersinger von nürnberg act 3 prelude
0090   0392

parsifal prelude
0399   0604   0840   1138

parsifal karfreitagszauber
0604

rhine journey/götterdämmerung
0195   0232   0370   0505   0558

rienzi overture
0194   0399   0717   1138

siegfried idyll
0097   0370   0380   0534   0818   0880
1333

tannhäuser overture
0370   0472   0476   0717   1138   1333

wagner tannhäuser venusberg music
0476   0717

tristan und isolde prelude and liebestod
0604   0655   0880   0993   1167   1333

wesendonk-lieder
0557

weber symphony no 1
1106

konzertstück
0572

aufforderung zum tanz
0666   0674   1106

abu hassan overture
0014   0203   1106

beherrscher der geister overture
1106

euryanthe overture
0247a   0326   0432   0505   1106

der freischütz overture
0173   0236   0505   0520   1162

jubel overture
0032

oberon overture
0184   0392   0432   0468   0632

peter schmoll overture
0032   0043   0432

preciosa overture
0432   0852

*0001/1905-1907/g & t sessions

wagner
parsifal
excerpt
(nur eine
waffe taugt)

unnamed
conductor
schmedes

1905 version
g & t 3-42049
1907 version
g & t 3-42852
lp: emi 1C049 30679M/
    1C181 30669-30678M
lp: preiser CO 365
other operatic arias possibly also recorded

*0002/ june 1910/g & t session

weingartner
frühlings-
gespenster

**weingartner
marcel**

g & t/grammophon 2-43385

weingartner
schäfers
sonntagslied

g & t/grammophon 2-43384
lp: rococo 5370

0003. 17 january 1924/odeon session

verdi   **boschetti**   odeon 80202
rigoletto   gerhart   cd: preiser 89191
excerpt   *sung in german*
(caro nome)

puccini   odeon 80202
madama
butterfly
excerpt
(un bel di)

weber   **boschetti**   odeon 80203-80204/8076
abu hassan   gerhart   cd: preiser 89191
excerpt
(wird philomele
trauern?)

strauss   odeon 80205-80206/8005
ariadne   cd: preiser 89191
auf naxos
excerpt
(grossmächtige
prinzessin)

wagner   **boschetti**   odeon 80186
tannhäuser   duhan
excerpt
(o du mein holder
abendstern)

rossini   **boschetti**   odeon 80184/8084
il barbiere   duhan
di siviglia   *sung in german*
excerpt
(largo al
factotum)

puccini   odeon 80188/8084
tosca
excerpt
(3 sbirri!)

0004. 18 january 1924/odeon session

mozart **boschetti** odeon 80196
le nozze di gerhart cd: orfeo C394 101B/C408 955R
figaro duhan *also in a private lp edition by preiser*
excerpt *sung in german*
(crudel
perche finora!)

mozart   odeon 80197
don giovanni
excerpt
(la ci darem
la mano)

verdi   odeon 80198
il trovatore
excerpt
(mira d'acerbe
lagrime)

verdi   odeon 80199
rigoletto   lp: emi EX 29 01313
excerpt
(tutte le feste)

0005/22-23 january 1924/odeon sessions

mozart zauberflöte excerpt (dies bildnis)	**kaiser** grosavescu	odeon 80891/8588
wagner meistersinger von nürnberg excerpt (morgenlich leuchtend); verdi aida excerpt (celeste aida)		odeon 80892/8600
puccini madama butterfly excerpt (addio fiorito asil)		odeon 80885/8505
verdi rigoletto excerpt (ella mi fu rapita)	**kaiser** grosavescu *sung in german*	odeon 80645/8596/8600
puccini tosca excerpt (recondita armonia)		odeon 80886/8505

0005/concluded

puccini   **kaiser**   odeon 80886/8505
la boheme   grosavescu
excerpt
(che gelida
manina)

leoncavallo   odeon 80887/80949/8506
i pagliacci   *also in a private lp edition by preiser*
excerpt
(un tal gioco)

leoncavallo   odeon 80888/80951/8506
i pagliacci
excerpt
(vesti la giubba)

puccini   odeon 80889/8596
tosca
excerpt
(e lucevan le
stelle)

verdi   odeon 80890/80953
rigoletto
excerpt
(la donna e
mobile)

bizet   odeon 80893/8588
carmen
excerpt
(la fleur que tu
m'avais jetée)

orchestral accompaniments for all recordings in these 22-23 january 1924 sessions were re-recorded in berlin with a berlin orchestra; certain catalogue numbers may therefore refer to the re-recorded versions

0006/1924/grammophon sessions

schubert symphony no 9, second movement	**foch**	grammophon 66342-66343/ 69781-69782/B 20513-20516 *B 20513-20516 was a single-sided not published until 1926*
strauss dance of the 7 veils/salome		grammophon 66065

jürgen schmidt mentions that a tchaikovsky work may also have been recorded at these session

0007/autumn 1924/grammophon sessions

j.strauss an der schönen blauen donau waltz	**klein**	grammophon 66053/66056 cd: toshiba shinseido SGR 8243
j.strauss wiener blut waltz		grammophon 66053 cd: toshiba shinseido SGR 8243
josef strauss dorfschwalben aus österreich; j.strauss g'schichten aus dem wienerwald waltzes		grammophon 66054
josef strauss delirien; sphärenklänge waltzes		grammophon 66055 cd: toshiba shinseido SGR 8243
j.strauss wein weib und gesang waltz		grammophon 66056
lanner wienerwalzer; j.strauss wienerwalzer arranged by bayer		grammophon 66066

these strauss waltzes were recorded in abbreviated form

0008/28 november 1924/odeon session

wagner der fliegende holländer excerpt (die frist ist um)	**boschetti** schipper	odeon 80792/8587 cd: preiser 89218 *part one of the aria only*
wagner meistersinger von nürnberg excerpt (verachtet mir die meister nicht!)		odeon 80794/8586 cd: preiser 89218
marschner hans heiling excerpt (an jenem tag)		odeon 80795/8586 cd: preiser 89218

orchestral accompaniment for the items in this session were later re-recorded in berlin with a berlin orchestra; certain catalogue numbers may therefore refer to the re-recorded versions

0009/2-6 december 1924/odeon sessions

verdi
il trovatore
excerpt
(stride
la vampa)
boschetti
olszewska
sung in german
odeon 80790/8529

bizet
carmen
excerpt
(en vain pour
éviter)
odeon 80791/8529

wagner
der fliegende
holländer
excerpt
(die frist ist um)
boschetti
schipper
odeon 80792-80793/8587
cd: preiser 89218
parts two and three of the aria

j.strauss
frühlings-
stimmen
waltz;
adam
variations on
a mozart air
boschetti
gerhart
odeon 80252/8068

mozart
le nozze di
figaro
excerpt
(deh vieni
non tardar);
verdi
un ballo in
maschera
excerpt
(saper vorreste)
boschetti
gerhart
sung in german
odeon 80253/8068

the titles in these sessions sung by gerhart may not all have been published; orchestral accompaniments for the titles sung by olszewska and schipper were later re-recorded in berlin with a berlin orchestra, so that certain catalogue numbers may refer to the re-recorded versions

*0010/1927/grammophon sessions

wagner
der fliegende
holländer
excerpt
(traft ihr
das schiff);
tannhäuser
excerpt
(dich teure
halle!)

unnamed
conductor
nemeth

grammophon 66620
cd: pearl GEMMCD 9198

verdi
il trovatore
excerpt
(tacea la notte)

grammophon 66621
cd: pearl GEMMCD 9198

puccini
turandot
excerpt
(in questa
reggia);
korngold
die tote stadt
excerpt
(glück, das mir
verblieb)

grammophon 66623
cd: pearl GEMMCD 9198

verdi
un ballo in
maschera
excerpts
(ma dall' arido;
morro ma prima
in grazia)

grammophon 66624
cd: pearl GEMMCD 9198

wagner
lohengrin
excerpts
(einsam in
trüben tagen;
euch lüften)

grammophon 66626
cd: pearl GEMMCD 9198

0011/4-13 april 1928/konzerthaus/hmv sessions

beethoven symphony no 6 "pastoral"	**schalk**	78: hmv D 1473-1477 78: hmv (austria) ES 443-447 cd: emi CDH 764 2962/CHS 764 2942 cd: preiser 90111 cd: dante LYS 236-237 *issued on lp in japan by artisco*
beethoven symphony no 8		78: hmv D 1481-1483 78: hmv (austria) ES 450-452 78: hmv (italy) AW 16-18 lp: melodiya M10 43875-43876 cd: preiser 90111 cd: dante LYS 236-237 *issued on lp in japan by artisco*
beethoven leonore no 3 overture		78: hmv D 1614-1615 78: hmv (austria) ES 448-44 lp: melodiya M10 43875-43876 cd: dante LYS 236-237 *issued on lp in japan by artisco*

0012/25-26 april 1928/konzerthaus/hmv sessions

wagner siegfried opening of act three (prelude; wache wala!; stark ruft das lied!)	**alwin** olszewska schipper	78: hmv D 1533-1534 78: hmv (austria) ES 440-441 lp: preiser LV 39 cd: preiser 89218 *second part only* lp: emi EX 29 01313

0013/15 october 1928/konzerthaus/hmv session

handel joshua excerpt (o had i jubal's lyre!)	**alwin** schumann *sung in german*	78: hmv D 1632 78: hmv (austria) ES 555 78: electrola EJ 432 78: victor 7209 lp: preiser LV 218 lp: emi EX 29 05413 lp: angel IB 6144 cd: pearl GEMMCD 9379
strauss die heil'gen 3 könige	**alwin** schumann	78: hmv D 1632 78: hmv (austria) ES 555 78: electrola EJ 432 78: victor 7209 lp: preiser LV 218 cd: pearl GEMMCD 9379
strauss muttertändelei		78: hmv (austria) ER 304 78: electrola E 532 78: victor 1661 lp: preiser LV 218 cd: pearl GEMMCD 9379
marx marienlied		78: hmv (austria) ER 304 78: electrola E 532 78: victor 1661 lp: emi EX 29 01693 cd: pearl GEMMCD 9379 cd: testament SBT 0132

1928 sessions at which tauber sang operetta arias by lehar, with the conductor ernst hauke, and described on a pearl CD reissue as being made in vienna with staatsoper orchestra, probably took place in berlin with the staatskapelle

0014/9-25 january 1929/konzerthaus/hmv sessions

beethoven   **heger**   hmv unpublished
könig stephan   *recording published from later*
overture   *sessions in september 1929*

mozart   hmv unpublished
idomeneo   *recording published from later*
overture   *sessions in september 1929*

mozart   78: hmv C 1796
der schauspiel-   78: hmv (austria) AN 437
direktor
overture

weber   78: hmv B 3101
abu hassan   78: hmv (austria) AM 1896
overture

haydn   78: hmv B 3101
overture in d   78: hmv (austria) AM 1896

suppé   78: hmv C 1677
pique dame   78: hmv (france) L 834
overture   78: electrola EH 293
                                                  78: victor 11346
                                                  lp: turnabout THS 65066
                                                  cd: toshiba shinseido SGR 8243

goldmark   78: hmv C 2352-2356
rustic wedding   78: hmv (austria) AN 263-267
symphony   78: victor M 103

strauss   78: hmv C 1841
love scene/   78: hmv (austria) AN 269
feuersnot   78: electrola EH 292

suppé   78: hmv C 1667
morning noon   78: hmv (france) L 767
and night   78: hmv (italy) S 10074
in vienna   78: electrola EH 291
overture   78: victor 36004

0015/20 january-14 february 1929/konzerthaus/hmv sessions

bizet   **alwin**   78: hmv (austria) BB 207
carmen   hammes
excerpt   *sung in german*
(votre toast!)

bach   **alwin**   78: hmv D 1664
matthäus-   anday   78: hmv (austria) ES 506
passion   78: electrola EJ 437
excerpt   cd: preiser 89046
(erbarme dich);
handel
dank sei dir herr!

gounod   **alwin**   hmv unpublished
faust   anday
excerpt   *sung in german*
(si le bonheur)

donizetti   78: hmv (austria) ES 729
la favorita   lp: emi EX 29 01313
excerpt   cd: preiser 89046
(o mio fernando!)

0016/1-3 february 1929/konzerthaus/hmv sessions

josef strauss   **kleiber**   78: hmv C 1685
dorfschwalben   78: hmv (italy) S 10801
aus österreich   78: electrola EH 323
waltz   78: victor C 15
                                               cd: emi CDH 764 2992/CHS 764 2942
                                               cd: preiser 90115

j.strauss   78: hmv C 1697
künstlerleben   78: hmv (austria) AN 272
waltz   78: electrola EH 324
                                               78: victor C 15
                                               lp: emi 1C147 30226-30227M
                                               cd: preiser 90115
                                               cd: archiphon ARC 102
                                               cd: biddulph WHL 002
                                               cd: dg 459 7342

mozart   78: hmv C 1686-1688/
symphony   C 7234-7236 auto
no 38   78: hmv (austria) AN 274-276
"prague"   78: electrola EH 325-327
                                               lp: discocorp BWS 1021
                                               cd: preiser 90115
                                               cd: musica classica 2003-2004
                                               cd: grammofono AB 78609

j.strauss   78: hmv C 1676
du und du   78: hmv (austria) AN 273
waltz   78: electrola EH 289
                                               78: victor M 907
                                               lp: turnabout THS 65066
                                               cd: dg 435 3352/459 7342
                                               cd: preiser 90115
                                               cd: archiphon ARC 102
                                               cd: biddulph WHL 002

0017/24 april-24 may 1929/konzerthaus/hmv sessions

wagner lohengrin excerpts (dank könig dir!; trugbetörte fürsten!)	**alwin** schipper	78: hmv (austria) ES 579 78: electrola EJ 435 cd: preiser 89218
d'albert tiefland excerpt (hüll' in die mantille!)		78: hmv (austria) ER 311 78: electrola EW 74 cd: preiser 89218/89999
verdi rigoletto excerpts (cortigiani!; pari siamo)	**alwin** schipper *sung in german*	78: hmv (austria) ES 587 cd: preiser 89218
verdi aida excerpt (ciel, mio padre!)	**alwin** nemeth schipper *sung in german*	78: hmv (austria) ES 588 78: electrola EJ 491 lp: preiser LV 39 cd: preiser 89218

0018/4-5 june 1929/konzerthaus/hmv sessions

humperdinck königskinder excerpt (vater, mutter, hier will ich knien!); es ist alles wie ein wunderbarer garten)	**heger** achsel	78: hmv (austria) AM 2181
j.strauss die fledermaus excerpt (czardas)		hmv unpublished
j.strauss der zigeunerbaron excerpt (so elend und treu); lehar zigeunerliebe excerpt (war einst ein mädel)		78: hmv (austria) AM 2183
wagner der fliegende holländer excerpt (traft ihr das schiff)		78: hmv (austria) AM 2182
verdi il trovatore excerpt (tacea la notte)	**heger** achsel *sung in german*	78: hmv (austria) AM 2182

0019/6-25 june 1929/hmv sessions

gluck iphigenie in aulis excerpts (o artemis, entzürnte!; o du, die ich so innig liebte!)	**alwin** schipper	78: hmv (austria) ES 586 78: electrola EJ 490 lp: preiser LV 95 cd: preiser 89218
gounod faust excerpt (avant de quitter)	**alwin** schipper *sung in german*	78: hmv (austria) ES 734 cd: preiser 89218
puccini il tabarro excerpt (nulla! silenzio!)		78: hmv (austria) ER 311 78: electrola EW 74 cd: preiser 89218
gluck orfeo ed euridice excerpt (che faro)	**alwin** anday *sung in german*	hmv unpublished
mozart la clemenza di tito excerpt (parto, parto)		lp: emi EX 29 01693 cd: testament awaiting publication *unpublished hmv 78rpm recording*
verdi il trovatore excerpt (d'amor sull' alli rosee)	**alwin** nemeth *sung in german*	78: hmv (austria) ES 569 78: electrola EJ 498 lp: hungaroton LPX 11687 cd: preiser 89109/89999

0019/continued

verdi la forza del destino excerpt (madre pietosa vergine)	**alwin** nemeth	78: hmv HMS 13 78: hmv (austria) ES 571 lp: preiser LV 248 lp: hungaroton LPX 11687 lp: emi EX 29 01313 cd: preiser 89109 cd: pearl GEMMCD 9198
verdi la forza del destino excerpt (pace, pace!)		78: hmv (austria) ES 571 lp: hungaroton LPX 11687 cd: preiser 89109 cd: pearl GEMMCD 9198
verdi la forza del destino excerpt (la vergine degli angeli)		hmv unpublished
weber oberon excerpt (ozean du ungeheuer!)		78: hmv D 1717 78: hmv (austria) ES 572 78: electrola EJ 499 lp: hungaroton LPX 11687 cd: preiser 89109 cd: pearl GEMMCD 9198
wagner der fliegende holländer excerpts (summ und brumm!; trafft ihr das schiff)	**alwin** vienna opera chorus nemeth kittel	78: hmv (austria) lp: hungaroton LPX 11687

0019/concluded

mozart entführung aus dem serail excerpt (ach ich liebte)	**alwin** nemeth	78: electrola EJ 498 lp: preiser LV 248 lp: hungaroton LPX 11687
mozart entführung aus dem serail excerpt (martern aller arten)		78: hmv D 2023 78: electrola EJ 497 cd: pearl GEMMCD 9198
goldmark die königin von saba excerpt (der freund ist dein)		78: hmv D 1720/VB 13 78: hmv (austria) ES 516 lp: emi EX 29·01693 cd: preiser 89109 cd: pearl GEMMCD 9198 cd: testament SBT 0132
goldmark die königin von saba excerpt (doch eh' ich in des todes tal)		78: hmv D 1720/VB 13 78: hmv (austria) ES 516 lp: hungaroton LPX 11687 lp: emi EX 29 01313 cd: preiser 89109 cd: pearl GEMMCD 9198 *also in a private lp edition by preiser*
mozart entführung aus dem serail excerpt (ach ich liebte)	**alwin** perras	78: hmv DB 4439 78: victor 12007 cd: orfeo C394 101B/C408 955R
mozart entführung aus dem serail excerpt (martern aller arten)		78: hmv DB 4439 78: victor 12007

0020/12-13 june 1929/konzerthaus/hmv sessions

brahms   **krauss**   78: hmv B 3145
hungarian   78: hmv (austria) AM 2279
dances   78: hmv (italy) HN 481
nos 1 and 3   cd: preiser 90258

haydn   78: hmv E 539-541/E 7003-7005 auto
symphony   78: hmv (austria) AM 2280-2282
no 88   78: electrola EW 71-73
                                  78: victor 4189-4191
                                  cd: preiser 90104/90112
                                  cd: koch 3-7011-2
                                  recording completed on 2 july 1929

0021/2-3 july 1929/konzerthaus/hmv sessions

j.strauss   **krauss**   78: hmv B 3149
perpetuum   78: hmv (austria) AM 2283
mobile   78: electrola EG 1626
                                       lp: emi 1C147 30226-30227M/
                                                   1C053 01534M
                                       cd: emi CDH 764 2992/CHS 764 2942
                                       cd: preiser 90112/90139
                                       cd: radio years RY 57
                                       cd: biddulph WHL 001
                                       cd: arlecchino ARL 83-85

j.strauss   78: hmv B 3149
annen polka   78: hmv (austria) AM 2283
                                       78: electrola EG 1626
                                       lp: emi 1C053 01534M
                                       cd: dg 435 3352
                                       cd: preiser 90112/90139
                                       cd: radio years RY 57
                                       cd: biddulph WHL 001
                                       cd: arlecchino ARL 83-85

j.strauss   78: hmv C 1756
morgenblätter   78: electrola EH 416
waltz   78: victor M 907
                                       lp: emi 1C053 01534M
                                       cd: preiser 90090/90112/90139
                                       cd: radio years RY 57
                                       cd: biddulph WHL 001
                                       cd: arlecchino ARL 83-85

j.strauss   78: hmv C 1755
die fledermaus   78: hmv (austria) AN 377
overture   cd: emi CDH 764 2992/CHS 764 2942
                                       cd: preiser 90112/90139
                                       cd: dg 459 7342
                                       459 7342 incorrectly dated 1930

bruckner   78: hmv C 1789
scherzo/   78: electrola EH 392
symphony   cd: emi CHS 566 6602
no 4   cd: preiser 90258

*0022/6 september 1929/konzerthaus/hmv session

zeller	**alwin**	78: hmv E 554/DA 6037
vogelhändler	schumann	78: hmv (austria) ER 338
excerpt		78: electrola EW 83
(wie mein		cd: romophone 810192
ahn'l 20 jahr)		*additional unpublished take of the aria was also recorded*
j.strauss		78: hmv E 545
die fledermaus		78: hmv (austria) ER 319
excerpt		78: hmv (france) P 853
(spiel' ich die		78: electrola EW 82
unschuld)		lp: emi EX 29 05413
		lp: angel 1B-6144
		cd: romophone 810192
vlies		hmv unpublished
schlafe mein		
prinzchen		

0023/7 september 1929/konzerthaus/hmv session

mozart	**heger**	78: hmv C 1796
idomeneo		78: hmv (austria) AN 437
overture		
beethoven		78: hmv C 1795
könig stephan		78: hmv (austria) AN 435
overture		cd: toshiba shinseido SGR 8243
		recording completed on 17-18 september 1929

0024/9 september 1929/konzerthaus/hmv session

wagner	**alwin**	78: hmv C 1772
kaisermarsch		78: hmv (austria) AN 404
		78: electrola EH 425

mozart — 78: hmv B 3188
rondo alla — 78: hmv (austria) AM 2379
turca — 78: hmv (france) K 5848
arranged by — 78: victor 82-5018
herbeck

beethoven — 78: hmv B 3188
turkish march/ — 78: hmv (austria) AM 2379
die ruinen — 78: hmv (france) K 5848
von athen

0025/11-12 september 1929/konzerthaus/hmv sessions

auber **krauss** 78: hmv C 1785
fra diavolo — 78: hmv (austria) AN 436
overture

beethoven — 78: hmv C 2030-2033
symphony — 78: hmv (austria) AN 581-584
no 2 — 78: hmv (italy) S 10246-10249
— 78: victor M 131
— cd: preiser 90258

0026/13 september 1929/konzerthaus/hmv session

j.strauss : **heger** 78: hmv (austria) AM 2330
eine nacht achsel *also in a private lp edition by preiser*
in venedig gallos
excerpts
(kommt und
kauft; versäume
nicht!)

0027/9 october 1929/konzerthaus/hmv session

j.strauss einzugsmarsch/ zigeunerbaron	**krauss**	78: hmv B 3221 78: hmv (austria) AM 2496 78: electrola EG 1780 lp: emi 1C053 01534M cd: wing (japan) WCD 8 cd: preiser 90112
j.strauss leichtes blut polka		78: hmv B 3221 78: hmv (austria) AM 2496 78: electrola EG 1780 lp: emi 1C053 01534M cd: preiser 90112

0028/15-17 october 1929/konzerthaus/hmv sessions

goldmark das heimchen am herd overture	**krauss**	78: hmv (austria) AN 451 lp: past masters PM 36
goldmark im frühling overture		78: hmv C 1802 78: hmv (austria) AN 438
goldmark sakuntala overture		78: hmv C 1820-1821 78: hmv (austria) AN 439-440 lp: past masters PM 36
hérold zampa overture		78: hmv C 1803 78: hmv (austria) AN 441 78: hmv (italy) S 10231

0029/26-28 october 1929/konzerthaus/hmv sessions

beethoven symphony no 5	**schalk**	78: hmv C 2022-2025/C 7298-7301 auto 78: hmv (austria) AN 589-592 cd: dante LYS 236-237 *issued on lp in japan by preiser*

0030/28-29 october 1929/konzerthaus/hmv sessions

strauss	**krauss**	78: hmv C 2034-2037
der bürger		78: hmv (austria) AN 585-588
als edelmann		78: victor M 101
suite		cd: koch 3-7129-2

0031/3-10 january 1930/konzerthaus/hmv sessions

zeller **alwin** hmv unpublished
vogelhändler schumann
excerpt
(wie mein
ahn'l 20 jahr);
der obersteiger
excerpt
(sei nicht bös);
vlies
schlafe mein
prinzchen

verdi **alwin** 78: hmv (austria) EG 1824
rigoletto kalenberg
excerpt *sung in german*
(questa o
quella);
il trovatore
excerpt
(di quella pira)

puccini 78: hmv (austria) EG 1823
tosca
excerpt
(e lucevan
le stelle)

0032/15-21 january 1930/konzerthaus/hmv sessions

weber jubel overture	**krauss**	78: hmv C 2193 78: hmv (austria) AN 665 78: hmv (italy) S 10289 *recording completed on 17 january 1931*
weber peter schmoll overture		hmv unpublished *recording published from later sessions in september 1931*
brahms symphony no 3		78: hmv C 2026-2029/C 7129-7132 auto 78: hmv (austria) AN 577-580 cd: koch 3-7129-2 cd: preiser 90258 cd: biddulph WHL 052 *recording completed on 20 march 1930*

0033/22 january 1930/konzerthaus/hmv session

wagner tannhäuser excerpt (o du mein holder abendstern)	**alwin** hammes	78: hmv (austria) AN 471 lp: emi 1C181 30669-30678M/ EX 29 01313
thomas mignon excerpt (connais-tu le pays?)	**alwin** anday *sung in german*	78: hmv (austria) *recording completed in february 1930*
verdi il trovatore excerpt (stride la vampa)		78: hmv (austria) ES 729 cd: preiser 89046

0034/7 october 1930/konzerthaus/hmv session

korngold **alwin** 78: hmv (austria) BB 207/AN 618
die tote hammes lp: emi EX 29 01693
stadt   cd: testament SBT 0132
excerpt
(mein sehnen,
mein wähnen)

weinberger   78: hmv (austria) AM 3080
schwanda der   lp: emi EX 29 01313
dudelsackpfeifer   *also in a private lp edition by preiser*
excerpt
(ich bin
schwanda!)

0035/9 october 1930/konzerthaus/hmv session

j.strauss **krauss** 78: hmv C 2093
1001 nacht   78: hmv (austria) AN 630
waltz   78: electrola EH 484
    lp: emi 1C053 01534M
    lp: turnabout THS 65066
    cd: preiser 90112
    cd: radio years RY 57
    cd: biddulph WHL 001
    cd: dg 459 7342
    cd: arlecchino ARL 83-85

0036/17 january 1931/konzerthaus/hmv session

mozart **krauss** 78: hmv C 2194
le nozze di   78: hmv (austria) AN 666
figaro   78: electrola EW 1229
overture   78: victor 11-242
    lp: emi 1C187 29225-29226M

ziehrer   78: hmv C 2195
weana mad'ln   78: electrola EH 491
waltz   lp: emi 1C053 01534M
    cd: emi CDH 764 2992/CHS 764 2942
    cd: preiser 90112

0037/29-30 january 1931/konzerthaus/hmv sessions

mozart	**krauss**	78: hmv C 2194
entführung		78: hmv (austria) AN 666
aus dem		78: hmv (italy) S 10290
serail		78: victor M 584
overture		

mozart
cosi fan tutte
overture
78: hmv C 2233
78: hmv (austria) AN 724
78: hmv (italy) S 10295
cd: emi CDH 764 2952/CHS 764 2942

josef strauss
sphärenklänge
waltz
78: hmv C 2195
78: hmv (austria) AN 667
78: electrola EH 491
lp: emi 1C053 01534M
cd: preiser 90112
cd: radio years RY 57
cd: biddulph WHL 001
cd: arlecchino ARL 83-85

j.strauss
liebeslieder
waltz
78: hmv C 2239
78: electrola EH 829
78: victor M 907
lp: emi 1C053 01534M
cd: preiser 90112
cd: radio years RY 57
cd: biddulph WHL 001
cd: arlecchino ARL 83-85
recording completed on 2 september 1931

0038/16 april 1931/konzerthaus/hmv session

schubert   **krauss**   78: hmv C 2233
rosamunde   78: hmv (austria) AN 724
ballet music   78: electrola EH 494
in g

0039/16 april 1931/konzerthaus/hmv session

beethoven   **schalk**   hmv unpublished
symphony   *re-make of the 1928 recording*
no 8

beethoven   hmv unpublished
symphony   *proposed re-make of the 1929 recording*
no 5, opening
of first
movement

0040/26-27 june 1931/konzerthaus/hmv sessions

strauss   **alwin**   78: hmv C 2294-2295
rosenkavalier   78: hmv (austria) AN 722-723
suite   78: victor 11217-11218
arranged by   cd: toshiba shinseido SGR 8243
nambuat

j.strauss   78: hmv C 2338
wo die zitronen   78: hmv (austria) AN 728
blüh'n   78: electrola EH 771
waltz

0041/8 august 1931/salzburg festspielhaus

mozart   **walter**   lp: danacord DACO 131-133
zauberflöte   gerhart
fragments   mayr

0042/21 september 1931/konzerthaus/hmv session

strauss waltz/ intermezzo	**alwin**	78: hmv C 2343 78: hmv (austria) AN 740 78: hmv (italy) S 10407 78: victor 11430
saint-saens samson et dalila excerpt (amour, viens aider ma faiblesse)	**alwin** anday *sung in german*	78: electrola EG 2340 cd: preiser 89046/89999
saint-saens samson et dalila excerpt (mon coeur s'ouvre a ta voix)		78: electrola EG 2340 cd: preiser 89046
bizet carmen excerpt (l'amour est un oiseau rebelle)		78: electrola EH 695 cd: preiser 89046 *also in a private lp edition by preiser*
bizet carmen excerpt (card scene)		78: electrola EH 695 cd: preiser 89046

0043/22 september 1931/konzerthaus/hmv session

weber peter schmoll overture	**krauss**	78: hmv C 2344 78: hmv (austria) AN 739 78: victor 11429
lanner die kosenden; die romantiker waltzes		78: hmv C 2337

0044/5 august 1932/mainz

josef and johann strauss pizzicato polka   **krauss**   unpublished radio broadcast
berlin radio transcription disc

0045/20 january 1933/staatsoper

wagner
meistersinger
von nürnberg
excerpts
including
overture

krauss
vienna opera
chorus
ursuleac
rünger
kalenberg
zimmermann
bockelmann
zec
wiedemann

cd: koch 3-1464-2

0046/22 january 1933/staatsoper

strauss
rosenkavalier
fragments

krauss
ursuleac
gerhart
hadrabova
pataky
mayr

cd: koch 3-1451-2
excerpts
lp: ed smith UORC 346
cd: koch 3-1450-2

0047/25 february 1933/staatsoper

verdi
don carlo
fragments

krauss
ursuleac
rünger
völker
manowarda
schipper
jerger
sung in german

cd: koch 3-1466-2
excerpts
lp: teletheater 120.747

0048/26 february 1933/staatsoper

wagner
meistersinger
von nürnberg
excerpts from
acts 2 and 3
including
quintet

krauss
vienna opera
chorus
ursuleac
paalen
lorenz
zimmermann
jerger
zec
wiedemann

cd: koch 3-1456-2

0049/28 february 1933/staatsoper

wagner
das rheingold
fragments

krauss
ursuleac
paalen
graarud
zimmermann
kalenberg
manowarda

cd: koch 3-1464-2
excerpts
lp: teletheater 120.747

0050/1 march 1933/staatsoper

wagner
die walküre
excerpts
(heilig ist
mein herd;
winterstürme)

krauss
ursuleac
völker
mayr

cd: koch 3-1466-2
excerpts
lp: ed smith UORC 437
lp: teletheater 120.747

0051/7 march 1933/staatsoper

wagner
götter-
dämmerung
fragments
from acts
1 and 3

krauss
trundt
anday
kalenberg
manowarda
schipper

cd: koch 3-1464-2
excerpts
cd: koch 3-1450-2

0052/4 april 1933/staatsoper

giordano andrea excerpt (cosi fui sola!) | **heger** lehmann *sung in german* | cd: koch 3-1462-2

0053/13 april 1933/staatsoper

wagner
parsifal
excerpts from
acts 2 and 3

krauss
vienna opera
chorus
rünger
graarud
manowarda
schipper
wiedemann

cd: koch 3-1464-2
excerpts
lp: ed smith EJS 460
lp: teletheater 120.747
excerpts on EJS 460 incorrectly described as conducted by weingartner

0054/14 april 1933/staatsoper

wagner
der fliegende
holländer
fragments
from act 2

heger
vienna opera
chorus
nemeth
paalen
kalenberg
jerger
norbert

cd: koch 3-1454-2

0055/29 april 1933/staatsoper

strauss
salome
fragments

reichenberger
jeritza
paalen
maikl
graarud
schipper

lp: ed smith EJS 334
cd: koch 3-1462-2

0056/1 may 1933/staatsoper

wagner	**krips**	cd: koch 3-1453-2
götter-	vienna opera	
dämmerung	chorus	
fragments	trundt	
from acts	angerer	
1 and 3	kalenberg	
	schipper	
	manowarda	

0057/10 may 1933/staatsoper

wagner	**krips**	lp: ed smith EJS 332
der freischütz	vienna opera	cd: koch 3-1453-2
excerpts	chorus	
including	rethberg	
durch die wälder;	völker	
leise leise;	manowarda	
und ob die wolke	ettl	

0058/15 may 1933/staatsoper

wagner	**krips**	cd: koch 3-1466-2
rienzi	anday	*excerpts*
fragments	völker	lp: teletheater 120.747
including	gallos	cd: koch 3-1450-2
erstehe hohe	ettl	
roma neu!;		
allmächt'ger		
vater!		

0059/1 june 1933/staatsoper

strauss	**krauss**	cd: koch 3-1466-2
die frau ohne	vienna opera	*excerpts*
schatten	chorus	lp: ed smith UORC 345
fragments	ursuleac	lp: teletheater 120.747
	rünger	
	völker	

0060/3 june 1933/staatsoper

wagner
lohengrin
fragments
from acts
1 and 2

rühlmann
vienna opera
chorus
zika
rünger
völker
manowarda
schipper

cd: koch 3-1466-2

0061/11 june 1933/staatsoper

wagner
die walküre
excerpts

krauss
jeritza
hüni-mihacsek
völker
schorr
mayr

cd: koch 3-1464-2
excerpts
lp: teletheater 120.747

0062/13 june 1933/staatsoper

wagner
siegfried
fragments

heger
kappel
schubert
zimmermann

cd: koch 3-1459-2

0063/15 june 1933/staatsoper

wagner
götter-
dämmerung
excerpts
including
rhine journey
and immolation

heger
vienna opera
chorus
kappel
achsel
anday
kalenberg
schipper
manowarda

lp: ed smith EJS 460
cd: koch 3-1459-2

0064/14 september 1933/staatsoper

wagner
die walküre
excerpts

krauss
jeritza
lehmann
völker
schorr

cd: koch 3-1462-2

0065/20 september 1933/staatsoper

strauss	**krauss**	cd: koch 3-1455-2
die ägyptische	vienna opera	*excerpts*
helena	chorus	lp: teletheater 120.747
excerpts	ursuleac	
	bokor	
	völker	
	rosvaenge	
	jerger	

0066/20-24 september 1933/konzerthaus/hmv sessions

strauss	**heger**	78: hmv DB 2060-2072/
rosenkavalier	vienna opera	DB 7547-7559 auto
abridged	chorus	78: odeon PXO 1014
version	lehmann	78: victor M 196
	schumann	45: victor WCT 6005
	olszewska	lp: hmv COLH 110-111
	madin	lp: hmv (france) FALP 50014-50015
	mayr	lp: electrola E 80630-80631/
		WCLP 697-698
		lp: victor LCT 6005
		lp: angel 1C-6041
		lp: world records SH 181-182
		lp: emi RLS 7704/143 2943/
		1C143 43294-42395M
		cd: emi CHS 764 4872
		cd: pearl GEMMCDS 9365
		cd: grammofono AB
		excerpts
		78: victor M 329/M 633
		45: victor WCT 5
		lp: victor LCT 1
		lp: emi 1C147 29116-29117M/
		1C187 29225-29226M
		cd: rca/bmg 74321 694272/
		74321 694282
		excerpts also on private lp by preiser

0067/25 september 1933/staatsoper

wagner   **heger**   cd: koch 3-1462-2
tannhäuser   vienna opera
excerpts   chorus
from act 2   lehmann
    kalenberg
    maikl
    mayr
    schorr

0068/26 september 1933/staatsoper

mascagni   **reichenberger**   cd: koch 3-1462-2
cavalleria   vienna opera   *excerpts*
rusticana   chorus   lp: ed smith EJS 334
excerpts   jeritza   cd: koch 3-1450-2
    paalen
    bokor
    rosvaenge
    schipper
    sung in german

0069/17 october 1933/staatsoper

saint-saens   **reichenberger**   cd: koch 3-1454-2
samson   anday
et dalila   maison
excerpts
(salut a mon
maitre; mon
coeur s'ouvre
a ta voix)

0070/29 october 1933/staatsoper

strauss   **krauss**   cd: koch 3-1465-2
arabella   vienna opera   *excerpts*
excerpts   chorus   lp: teletheater 120.841
    ursuleac
    bokor
    kern
    rünger
    jerger
    mayr

0071/30 october 1933/staatsoper

verdi	**reichenberger**	cd: koch 3-1451-2
aida	rünger	
excerpt	lauri-volpi	
(e trono e		
vita, tutto		
darei per te)		

0072/15 november 1933/staatsoper

wagner	**krips**	cd: koch 3-1466-2
götter-	a.konetzni	
dämmerung	pölzer	
fragments	manowarda	
	schipper	

0073/5 december 1933/staatsoper

d'albert	**alwin**	cd: koch 3-1451-2
tiefland	pauly	
excerpts	pölzer	
(ich grüss'		
noch einmal		
meine berge;		
mein leben		
wagt' ich drum)		

0074/15 december 1933/staatsoper

verdi	**krauss**	cd: koch 3-1466-2
otello	ursuleac	*excerpts*
fragments	völker	lp: teletheater 120.841
	manowarda	
	sung in german	

0075/11 january 1934/konzerthaus/odeon session

lehar	**lehar**	78: odeon 4536
giuditta	tauber	78: parlophone RO 20289/PO 178
excerpt		78: decca (usa) D 20341
(du bist		lp: emi 1C147 30639-30640M
meine sonne)		cd: preiser 90150
		cd: emi CDC 754 8382
		cd: bel age BLA 103.352
		cd: pearl GEMMCD 9310

lehar		78: odeon 4536
giuditta		78: parlophone RO 20289/PO 178
excerpt		78: decca (usa) D 20341
(freunde, das		lp: electrola HZE 226
leben ist		lp: emi 1C147 30639-30640M
lebenswert!)		cd: preiser 90150
		cd: emi CDC 754 8382
		cd: bel age BLA 103.352
		cd: pearl GEMMCD 9310

lehar	**lehar**	78: odeon 4535
giuditta	novotna	78: parlophone RO 20290/PO 177
excerpts	tauber	78: decca (usa) D 20342
(schönste		lp: emi 1C147 30639-30640M
der frauen;		cd: preiser 90150
so wie in dem		cd: emi CDC 754 8382
sonnenball)		cd: bel age BLA 103.352
		cd: pearl GEMMCD 9310

lehar		78: odeon 4537
giuditta		78: parlophone RO 20290/PO 167
excerpt		78: decca (usa) D 20343
(schön wie		lp: emi 1C147 30639-30640M
die blaue		cd: preiser 90150
sommernacht)		cd: emi CDC 754 8382
		cd: bel age BLA 103.352
		cd: pearl GEMMCD 9310
		also in a private lp edition by preiser

lehar	**lehar**	78: odeon 4537/26316
giuditta	novotna	78: parlophone RO 20291/PO 167
excerpt		78: decca (usa) D 20343
(meine lippen		lp: emi1C14730639-30640M/EX 29 01313
sie küssen		cd: preiser 90150
so heiss!)		cd: emi CDC 754 8382
		cd: bel age BLA 103.352
		cd: pearl GEMMCD 9310

0076/19 january 1934/staatsoper

leoncavallo	**alwin**	cd: koch 3-1466-2
i pagliacci	vienna opera	
excerpts	chorus	
(pagliacco	achsel	
non son!;	völker	
ah tu mi	schipper	
s'fidi)	hammer	
	sung in german	

0077/20 january 1934/staatsoper

lehar	**lehar**	lp: ed smith EJS 532
giuditta	novotna	cd: koch 3-1451-2
(meine lippen		
sie küssen		
so heiss!)		

0078/13 april 1934/staatsoper

wagner	**krauss**	cd: koch 3-1460-2
meistersinger	vienna opera	
von nürnberg	chorus	
excerpts	ursuleac	
from acts	szantho	
2 and 3	völker	
including	zimmermann	
quintet	jerger	

0079/12-14 june 1934/konzerthaus/columbia sessions

bach	**dobrowen**	78: columbia LX 408-410/
violin	huberman	LX 8183-8185 auto
concerto		78: columbia (france) LFX 411-413
in e		78: columbia (usa) M 235
bwv 1042		cd: pearl GEMMCD 9341
		cd: strings QT 99369
		issued on lp in japan by artisco

bach	78: columbia LX 329-330
violin	78: columbia (usa) X 45
concerto	cd: pearl GEMMCD 9341
in a minor	*issued on lp in japan by preiser*
bwv 1041	

mozart	78: columbia LX 494-496/
violin	LX 8243-8245 auto
concerto	78: columbia (australia) LOX 319-321
no 3	78: columbia (usa) M 258
	cd: pearl GEMMCD 9341

0080/18-22 june 1934/konzerthaus/columbia sessions

beethoven	**szell**	78: columbia LX 509-513/
violin	huberman	LX 8256-8260 auto
concerto		lp: columbia (usa) ML 4769
		lp: rococo 2033
		lp: emi 143 5341
		cd: emi CDH 763 1942
		cd: preiser 90118
		cd: magic talent CD 48023
		cd: arlecchino ARL 153-154
		cd: appian APR 5506
		also on lp in japan by artisco

lalo	78: columbia LX 347-349/LCX 201-203/
symphonie	LX 8129-8131 auto
espagnole	78: columbia (france) LFX 370-372
	78: columbia (usa) M 214
	lp: rococo 2002
	lp: emi 1C053 01419M
	cd: appian APR 5506
	also on lp in japan by artisco

0081/23 june 1934/konzerthaus/hmv session

j.strauss   **szell**   78: hmv C 2686
an der schönen   78: hmv (italy) S 10460
blauen donau   78: hmv (switzerland) FKX 26
waltz   78: victor M 805
                              45: victor WBC 1008
                              lp: victor LBC 1008
                              lp: turnabout THS 65066
                              cd: dg 435 3352/459 7342
                              cd: preiser 90115/90118/90139

j.strauss   78: hmv C 2687
tritsch-tratsch   45: victor WBC 1008
polka   lp: victor LBC 1008
                              cd: emi CDH 764 2992/CHS 764 2942
                              cd: preiser 90115/90139
                              cd: dg 459 7342

j.strauss   78: hmv C 2687
frühlingsstimmen   78: victor 13597
waltz   45: victor WBC 1008
                              lp: victor LBC 1008
                              cd: emi CDH 764 2992/CHS 764 2942
                              cd: preiser 90115/90118/90139

josef and   78: hmv C 2687
johann strauss   45: victor WBC 1008
pizzicato polka   lp: victor LBC 1008
                              cd: preiser 90115/90139

**0082/23 june 1934/konzerthaus/hmv session

josef strauss sphärenklänge waltz	**rosenek** schumann	78: hmv DA 1395/DA 4435 78: hmv (ireland) IR 281 78: victor (japan) JE 12 lp: emi EX 29 05413 lp: angel 1B-6144 cd: pearl GEMMCD 9379
mendelssohn auf flügeln des gesanges arrangement		78: hmv DA 1395 78: victor M 383 78: victor (japan) JE 12 cd: romophone 810182
schubert ave maria arrangement		78: hmv DB 2291 78: victor 8423 78: victor (japan) JD 49 cd: emi CHS 763 0402
stölzel bist du bei mir		78: hmv DB 2291 78: victor 8423 78: victor (japan) JD 49 lp: emi EX 29 05413 lp: angel 1B-6144 cd: pearl GEMMCDS 9900

0083/26 august 1934/salzburg festspielhaus

wagner siegfried's funeral march/ götter- dämmerung	**toscanini**	lp: melodram MEL 012 lp: discocorp ATRA 3008

0084/30 september 1934/staatsoper

wagner götter- dämmerung excerpts (mehr gabst du, wunderfrau!; helle wehr, heilige waffe!)	**weingartner** a.konetzni melchior manowarda	cd: koch 3-1451-2 *excerpts* lp: teletheater 120.841

0085/10-11 october 1934/konzerthaus/columbia sessions

beethoven	**walter**	78: columbia LX 342-346
piano	gieseking	78: columbia (germany) LWX 83-87
concerto		78: columbia (france) LFX 359-363
no 5		78: columbia (usa) M 243
"emperor"		lp: rococo 2019
		lp: turnabout THS 65011
		lp: emi 3C153 52700-52705M/
		1C147 50149-50151M
		cd: grammofono AB 78506
		cd: appian APR 5512
		appian dated september 1934; also issued
		on lp in japan by toshiba

0086/1 november 1934/staatsoper

wagner	**krauss**	cd: koch 3-1466-2
die walküre	ursuleac	
fragments	völker	
(wo bist du,		
siegmund?;		
zauberfest		
bezähmt		
ein schlaf)		

0087/19 november 1934/staatsoper

wagner	**krauss**	cd: koch 3-1466-2
götter-	vienna opera	
dämmerung	chorus	
fragments	rünger	
	anday	
	szantho	
	manowarda	
	schipper	

0088/23 november 1934/staatsoper

tchaikovsky   **reichenberger**   cd: koch 3-1451-2
evgeny   kullmann
onegin   *sung in german*
excerpt
(where have
you gone?)

0089/14 december 1934/staatsoper

puccini   **reichenberger**   cd: koch 3-1451-2
turandot   nemeth
fragments   kiepura
including   *sung in german*
nessun dorma

0090/30 december 1934/staatsoper

wagner   **weingartner**   cd: koch 3-1451-2
meistersinger
von nürnberg
act 3 prelude

fragments from a staatsoper performance of lohengrin, which took place in december 1934 under weingartner, may also survive; fragments from a 1934 performance of der fliegende holländer, conducted by walter, may also survive

0091/2-5 february 1935/konzerthaus/columbia sessions

beethoven	**weingartner**	78: columbia LX 413-420/
symphony	vienna opera	LX 8175-8182
no 9	chorus	78: columbia (germany) LWX 134-141
"choral"	helletsgruber	78: columbia (italy) GQX 10782-10789
	anday	78: columbia (usa) M 227
	maikl	78: columbia (canada) D 4
	mayr	lp: columbia COLC 27-28
		lp: columbia (usa) ML 165/SL 165/
		E7L-55/RL 6636-6642
		cd: preiser 90193
		cd: pearl GEMMCD 9047
		cd: arkadia 78508
		cd: grammofono AB 78012-78016
		cd: avid AMSC 583
		cd: dante LYS 174

also issued in japan by artisco, toshiba and toshiba shinseido

0092/10 february 1935/staatsoper

wagner	**weingartner**	lp: teletheater 643.333
meistersinger		cd: koch 3-1451-2
von nürnberg		
overture		

act 3 prelude recorded at this performance may also survive

0093/14 february 1935/staatsoper

lehar **lehar** cd: koch 3-1451-2
giuditta tauber
excerpt
(du bist
meine sonne)

0094/14 march 1935/staatsoper

bellini **del campo** cd: koch 3-1451-2
la sonnambula dal monte
fragments sinnone

0095/19 march 1935/staatsoper

rossini **del campo** cd: koch 3-1451-2
il barbiere dal monte
di siviglia sinnone
fragments montesanto
including
largo al
factotum and
rosina's
insert aria

0096/7 june 1935/staatsoper

verdi **de sabata** lp: teletheater 643.333
otello vienna opera cd: koch 3-1451-2
excerpt chorus
(fuoco di *sung in german*
gioia!)

0097/16 june 1935/konzerthaus/hmv session

wagner **walter** 78: hmv DB 2634-2635
siegfried 78: victor G 21
idyll lp: world records SH 193-194
  lp: turnabout THS 65163
  cd: emi CDH 764 2982/CHS 764 2942
  cd: preiser 90157
  cd: palladio PD 4169
  cd: grammofono AB 78546

0098/20-22 june 1935/musikvereinssaal/hmv sessions

wagner	**walter**	78: hmv DB 2636-2643/
die walküre	lehmann	DB 8039-8046 auto
act 1	melchior	78: columbia (germany) LWX 105-112
	list	78: columbia (italy) GQX 10889-10896

78: victor M 298
45: victor WCT 58
lp: hmv COLH 133
lp: hmv (france) FALP 50013
lp: electrola E 80686-80688
lp: victor LVT 1003/LCT 1033
lp: angel 60190
lp: emi 2C051 03023/29 01313/
   1C049 03023M
lp: danacord DACO 171-176
cd: danacord DACOCD 317-318
cd: emi CDH 761 0202
cd: arkadia AB 78526
excerpts
78: victor M 329/M 633
45: victor WCT 2
lp: victor LCT 1/LCT 1001
lp: top classic TC 9049
lp: emi 1C147 01259-01260M/
   1C149 29116-29117M/
   1C147 30636-30637M

0098/concluded

wagner	**walter**	78: hmv DB 3724-3725 and 3728
die walküre	lehmann	78: victor M 582
act 2	flesch	lp: electrola E 80686-80688
scenes	melchior	lp: turnabout THS 65163
3 and 5	list	lp: emi EX 29 02123
	jerger	lp: danacord DACO 171-176
		cd: danacord DACOCD 317-318
		cd: emi CDH 764 2552
		excerpts
		lp: emi RLS 7711/EX 29 01313/ 1C137 54390-54396M
		these scenes were added to recordings made in berlin in 1938, in which the berlin staatskapelle was conducted by seidler-winkler, to constitute a complete edition of the second act of die walküre

0099/28 july 1935/salzburg festspielhaus

beethoven **weingartner** unpublished radio broadcast
symphony
no 3
"eroica"

0100/1 august 1935/salzburg festspielhaus

mozart **walter** unpublished radio broadcast
don giovanni arangi-lombardi
fragment
from act 1

0101/16 september 1935/staatsoper

gounod	**alwin**	cd: koch 3-1451-2
faust	kullmann	
excerpts	pinza	
(le veau d'or;	*sung in german*	
salut demeure)	*(kullmann) and*	
	french (pinza)	

0102/20 september 1935/staatsoper

wagner	**weingartner**	lp: teletheater 643.333
meistersinger	lehmann	cd: koch 3-1462-2
von nürnberg	thorborg	
excerpts	laholm	
(jerum! jerum!;	wernigk	
selig wie	hofmann	
die sonne)	wiedemann	

0103/29 september 1935/ravag

lehar	**lehar**	cd: eklipse EKRCD 36
paganini	jeritza	
excerpt		
(liebe, du himmel		
auf erden);		
bond		
i love you truly		

0104/13 october 1935/staatsoper

wagner	**furtwängler**	lp: ed smith UORC 242
tannhäuser	vienna opera	lp: teletheater 643.333
fragments	chorus	*excerpts*
	bathy	lp: acanta 40.23520
	pistor	cd: acanta 44.1055
	maikl	cd: koch 3-1470-2
	hofmann	
	sved	
	markhoff	
	wernigk	
	ettl	

0105/15 october 1935/staatsoper

wagner	**furtwängler**	cd: koch 3-1454-2
tannhäuser	sved	
excerpt		
(als du in		
kühnem sange)		

0106/18 october 1935/staatsoper

wagner	**furtwängler**	lp: ed smith UORC 242
tannhäuser	sved	lp: teletheater 643.333
excerpt		cd: koch 3-1454-2
(wohl wusst'		
ich hier/o du		
mein holder		
abendstern)		

0107/28 october-6 november 1935/staatsoper

nicolai	**weingartner**	cd: koch 3-1460-2
die lustigen	vienna opera	
weiber von	chorus	
windsor	majkut	
including	bollhammer	
als büblein	hofmann	
klein	jerger	

0108/9 january 1936/staatsoper

wagner	**furtwängler**	lp: teletheater 643.333
tannhäuser	vienna opera	cd: koch 3-1470-2
excerpts	chorus	
including	müller	
dich teure	lorenz	
halle!		

0109/11 february 1936/staatsoper

wagner	**krips**	cd: koch 3-1451-2
lohengrin	hussa	
excerpt	ralf	
(höchstes		
vertrau'n)		

0110/13-17 february 1936/staatsoper

wagner	**furtwängler**	cd: dante LYS 217-218
die walküre	a.konetzni	cd: koch 3-1470-2
excerpts	müller	*excerpts*
	hadrabova	lp: ed smith EJS 451/EJS 543
	völker	*ed smith incorrectly dated december 1937*
	grossmann	
	jerger	

0111/24-26 february 1936/musikvereinssaal/columbia sessions

beethoven
symphony
no 7
	weingartner	78: columbia LX 484-488/
		    LX 8235-8239 auto
		78: columbia (usa) M 260
		lp: columbia (usa) ML 4507/E7L-55/
		    RL 6336-6342
		cd: grammofono AB 78012-78016
		issued in japan by artisco, toshiba
		and toshiba shinseido

beethoven
symphony
no 8
		78: columbia LX 563-565/
		    LX 8295-8297 auto
		78: columbia (usa) M 292
		78: columbia (canada) D 8
		78: columbia (argentina) 264962-264964
		lp: columbia COLC 28
		lp: columbia (usa) ML 165/SL 165/
		    E7L-55/RL 6336-6342
		cd: preiser 90113
		cd: grammofono AB 78012-78016
		issued in japan by artisco, toshiba
		and toshiba shinseido

beethoven die geschöpfe des prometheus overture		78: columbia LX 488/LX 8235 78: columbia (france) LFX 428 78: columbia (italy) GQX 10781 78: columbia (usa) M 260/72634D 78: columbia (australia) LOX 287 lp: columbia (usa) ML 4647 cd: grammofono AB 78856-78857 cd: toshiba shinseido SGR8243/SGR8531 *issued in japan by artisco and toshiba;* *toshiba shinseido has published an additional* *cd(BCD 0048) containing a completely* *different take of the overture*

0112/11 april 1936/staatsoper

wagner	**weingartner**	lp: ed smith EJS 460
parsifal	thorborg	cd: koch 3-1451-2
fragments	graarud	
	kipnis	

0113/18 april 1936/staatsoper

wagner	**knappertsbusch**	cd: koch 3-1456-2/3-1474-2
siegfried	szantho	
excerpts	kalenberg	
from acts	zimmermann	
1 and 3	schipper	

0114/21 april 1936/staatsoper

verdi	**de sabata**	cd: koch 3-1454-2
aida	vienna opera	
excerpts	chorus	
	nemeth	
	anday	
	pataky	
	sved	
	zec	
	sung in german	

0115/22 april 1936/staatsoper

strauss	**knappertsbusch**	cd: koch 3-1462-2
rosenkavalier	vienna opera	*excerpts*
excerpts	chorus	lp: ed smith EJS 332
including	lehmann	lp: teletheater 763.3589
trio	schumann	
	hadrabova	
	sternek	
	madin	

0116/18-21 may 1936/musikvereinssaal/hmv sessions

brahms   **walter**   78: hmv DB 2933-2936/
symphony   DB 8169-8172 auto
no 3   78: victor M 341
                                    lp: discocorp BWS 803
                                    cd: koch 3-7120-2
                                    also private lp edition by preiser
                                    and toshiba in japan

schubert   78: hmv DB 2937-2939/
symphony   DB 8187-8189 auto
no 8   78: victor G 9
"unfinished"   cd: emi CDH 764 2962/CHS 764 2942
                                   cd: palladio PD 4169
                                   issued on lp by toshiba in japan

beethoven   78: hmv DB 2885-2886
leonore   78: victor M 359
no 3   cd: preiser 90157
overture   cd: koch 3-7011-2
                                    cd: grammofono AB 78517
                                    cd: phonographe PH 5031-5032
                                    also private lp edition by preiser
                                    and toshiba in japan

0117/22-23 may 1936/musikvereinssaal/columbia sessions

beethoven   **weingartner**   78: columbia LX 532-537/
symphony   LX 8273-8278 auto
no 3   78: columbia (usa) M 285
"eroica"   78: columbia (canada) D 7
                                    lp: columbia (usa) ML 4503/E7L-55/
                                         RL 6336-6342
                                    lp: emi RLS 717/1C053 01481M/
                                        1C147 01759-01761M
                                    cd: preiser 90113
                                    cd: grammofono AB 78012-78016
                                    issued in japan by artisco, toshiba
                                    and toshiba shinseido

0118/23 may 1936/musikvereinssaal/hmv session

beethoven	**rosé**	78: hmv DB 2886
die ruinen		78: victor M 359/M 426
von athen		
overture		

0119/24 may 1936/musikvereinssaal

mahler	**walter**	78: columbia ROX 165-171/
das lied	thorborg	ROX 8025-8031 auto
von der	kullmann	78: columbia (usa) M 300
erde		78: columbia (canada) D 124
		lp: perennial 2004
		lp: angel 60191
		lp: emi HLM 7007/1C047 01204M
		cd: emi CDH 764 2972/CHS 764 2942
		cd: palladio PD 4172-4173
		cd: grammofono AB 78553
		cd: dutton CDEA 5014
		cd: pearl GEMMCD 9413
		cd: music and arts CD 749/CD 4749

mahler	**walter**	78: columbia LB 44/LC 23
ich bin der	thorborg	78: columbia (usa) 4201M
welt abhanden		lp: parnassus 4
gekommen		lp: angel 60191
		lp: emi HLM 7017/1C047 01204M
		cd: emi CDH 764 2972/CHS 764 2942
		cd: dutton CDEA 5014
		cd: pearl GEMMCD 9413
		cd: music and arts CD 4749

0120/7 june 1936/staatsoper

verdi	**de sabata**	cd: koch 3-1454-2
aida	vienna opera	*excerpts*
excerpts	chorus	lp: ed smith EJS 337/EJS 405
	nemeth	lp: teletheater 762.3589
	thorborg	
	björling	
	sved	
	hofmann	
	sung in german	
	except björling	
	(swedish)	

0121/8 august 1936/salzburg festspielhaus

wagner	**toscanini**	lp: ed smith UORC 257
meistersinger	vienna opera	lp: MR 2003
von nürnberg	chorus	cd: eklipse EKRCD 54
act 1	lehmann	
	thorborg	
	kullmann	
	sallaba	
	nissen	
	alsen	
	wiedemann	

0122/16 august 1936/salzburg festspielhaus

beethoven	**toscanini**	lp: ed smith UORC 218
fidelio	lehmann	cd: radio years RY 70
act 1	helletsgruber	cd: grammofono AB 78702/
nos. 1-9	gallos	AB 78017-78025
only	jerger	*radio years incorrectly dated 25 july 1936;*
	baumann	*grammofono incorrectly dated 1935*

0123/11 september 1936/staatsoper

wagner	**weingartner**	lp: teletheater 762.3589
götter-	flagstad	cd: koch 3-1451-2
dämmerung		
excerpt		
(starke scheite)		

siegfried's rhine journey from this 11 september performance may also survive

0124/14 september 1936/staatsoper

strauss
rosenkavalier
excerpts
(prelude;
wie du warst;
leopold, wir
geh'n!)

knappertsbusch
a.konetzni
schumann
flesch
sternek

cd: koch 3-1467-2
excerpts
lp: teletheater 762.3589

0125/30 september 1936/staatsoper

strauss
elektra
excerpts
(weh, ach
ganz allein!;
es rührt sich
niemand)

knappertsbusch
pauly
schipper

lp: teletheater 762.3589
cd: koch 3-1467-2

0126/8 october 1936/staatsoper

wagner
lohengrin
excerpt
(durch
gottes sieg)

knappertsbusch
vienna opera
chorus
helletsgruber
a.konetzni
ralf
hofmann
schipper

cd: koch 3-1451-2

0127/13 october 1936/staatsoper

wagner
die walküre
excerpts

walter
merker
h.konetzni
thorborg
völker
hofmann
alsen

cd: koch 3-1459-2

0128/19 october 1936/staatsoper

wagner	**knappertsbusch**	cd: koch 3-1460-2
meistersinger	vienna opera	
von nürnberg	chorus	
excerpts	mansinger	
including	thorborg	
quintet	kalenberg	
	sallaba	
	hofmann	
	alsen	
	wiedemann	

0129/10 november 1936/staatsoper

gounod	**krips**	lp: ed smith UORC 242
faust	helletsgruber	lp: teletheater 762.3589
fragments	rosvaenge	cd: koch 3-1462-2
from acts	berglund	
1 and 3	sved	
	sung in german	
	except berglund	
	(swedish)	

0130/5-18 december 1936/musikvereinssaal/hmv sessions

beethoven symphony no 6 "pastoral"	**walter**	78: hmv DB 3051-3055/ DB 8219-8223 auto 78: victor G 20 lp: turnabout THS 65042 lp: emi 1C147 50149-50151M cd: preiser 90157 cd: avid AMSC 583 *also private lp edition by preiser and lp issue in japan by toshiba*
mozart eine kleine nachtmusik		78: hmv DB 3075-3076 78: victor M 364 lp: victor CAL 253 lp: turnabout THS 65036 lp: emi 1C147 50178-50180M cd: emi CHS 763 9122 cd: grammofono AB 78528 cd: arkadia 78528 *issued on lp in japan by toshiba*
mozart symphony no 38 "prague"		78: hmv DB 3112-3114/ DB 8302-8303 auto 78: victor M 457 lp: hmv COLH 37 lp: victor CAL 237 lp: turnabout THS 65033-65035 lp: emi 1C147 50178-50160M/MFP 2061 cd: emi CHS 763 9122 cd: grammofono AB 78793 cd: arkadia 78505 *issued on lp in japan by toshiba*

0131/16 december 1936-5 january 1937/staatsoper

verdi don carlo excerpts	**walter** vienna opera chorus h.konetzni nikolaidi völker kipnis ardelli *sung in german*	cd: koch 3-1460-2 *excerpts* lp: ed smith EJS 334

0132/19 december 1936/staatsoper

wagner	**knappertsbusch**	lp: teletheater 762.3589
lohengrin	vienna opera	cd: koch 3-1467-2
excerpts	chorus	cd: radio years RY 98
	teschemacher	
	a.konetzni	
	kötter	
	alsen	

0133/13 january 1937/odeon session

paumgartner	**krips**	78: odeon 4852
rossini in neapel	tauber	lp: emi 1C137 78130-78133M
excerpts		
(schon die		
halbe nacht;		
auch manch'		
vergang'ne		
nacht)		

0134/14 january 1937/staatsoper

wagner	**krips**	cd: koch 3-1453-2
meistersinger	vienna opera	
von nürnberg	chorus	
fragments	reich	
	kalenberg	
	prohaska	
	wiedemann	

0135/18 january 1937/staatsoper

wagner	**krips**	cd: koch 3-1459-2
das rheingold	a.konetzni	
fragments	prohaska	
	zec	
	alsen	

0136/22 january 1937/staatsoper

wagner
siegfried
fragments

krips
helletsgruber
anday
lorenz
wernigk
prohaska

cd: koch 3-1453-2

0137/24 january 1937/staatsoper

wagner
götter-
dämmerung
fragments

knappertsbusch
vienna opera
chorus
a.konetzni
paalen
achsel
anday
lorenz
destal
prohaska

cd: koch 3-1474-2

0138/5 february 1937/staatsoper

leoncavallo
i pagliacci
excerpts
(vesti la
giubba;
sperai tanto
il delirio)

alwin
vienna opera
chorus
piccaver
monthy
sung in german

cd: koch 3-1463-2

0139/7 march 1937/staatsoper

gounod
faust
fragments

krips
rethy
björling
sved
kipnis
*sung in german
excerpt björling
(swedish)*

lp: ed smith EJS 337/UORC 242
lp: historical recording enterprises
  HRE 376
cd: koch 3-1454-2

0140/12 march 1937/staatsoper

leoncavallo	**alwin**	lp: ed smith EJS 337
i pagliacci	vienna opera	cd: koch 3-1454-2
fragments	chorus	
	bokor	
	björling	
	ginrod	
	sung in german	
	except björling	
	(swedish)	

0141/19 march 1937/staatsoper

wolf-ferrari	**knappertsbusch**	lp: teletheater 762.3596-3597
i gioielli	vienna opera	cd: koch 3-1467-2
della madonna	chorus	
excerpts	bokor	
	maikl	
	ardelli	
	jerger	
	ettl	
	sung in german	

0142/3-5 may 1937/musikvereinssaal/hmv sessions

brahms symphony no 1	**walter**	78: hmv DB 3277-3281 78: victor M 470 cd: preiser 90114 cd: grammofono AB 78517 cd: avid AMSC 603 *issued on lp in japan by toshiba*
mozart 3 german dances k605		78: hmv DA 1570 78: victor 4564 lp: turnabout THS 65036 lp: emi 1C147 50178-50180M cd: emi CHS 763 9122 cd: pearl GEMMCD 9940
haydn symphony no 96 "miracle"		78: hmv DB 3282-3284/ DB 8359-8361 auto 78: victor M 885 lp: victor LCT 6015 lp: emi 1C053 01456M lp: turnabout THS 65020 lp: discocorp BWS 1002 cd: preiser 90114 cd: pearl GEMMCD 9945 *also private lp edition by preiser*

0143/5 may 1937/staatsoper

puccini   **duhan**   cd: koch 3-1463-2
la fanciulla   piccaver
del west   *sung in german*
excerpt
(ch' ella
mi creda)

0144/7 may 1937/musikvereinssaal/hmv sessions

mozart	**walter**	78: hmv DB 3273-3276/
piano	conductor	DB 8544-8547 auto
concerto	and pianist	78: victor M 420
no 20		lp: victor LM 6130
		lp: rococo 2065
		lp: turnabout THS 65036
		lp: emi 1C147 50178-50180M
		cd: emi CHS 763 9122
		cd: preiser 90141
		cd: pearl GEMMCD 9940
		cd: wing (japan) WCD 50
		also private lp edition by preiser

0145/10 may 1937/staatsoper

mascagni	**alwin**	cd: koch 3-1463-2
cavalleria	vienna opera	
rusticana	chorus	
excerpts	piccaver	
(viva il vino!;	schipper	
io so che il	*sung in german*	
torto e mio!)		

leoncavallo	**alwin**	cd: koch 3-1463-2
i pagliacci	schumann	
excerpt	*sung in german*	
(stridono		
lassu)		

0146/23 may 1937/staatsoper

verdi	**alwin**	cd: koch 3-1463-2
aida	vienna opera	*excerpts*
excerpts	chorus	lp: ed smith EJS 336
including	nemeth	
celeste aida;	anday	
o terra addio)	gigli	
	zec	
	sved	
	kipnis	
	sung in german	
	except gigli	
	(italian)	

0147/10 june 1937/staatsoper

wagner
das rheingold
excerpt
(abendlich
strahlt)

knappertsbusch
szantho
hofmann

cd: koch 3-1474-2

0148/12 june 1937/staatsoper

wagner
die walküre
excerpt
(nun zäume
dein ross)

knappertsbusch
a.konetzni
hofmann

lp: ed smith EJS 332
cd: koch 3-1456-2

0149/13 june 1937/staatsoper

strauss
rosenkavalier
excerpts
including
mir ist
die ehre
widerfahren)

knappertsbusch
h.konetzni
schumann
bokor
michalsky

lp: ed smith EJS 332
cd: koch 3-1467-2
ed smith incorrectly names singer of oktavian as novotna

0150/16 june 1937/staatsoper

wagner
siegfried
fragments

knappertsbusch
szantho
schumann
lorenz
wernigk
hofmann
zec

cd: koch 3-1460-2/3-1474-2
excerpts
lp: ed smith EJS 444

0151/19 june 1937/staatsoper

wagner
götter-
dämmerung
fragments

knappertsbusch
a.konetzni
achsel
paalen
szantho
anday
kipnis

cd: koch 3-1474-2

0152/29 june 1937/paris théatre du champs-elysées

mozart	**walter**	lp: emi EG 29 07811
requiem	vienna opera	cd: emi CHS 763 9122
	chorus	cd: grammofono AB 78546
	schumann	cd: arkadia 78528
	thorborg	
	dermota	
	kipnis	
bruckner		cd: toshiba promotional issue in
te deum		japan only

0153/30 july 1937/salzburg festspielhaus

mozart	**toscanini**	lp: toscanini society ATS 1025-1027
zauberflöte	vienna opera	lp: mrf records MRF 71
	chorus	lp: estro armonico EA 056
	novotna	lp: cetra LO 44
	osvath	cd: melodram MEL 37040
	komarek	cd: grammofono AB 78017-78025/
	rosvaenge	AB 78528-78529
	domgraf-fassbänder	cd: 40s label FTO 321-322
	kipnis	cd: naxos 811.0828-811.0829
	jerger	*excerpts*
		lp:pearl GEMM 261-262/GEMM 277-278
		cd: pearl GEMMCD 9467
		cd: amadeo 427 0892
		cd: orfeo C394 101B/C408 955R
		cd: salzburg festival/orfeo SF 001

0154/2 august 1937/salzburg festspielhaus

mozart	**walter**	lp: discocorp
don giovanni	vienna opera	cd: radio years RY 83-85
	chorus	cd: eklipse EKRCD 43
	rethberg	*excerpts*
	helletsgruber	cd: orfeo C394 101B/C408 955R
	bokor	
	borgioli	
	pinza	
	lazzari	
	ettl	
	alsen	

0155/5 august 1937/salzburg festspielhaus

wagner	**toscanini**	lp: toscanini society ATS 1062-1066
meistersinger	vienna opera	lp: mrf records MRF 16
von nürnberg	chorus	lp: MR 2003
	reining	lp: accent ACC 150040
	thorborg	lp: melodram MEL 012
	noort	cd: melodram MEL 47041
	sallaba	cd: eklipse EKRCD 54
	nissen	cd: grammofono AB 78703-78706/
	alsen	AB 78017-78025
	wiedemann	*excerpts*
		lp: historia H 700-701

grammofono incorrectly dated 8 august

0156/11 august 1937/salzburg festspielhaus

mozart	**walter**	lp: discocorp RR 801
le nozze di	vienna opera	cd: arkadia 50004
figaro	chorus	*excerpts*
	rautawaara	cd: orfeo C394 101B/C408 955R
	rethy	
	novotna	
	pinza	
	stabile	

0157/23 august 1937/salzburg festspielhaus

verdi	**toscanini**	lp: penzance records PR 37
falstaff	vienna opera	lp: toscanini society ATS 1067-1069
	chorus	lp: morgan records MOR 3701
	somigli	lp: cetra LO 46
	cravcenko	cd: di stefano GDS 21014
	vasari	cd: minerva MNA 36-37
	oltrabella	cd: arkadia CD 625/CDHP 625
	borgioli	cd: 40s label FTO 321-322
	stabile	cd: grammofono AB 78707-78708/
	biasini	AB 78017-78025
		excerpts
		lp: MR 2003

0158/16 september 1937/staatsoper

verdi	**walter**	cd: koch 3-1457-2
aida	vienna opera	
excerpts	chorus	
	nemeth	
	thorborg	
	mazarolli	
	sved	
	alsen	
	sung in german	

0159/14 october 1937/staatsoper

pfitzner	**walter**	cd: koch 3-1457-2
palestrina	vienna opera	
excerpts	chorus	
	bokor	
	rethy	
	witt	
	wernigk	
	jerger	
	alsen	

0160/18 october 1937/musikvereinssaal/hmv session

brahms	**walter**	78: hmv DB 3394
academic		78: victor 12190
festival		lp: victor CAL 242
overture		cd: avid AMSC 603
		issued on lp in japan by toshiba
j.strauss		78: hmv DB 3397
kaiserwalzer		78: victor M 805
		lp: turnabout THS 65066
		cd: dg 435 3352/459 7342
		cd: dante LYS 358
		cd: preiser 90139
		issued on lp in japan by toshiba

0161/18-20 october 1937/konzerthaus/columbia sessions

beethoven
symphony
no 1
	weingartner	78: columbia LX 677-679/
		   LX 8358-8360 auto
		78: columbia (france) LFX 523-525
		78: columbia (usa) M 321
		lp: columbia (usa) ML 4501/E7L-55/
		   RL 6336-6342
		cd: grammofono AB 78012-78016
		*issued in japan by artisco, toshiba
		and toshiba shinseido*

beethoven egmont overture		78: columbia LX 690 78: columbia (austria) LVX 14 78: columbia (usa) 69195D lp: columbia (usa) ML 4637 *issued in japan by artisco and toshiba shinseido*
beethoven triple concerto	**weingartner** odnoposoff auber morales	78: columbia LX 671-675/ LX 8353-8357 auto 78: columbia (france) LFX 518-522 78: columbia (austria) LVX 27-31 78: columbia (usa) M 327 78: columbia (italy) GQX 10915-10919 78: columbia (aregentina) 266408-266412 lp: columbia (usa) ML 2218 cd: pearl GEMMCD 9358 cd: grammofono AB 78012-78016 *issued in japan by toshiba shinseido*

0162/1 november 1937/staatsoper

wagner parsifal excerpts from acts 1 and 3	**knappertsbusch** vienna opera chorus nikolaidi alsen zec destal	cd: koch 3-1463-2

0163/7 november 1937/staatsoper

verdi	**walter**	cd: koch 3-1454-2
don carlo	vienna opera	*excerpts*
excerpts	chorus	lp: ed smith EJS 334
	reining	lp: teletheater 762.3596-3597
	tutsek	cd: koch 3-1450-2
	mazaroff	
	pierotic	
	alsen	
	sung in german	
	except mazaroff	
	(bulgarian)	

0164/20 november 1937/staatsoper

wagner	**knappertsbusch**	cd: koch 3-1467-2
tannhäuser	vienna opera	cd: radio years RY 98
excerpts	chorus	
	reining	
	a.konetzni	
	lorenz	
	maikl	
	alsen	
	schellenberg	

0165/25 november 1937/staatsoper

wagner	**furtwängler**	cd: koch 3-1470-2
meistersinger	vienna opera	*excerpts*
von nürnberg	chorus	lp: teletheater 762.8691-8692
excerpts	reining	
including	szantho	
overture and	lorenz	
quintet	zimmermann	
	kamann	
	alsen	
	wiedemann	

0166/22-27 december 1937/staatsoper

bizet
carmen
excerpts

walter
vienna opera
chorus
brems
rethy
mazaroff
arnold
pierotic
monthy
sung in german

cd: koch 3-1450-2/3-1456-2

0167/10-15 january 1938/musikvereinssaal/hmv sessions

haydn
symphony
no 100
"military"

walter

78: hmv DB 3421-3423/
　　DB 8445-8447 auto
78: victor M 472
lp: victor CAL 257
lp: turnabout THS 65029
lp: discocorp BWS 1002
lp: emi 1C053 01456M
cd: preiser 90141
cd: grammofono AB 78629
*also private lp edition by preiser
and in japan by toshiba*

mozart
symphony
no 41
"jupiter"

78: hmv DB 3428-3431/
　　DB 8135-8138 auto
78: victor M 253
lp: hmv COLH 37
lp: victor CAL 253
lp: emi 1C147 50178-50180M/MFP 2061
cd: emi CHS 763 9122
cd: palladio PD 4169
cd: grammofono AB 78793
cd: preiser 90141
cd: arkadia 78505
*also private lp edition by preiser
and in japan by toshiba*

mozart
la clemenza
di tito
overture

78: hmv DB 6032
78: victor 12506
lp: rococo 2065
lp: emi 1C147 50178-50180M
cd: emi CHS 763 9122
also on lp in japan by toshiba

0167/concluded

mozart la finta giardiniera overture	**walter**	78: hmv DB 3431/DB 6032/DB 8135 78: victor 12526 lp: rococo 2065 lp: emi 1C147 50178-50180M cd: emi CHS 763 9122 *also on lp in japan by toshiba*
mahler adagietto/ symphony no 5		78: hmv DB 3406 78: victor 12319 lp: emi 1C147 01402-01403M lp: world records SH 193-194 cd: preiser 90114 cd: pearl GEMMCD 9413 cd: dutton CDEA 5014 cd: music and arts CD 749/CD 4749 *also private lp edition by preiser and in japan by toshiba*

0168/15-16 january 1938/musikvereinssaal

mahler symphony no 9	**walter**	78: hmv DB 3613-3622 78: victor M 726 lp: victor LCT 6015 lp: emi 1C147 01402-01403M lp: world records SH 193-194 cd: emi CDH 763 0292 cd: palladio PD 4172-4173 cd: dutton CDEA 5005 *also on lp in japan by toshiba*

0169/18 january 1938/staatsoper

bizet carmen excerpts (ma mère je la vois; la fleur que tu m'avais jetée)	**alwin** rethy kiepura *rethy sings in german, kiepura in french*	cd: koch 3-1460-2

*0170/march 1938/odeon session

mozart	**alwin**	78: parlophone odeon RO 20386
zauberflöte	tauber	cd: nimbus NI 7801
excerpt		cd: preiser 89144
(dies bildnis)		cd: pearl GEMMCD9145/ GEMMCDS 9926

mozart		78: parlophone odeon RO 20386
entführung		cd: preiser 89144
aus dem		cd: pearl GEMMCD 9145
serail		
excerpt		
(o wie		
ängstlich!)		

0171/27 april 1938/staatsoper

salmhofer	**loibner**	cd: koch 3-1463-2
iwan	vienna opera	
sergejewitsch	chorus	
tarassenko	a.konetzni	
excerpts	mazaroff	
	jerger	
	monthy	
	ettl	

0172/20 may 1938/staatsoper

puccini	**loibner**	cd: koch 3-1460-2
gianni	rethy	
schicchi	with	
excerpts	wernigk	
including	godin	
o mio babbino	zec	
caro	ettl	
	sung in german	

0173/20 may 1938/odeon sessions

suppé die schöne galathea overture	**reichwein**	78: odeon 7840 78: parlophone E 11405 cd: schwann 311162
weber der freischütz overture		78: odeon 7842 78: parlophone E 11375
nicolai die lustigen weiber von windsor overture		78: odeon 7874 78: parlophone E 11378
thomas mignon overture		78: odeon 7875 78: parlophone E 11390
adam si j'étais roi overture		78: odeon 7876 78: parlophone E 11399
suppé dichter und bauer overture		78: odeon 7877 78: parlophone E 11381
flotow martha overture		78: odeon 7878 78: parlophone E 11392

0174/24 may 1938/staatsoper

mozart le nozze di figaro excerpts	**loibner** vienna opera chorus reining perras witt schöffler jerger *sung in german*	cd: koch 3-1463-2 *excerpts* cd: koch 3-1450-2

0175/19 june 1938/staatsoper

wagner	**tietjen**	cd: koch 3-1468-2
lohengrin	vienna opera	*excerpts*
excerpts	and berlin	cd: koch 3-1450-2
	staatsoper	*guest performance by soloists of*
	choruses	*berlin staatsoper*
	müller	
	klose	
	völker	
	manowarda	
	prohaska	

0176/23 june 1938/staatsoper

leoncavallo	**loibner**	cd: koch 3-1454-2
i pagliacci	vienna opera	
excerpts	chorus	
(a ventitre	michalski	
ore; ridi	monthy	
pagliaccio!;	mazaroff	
pagliaccio	*sung in german*	
non son!)		

another undated performance of the aria ridi pagliaccio, sung by rosvaenge with an unnamed conductor, can be heard on koch cd 3-1462-2

0177/8 august 1938/salzburg festspielhaus

beethoven	**knappertsbusch**	lp: melodram MEL 711
leonore no 3		cd: preiser 90260/90389
overture		*taken from a performance of the opera*
		fidelio; melodram incorrectly dated 1949

0178/5 september 1938/nürnberg operhaus

wagner	**furtwängler**	lp: ed smith UORC 224
meistersinger	vienna opera	lp: private issue (japan) JP 1143-1144
von nürnberg	and nürnberg	cd: palette (japan) PAL 2007-2008
extended	opera choruses	cd: koch 3-1452-2
fragments	lemnitz	*excerpts*
	berglund	lp: acanta 40.23520
	laholm	cd: acanta 44.1055
	zimmermann	cd: koch 3-1450-2
	bockelmann	cd: grammofono AB 78610
	fuchs	cd: iron needle IN 1364-1365
	manowarda	*this was a guest performance by the vienna staatsoper*

0179/19 september 1938/staatsoper

wagner	**knappertsbusch**	cd: koch 3-1469-2/3-1466-2
die walküre	rünger	
fragments	h.konetzni	
	pölzer	

0180/25 september 1938/staatsoper

wagner	**knappertsbusch**	cd: koch 3-1460-2/3-1466-2
götter-	rünger	
dämmerung	bugarinovic	
excerpts	with	
(norn scene;	rethy	
zu neuen taten)	pölzer	

0181/14 december 1938/staatsoper

schmidt	**loibner**	cd: koch 3-1463-2/3-1450-2
notre dame		
intermezzo		

0182/1 january 1939/staatsoper

weber	**moralt**	cd: koch 3-1463-2
der freischütz	vienna opera	
excerpts	chorus	
including	reining	
overture	rütgers	
and wolf's	pölzer	
glen scene	alsen	
	muzzarelli	
	monthy	
	ettl	

0183/6 january 1939/staatsoper

wagner	**reichwein**	cd: koch 3-1463-2
der fliegende	rode	
holländer	manowarda	
excerpts		
(nirgends		
ein grab;		
sie sei mein		
weib!)		

0184/25 january 1939/reichsrundfunk

weber	**kabasta**	unpublished radio broadcast
oberon		*kaiserwalzer may have been recorded*
overture;		*on another date*
mozart 5 german		
dances;		
j.strauss		
kaiserwalzer		

0185/6 april 1939/staatsoper

wagner	**knappertsbusch**	cd: koch 3-1452-2
parsifal	vienna opera	
excerpts	chorus	
including	a.konetzni	
prelude	grahl	
	alsen	
	wiedemann	

0186/7-8 may 1939/musikvereinssaal/telefunken sessions

bruckner	**jochum**	78: telefunken SK 3000-3007
symphony		lp: capitol P 8067-8068
no 7		cd: dante LYS 007-008
		dante incorectly dated 1935-1936

0187/16 may 1939/staatsoper

verdi	**loibner**	cd: koch 3-1460-2
falstaff	vienna opera	
excerpts	chorus	
	rethy	
	komarek	
	nikolaidi	
	dermota	
	jerger	
	monthy	
	sung in german	

0188/10 june 1939/staatsoper

strauss	**krauss**	cd: koch 3-1465-2
friedenstag	vienna opera	*excerpts*
	chorus	lp: acanta DE 23122-23123
	ursuleac	
	witt	
	dermota	
	hotter	
	alsen	
	wiedemann	

0189/3 august 1939/salzburg festspielhaus

weber	**knappertsbusch**	cd: koch 3-1467-2
der freischütz	vienna opera	cd: gebhardt JGCD 0015-1
excerpts	chorus	*excerpts*
	lemnitz	cd: radio years RY 70
	rütgers	cd: myto HO 11
	völker	
	bohnen	
	bissuti	

0190/13-21 august 1939/salzburg festspielhaus

mozart	**knappertsbusch**	lp: private issue (japan) M 1042
le nozze di	vienna opera	cd: radio years RY 75
figaro	chorus	cd: wing (japan) WCD 15
act 3	reining	
	rethy	
	rohs	
	pinza	
	stabile	

0191/20 october 1939/staatsoper

wagner	**reichwein**	cd: koch 3-1463-2
tannhäuser	schirp	
excerpts		
(ein furchtbares		
verbrechen; gar		
viel und schön)		

0192/23 october 1939/telefunken or odeon session

altnieder-	**lutze**	catalogue number not traced
ländisches		*according to jürgen schmidt this*
dankgebet		*session may also have included*
		recording of blue danube waltz

0193/april 1940/musikvereinssaal/electrola session

schubert	**böhm**	78: electrola DB 5588-5590
symphony		lp: emi 1C137 53032-53036M
no 8		cd: preiser 90922
"unfinished"		cd: dante LYS 407

0194/april 1940/musikvereinssaal/electrola sessions

verdi grand march/ aida	**knappertsbusch**	78: electrola DB 5608 cd: preiser 90116 cd: toshiba shinseido SGR 8228 cd: grammofono AB 78522
wagner rienzi overture		78: electrola DB 5607-5608 cd: preiser 90116 cd: toshiba shinseido SGR 8228 cd: archiphon ARC 110-111 cd: grammofono AB 78522/AB 78678
ziehrer weana mad'ln waltz		78: electrola EH 1299 lp: private issue (usa) P 1008 cd: preiser 90116 cd: toshiba shinseido SGR 8228

0195/12 may 1940/reichsrundfunk

wagner siegfried's rhine journey/ götter- dämmerung	**knappertsbusch**	cd: tahra TAH 309
mozart eine kleine nachtmusik		cd: tahra TAH 320-322

0196/may 1940/musikvereinssaal/electrola sessions

lehar die lustige witwe overture	**lehar**	78: electrola DB 5579 lp: emi 1C147 30639-30640M cd: emi CDC 754 8382/CDH 764 2992/ CHS 764 2942 cd: preiser 90150 cd: bel age BLA 103352
lehar musikalische memoiren rhapsody		78: electrola EH 1300-1301 lp: emi 1C147 30639-30640M cd: preiser 90150 cd: bel age BLA 103353
lehar paganini excerpt (liebe, du himmel auf erden!)	**lehar** rethy	78: electrola DA 4481 78: elite 21007 lp: emi 1C147 30639-30640M cd: emi CDC 754 8382 cd: preiser 90150 cd: bel age BLA 103351
lehar giuditta excerpt (meine lippen sie küssen so heiss)		78: electrola DA 4481 cd: preiser 90150 cd: toshiba shinseido SGR 8244

0197/17 october 1940/staatsoper

wagner der fliegende holländer excerpts including wie aus der ferne	**moralt** vienna opera chorus braun hotter manowarda	cd: koch 3-1472-2 *excerpts* cd: koch 3-1450-2

0198/5 november 1940/musikvereinssaal

beethoven missa solemnis	**krauss** vienna opera concert chorus eipperle willer patzak hann	cd: melodram CDM 28036 cd: dg 435 3212/435 3292 cd: grammofono AB 78846-78847

0199/7-8 november 1940/reichsrundfunk

jurek deutschmeister-regimentsmarsch;
josef strauss delirienwalzer;
j.strauss radetzky march;
an der schönen blauen donau;
cagliostro in wien overture;
g'schichten aus dem wienerwald;
wiener bonbons
        wacek
        unpublished radio broadcast

0200/21-22 december 1940/musikvereinssaal

bach brandenburg concerto no 5	**furtwängler** schneiderhan niedermayer furtwängler	lp: french furtwängler society SWF 8401-8402 lp: refrain (japan) AT 13-14

0201/12-14 january 1941/musikvereinssaal/telefunken sessions

j.strauss   **krauss**   78: telefunken SK 3187
rosen aus   lp: capitol P 8061
dem süden   cd: preiser 90291
waltz   cd: wing (japan) WCD 8
                                   cd: radio years RY 57
                                   cd: biddulph WHL 001
                                   cd: arlecchino ARL 83-85
                                   cd: teldec 3984 284112

strauss   78: telefunken SK 3139-3140
till eulenspiegels   lp: telefunken LGX 66032
lustige streiche   lp: capitol LGX 66032
                                   cd: preiser 90291
                                   cd: teldec 3984 284092

j.strauss   78: telefunken SK 3150
an der schönen   lp: capitol P 8061
blauen donau   cd: preiser 90291
waltz   cd: wing (japan) WCD 8
                                   cd: radio years RY 57
                                   cd: biddulph WHL 001
                                   cd: arlecchino ARL 83-85

j.strauss   78: telefunken SK 3241
ägyptischer   cd: preiser 90258
marsch   cd: radio years RY 57
                                   cd: biddulph WHL 001
                                   cd: arlecchino ARL 83-85
                                   cd: teldec 3984 284112

josef strauss   78: telefunken SK 3241
feuerfest   cd: preiser 90258
polka   cd: radio years RY 57
                                   cd: biddulph WHL 001
                                   cd: arlecchino ARL 83-85

0202/7 february 1941/staatsoper

borodin   **ludwig**   cd: koch 3-1471-2
prince igor   vienna opera   *excerpts*
excerpts   chorus   cd: koch 3-1450-2
                     braun
                     ilitsch
                     nikolaidi
                     dermota
                     schöffler
                     jerger
                     alsen
                     sung in german

0203/15 march 1941/reichsrundfunk

weber   **krauss**   unpublished radio broadcast in
abu hassan   clemens-krauss-archiv
overture

0204/18 march 1941/musikvereinssaal/telefunken sessions

j.strauss   **krauss**   78: telefunken SK 3161
die fledermaus   cd: preiser 90291
overture   cd: teldec 3894 284112

falla   78: telefunken SK 3329-3330
3 dances/   lp: telefunken LGM 65022
el sombrero   lp: capitol L 8096
de 3 picos   cd: preiser 90291

strauss   78: telefunken SK 3199
dance of the   78: capitol 89-81052
7 veils/   lp: capitol L 8096
salome   cd: preiser 90291
                                         excerpts
                                         cd: teldec 3894 269192

0205/20 march 1941/musikvereinssaal/telefunken session

mozart   **moralt**   78: telefunken E 3162
zauberflöte   dermota
excerpt
(dies bildnis)

mozart   **moralt**   78: telefunken E 3162
don giovanni   dermota
excerpt   *sung in german*
(dalla sua pace)

verdi   **moralt**   78: telefunken E 3189
rigoletto   öggl
excerpt   *sung in german*
(pari siamo);
la traviata
excerpt
(di provenza)

0206/2 june 1941/staatsoper

puccini moralt cd: koch 3-1454-2
turandot vienna opera
excerpts chorus
(l'egnimi sono nemeth
tre; nessun mazaroff
dorma) *sung in german*

0207/5-10 june 1941/staatsoper

verdi gui cd: koch 3-1458-2
aida vienna opera
excerpts chorus
  ilitsch
  nikolaidi
  svanholm
  hotter
  manowarda
  sung in german

0208/16 june 1941/staatsoper

wagner knappertsbusch lp: ed smith EJS 451
die walküre h.konetzni cd: koch 3-1469-2/3-1450-2
excerpts svanholm

0209/18 june 1941/staatsoper

weber knappertsbusch cd: koch 3-1469-2
der freischütz vienna opera
excerpt chorus
(o diese svanholm
sonne!) normann
  rus

0210/21 june 1941/staatsoper

wagner knappertsbusch cd: koch 3-1474-2
siegfried bugarinovic
excerpts kern
including svanholm
forest schöffler
murmurs

0211/27 june 1941/staatsoper

wagner götter- dämmerung fragments	**knappertsbusch** vienna opera chorus rütgers schürhoff bugarinovic svanholm alsen	cd: koch 3-1469-2

0212/2 august 1941/salzburg festspielhaus

mozart zauberflöte	**böhm** vienna opera chorus reining piltti anders weber böhme poell	cd: myto MCD 981.010

0213/18 august 1941/salzburg festspielhaus

mozart don giovanni	**knappertsbusch** vienna opera chorus h.konetzni braun rütgers dermota schöffler alsen krenn *sung in german*	unpublished radio broadcast

0214/19 september 1941/musikvereinssaal/telefunken session

j.strauss frühlings- stimmen waltz	**krauss**	78: telefunken SK 3160/E 1075/E 3861 lp: capitol P 8061 cd: preiser 90291 cd: wing (japan) WCD 8 cd: radio years RY 57 cd: biddulph WHL 001 cd: arlecchino ARL 83-85

0215/21 september 1941/reichsrundfunk

mozart symphony no 25	**kabasta**	unpublished radio broadcast
mozart concertone for 2 violins and orchestra	**kabasta** boskovsky barylli	unpublished radio broadcast

0216/8 october 1941/musikvereinssaal/reichsrundfunk

mozart symphony no 40	**krauss**	unpublished radio broadcast in clemens-krauss-archiv

0217/12 october 1941/staatsoper

wagner siegfried excerpts	**knappertsbusch** bugarinovic sattler wernigk hotter	cd: koch 3-1472-2

0218/16 october 1941/staatsoper

strauss ariadne auf naxos excerpts	**moralt** a.konetzni kern schulz svanholm jerger	cd: koch 3-1465-2 *excerpts* cd: preiser 89987

0219/17 october 1941/musikvereinssaal/reichsrundfunk

granados 3 dances	**krauss**	unpublished radio broadcast in clemens-krauss-archiv

0220/25 october-4 november 1941/staatsoper

verdi	**krauss**	cd: koch 3-1458-2
falstaff	vienna opera	
excerpts	chorus	
	rethy	
	kern	
	bugarinovic	
	nikolaidi	
	dermota	
	hann	
	kronenberg	
	sung in german	

0221/7 november 1941/redoutensaal

mozart	**böhm**	cd: koch 3-1460-2
le nozze di	reining	
figaro	cebotari	
fragments	rohs	
	ahlersmayer	
	sung in german	

0222/9 november 1941/reichsrundfunk

mozart	**knappertsbusch**	lp: hans-knappertsbusch-gesellschaft
symphony		(japan) HK 1006-1007/HKV 3
no 40		cd: music and arts CD 897
		cd: preiser 90951
mozart		cd: music and arts CD 897
symphony		cd: preiser 90951
no 41		
"jupiter"		

0223/21 november 1941/staatsoper

strauss	**knappertsbusch**	cd: koch 3-1466-2
elektra	vienna opera	
excerpts	chorus	
	rünger	
	h.konetzni	

0224/3 december 1941/staatsoper

mozart	**strauss**	cd: koch 3-1453-2
idomeneo	vienna opera	
arranged	chorus	
by strauss	böttcher	
excerpts	a.konetzni	
from act 2	rethy	
	sabel	
	kunz	
	sung in german	

0225/4 december 1941/staatsoper

mozart	**knappertsbusch**	cd: koch 3-1467-2
zauberflöte	vienna opera	*excerpts*
excerpts	chorus	cd: koch 3-1450-2
including	reining	
o isis und	berger	
osiris;	manowarda	
ach ich fühl's		

0226/25 december 1941/staatsoper

wagner	**furtwängler**	cd: koch 3-1456-2/3-1461-2
tristan und	a.konetzni	*excerpts*
isolde	klose	lp: ed smith EJS 399/UORC 267
excerpts	lorenz	lp: acanta HB 22.863
from act 2	monthy	cd: radio years RY 76

0227/1941/musikvereinssaal/reichsrundfunk
the recordings in this section could not be dated precisely

j.strauss indigo und die 40 räuber overture; vergnügungszug polka; klangfiguren waltz	**krauss**	unpublished radio broadcasts in clemens-krauss-archiv
mozart symphony no 41 "jupiter"		cd: refrain (japan) DR 92 0041 *incorrectly dated 1948*
smetana bartered bride overture		lp: melodiya M10 46981 001

0228/7 january 1942/staatsoper

beethoven fidelio excerpts (ha welch ein augenblick!; gott welch dunkel hier!)	**furtwängler** lorenz hotter	lp: ed smith UORC 242 *ha welch ein augenblick only; gott welch* *dunkel hier remains unpublished, as do* *certain other excerpts recently reported by* *johann gratz to have been traced*

0229/21 january 1942/musikvereinssaal/electrola sessions

wagner lohengrin excerpt (in fernem land)	**moralt** rosvaenge	78: electrola DB 5698 lp: preiser LV 43/LV 518 lp: emi RLS 7711/1C137 54390-54396M cd: grammofono AB 78668-78669
wagner lohengrin excerpt (mein lieber schwan)		78: electrola DB 5698 lp: electrola E 83382 lp: preiser LV 43/LV 518 lp: emi RLS 7711/EX 29 02123/ 1C137 54390-54396M cd: emi CMS 764 0082 cd: grammofono AB 78668-78669
puccini tosca excerpt (recondita armonia)	**moralt** rosvaenge *sung in german*	78: electrola DA 4504 lp: preiser LV 43/LV 520 cd: preiser 89018/90328 cd: cantus classics CACD 500024
puccini tosca excerpt (e lucevan le stelle)		78: electrola DA 4504 lp: preiser LV 43/LV 520 lp: emi 1C147 29240-29241M cd: preiser 89018/90328
donizetti l'elisir d'amore excerpt (una furtiva lagrima); verdi rigoletto excerpt (parmi veder)		electrola unpublished

0230/24 january 1942/musikvereinssaal/electrola session

wagner rienzi excerpts (erstehe hohe roma neu!; allmächtiger vater!)	**moralt** lorenz	lp: electrola E 60591 lp: emi 1C147 29154-29155M cd: preiser 89232 *unpublished electrola 78rpm recordings*
wagner tannhäuser excerpt (o fürstin!)	**moralt** reining lorenz	78: electrola DB 7624 lp: electrola E 60591 lp: emi 1C147 29154-29155M/ 　　EX 29 02123 lp: preiser LV 1315/LV 1333 cd: emi CMS 764 0082 cd: preiser 89065/89401/90213 *also a private lp edition by preiser*
wagner tannhäuser excerpt (allmächt'ge jungfrau!)	**moralt** reining	electrola unpublished

electrola sessions held in vienna on 26 january 1942, in which franz lehar conducted his own works with the soloists reining and rethy and which some re-issues described as being accompanied by wiener philharmoniker, did in fact use the wiener symphoniker as orchestra

0231/29-31 january 1942/musikvereinssaal/electrola sessions

mozart   **jerger**   78: electrola DA 4503
3 german
dances k605

jerger   78: electrola EH 1325
salzburger
hof- und
barockmusik

schubert   electrola unpublished
rosamunde
2 entr'actes

paganini   78: electrola EH 1324
moto perpetuo
arrangement;
handel
sixth movement
from concerto
op 3 no 5

tchaikovsky   78: electrola DB 7678-7680
serenade
for strings

jerger   electrola unpublished
partita

mozart   electrola unpublished
les petits riens
ballet music

mozart   **jerger**   electrola unpublished
clarinet   wlach
concerto

0232/31 january 1942/musikvereinssaal/electrola sessions

wagner tannhäuser excerpt (inbrunst im herzen)	**knappertsbusch** lorenz	78: electrola DB 7602 lp: electrola E 60591 lp: emi 1C147 29154-29155M cd: preiser 89232/90116 cd: toshiba shinseido SGR 8228
wagner siegfried's rhine journey/ götter- dämmerung	**knappertsbusch**	78: electrola DB 5699 cd: preiser 90116 cd: toshiba shinseido SGR 8228 cd: grammofono AB 78522/AB 78678
wagner siegfried's funeral march/ götter- dämmerung		cd: preiser 90116 cd: grammofono AB 78522/AB 78678 *unpublished electrola 78rpm recording*
komzak badner mad'ln waltz		78: electrola DB 7710 *orchestra on this issue may have been* *described as berlin philharmonic*
j.strauss leichtes blut polka		78: electrola DA 4487 lp: emi 1C147 30226-30227M cd: emi CDH 764 2992/CHS 764 2942 cd: dg 435 3352/459 7342 cd: preiser 90116/90090 cd: toshiba shinseido SGR 8228
johann and josef strauss pizzicato polka		78: electrola DA 4487 cd: emi CDH 764 2992/CHS 764 2942 cd: preiser 90116 cd: toshiba shinseido SGR 8228

0233/4-27 february 1942/staatsoper

orff
carmina
burana
excerpts

ludwig
vienna opera
chorus
rethy
michalski
schobe
söderquist
pichler
kronenberg
kunz

cd: koch 3-1471-2

0234/15 february 1942/staatsoper

strauss
salome
excerpts

strauss
schulz
schürhoff
witt
dermota
schöffler

lp: ed smith EJS 463
cd: koch 3-1453-2

0235/4 april 1942/staatsoper

wagner
parsifal
excerpts

reichwein
vienna opera
chorus
braun
lorenz
schöffler
vogel
roth

cd: koch 3-1456-2

0236/20-22 april 1942/kristall sessions

weber
der freischütz
overture,
ballet and
entr'acte

pfitzner

78: catalogue number unknown

0237/3 may 1942/staatsoper

egk
columbus
excerpts

ludwig
vienna opera
chorus
rethy
witt
kunz
schöffler

cd: koch 3-1471-2

0238/5 may 1942/staatsoper

pfitzner
palestrina
excerpta
from act 1
including
allein in
dunkler tiefe

moralt
schürhoff
witt
dermota
hotter

cd: koch 3-1471-2

0239/6 may 1942/staatsoper

strauss
salome
excerpts

strauss
schulz
bugarinovic
sattler
dermota
hotter

lp: ed smith EJS 463
cd: koch 3-1453-2

0240/8 may 1942/staatsoper

strauss
daphne
excerpts
including
closing scene

moralt
vienna opera
chorus
reining
dermota
rauch

cd: koch 3-1455-2

0241/9 may 1942/staatsoper

egk	**egk**	cd: koch 3-1471-2
joan von	vienna opera	
zarissa	chorus	
excerpts from		
the ballet		

0242/31 may 1942/staatsoper

wagner	**moralt**	cd: koch 3-1472-2
die walküre	braun	
excerpts	hotter	
from act 3		

excerpts from act 1 of an undated performance of the opera, conducted by martin and with h.konetzni and lorenz, can be heard on koch cd 3-1469-2

0243/7 june 1942/musikvereinssaal

haydn	**krauss**	lp: haydn society HSLP 2027
die jahreszeiten	vienna opera	lp: odeon ODX 111-113
	chorus	lp: parlophone PMA 1018-1020
	eipperle	cd: preiser 93053
	patzak	*parlophone edition was not published*
	hann	

0244/12-17 june 1942/kristall sessions

liszt	**weisbach**	78: catalogue number unknown
les préludes		
beethoven		78: catalogue number unknown
fidelio		
overture		
haydn		78: imperial 014.066-014.068
symphony		cd: schwann 311.162
no 104		*schwann incorrectly dated 1938*
"london"		

0244/concluded

mozart   **schüler**   78: imperial 014.071-014.073
symphony   78: pathé PDT 73-75
no 35
"haffner"

bizet   78: imperial 014.074
carmen
preludes
acts 1, 2
and 3

rossini   78: catalogue number unknown
la scala di seta
overture

mozart   78: imperial 014.073
der schauspiel-   78: pathé PDT 75
direktor
overture

weber   78: imperial 014.063
aufforderung
zum tanz

mozart   78: imperial 014.059-014.061
symphony
no 36
"linz"

haydn   78: imperial 014.054-014.056
symphony
no 100
"military"

0245/22 july 1942/musikvereinssaal/electrola session

mozart **moralt** electrola unpublished
entführung rosvaenge
aus dem
serail
excerpts
(o wie ängstlich!;
wenn der freude
tränen fliessen)

mozart **moralt** electrola unpublished
don giovanni rosvaenge
excerpts *sung in german*
(dalla sua pace;
il mio tesoro)

0246/5 august 1942/salzburg festspielhaus

mozart **krauss** cd: preiser 90203
le nozze di vienna opera cd: grammofono AB 78665-78667
figaro chorus *excerpts*
 braun cd: koch 3-1472-2
 beilke cd: orfeo C394 101B/C408 955R
 sommerschuh
 kunz
 hotter
 sung in german

0247/9 august 1942/salzburg festspielhaus

strauss **krauss** cd: myto MCD 92154
arabella vienna opera
 chorus
 ursuleac
 eipperle
 willer
 taubmann
 reinmar
 herrmann

0247a/13 august 1942/salzburg festspielhaus

weber **mengelberg** cd: tahra TAH 310
euryanthe
overture

0247b/16 august 1942/salzburg mozarteum

beethoven egmont overture	**mengelberg**	cd: tahra TAH 310

0248/27 august 1942/salzburg festspielhaus

respighi i pini di roma	**krauss**	lp: melodiya M10 46981 001 *a choral work by palestrina was also recorded at this concert but was probably performed by vienna opera chorus without orchestral accompaniment*

0249/10 september 1942/staatsoper

wagner götter- dämmerung excerpts including immolation scene	**reichwein** braun söderquist lorenz schöffler manowarda	cd: koch 3-1456-2/3-1472-2

0250/17-18 september 1942/musikvereinssaal/electrola sessions

brahms symphony no 2	**böhm**	78: electrola DB 7693-7698 cd: preiser 90922 cd: dante LYS 405

0251/22 september 1942/staatsoper

verdi aida excerpts including celeste aida; o patria mia; o terra addio!	**ludwig** vienna opera chorus ilitsch nikolaidi lorenz alsen ahlersmayer *sung in german*	cd: koch 3-1456-2 *excerpts* cd: koch 3-1450-2

0252/22-27 september 1942/musikvereinssaal/electrola sessions

wagner	**moralt**	78: electrola DB 7675-7676
die walküre	herrmann	lp: preiser LV 49
excerpt		cd: preiser 89076
(wotans abschied		
und feuerzauber)		

wagner		78: electrola DB 7645
der fliegende		lp: preiser LV 49
holländer		cd: preiser 89076
excerpt		
(die frist ist um)		

wagner	**moralt**	electrola unpublished
das rheingold	düren	*zur burg führt die brücke*
excerpt	michalsky	cd: preiser 89076
(closing scene)	schürhoff	
	witt	
	herrmann	
	monthy	

0253/27 september 1942/staatsoper

verdi	**böhm**	cd: koch 3-1458-2
un ballo in	vienna opera	*excerpts*
maschera	chorus	cd: koch 3-1450-2
excerpts	h.konetzni	*premiere performance of a new*
	noni	*production*
	nikolaidi	
	lorenz	
	ahlersmayer	
	sung in german	

0254/28 september 1942/staatsoper

wagner	**reichwein**	cd: koch 3-1469-2
der fliegende	nemeth	
holländer	svanholm	
fragments	berglund	
including		
wie aus der		
ferne		

0255/9 october 1942/reichsrundfunk

pergolesi	**moralt**	unpublished radio broadcast
la serva	kern	
padrona	pernerstorfer	
	sung in german	

0256/11 october 1942/staatsoper

wagner	**reichwein**	cd: koch 3-1469-2
tannhäuser	vienna opera	
excerpt	chorus	
(inbrunst im	tutsek	
herzen..to	svanholm	
end of opera)	poell	

excerpts from act 3 of an undated performance of tannhäuser, conducted by heger and with rünger, kalenberg and bockelmann, can be heard on koch cd 3-1451-2

0257/13 october 1942/musikvereinssaal/reichsrundfunk

smetana	**moralt**	lp: melodiya M10 46955 001
the bartered	vienna opera	cd: koch 3-1457-2
bride	chorus	*excerpts*
excerpts	rethy	cd: melodram CDM 26522
	nikolaidi	*this was a concert performance of the*
	dermota	*opera*
	pernerstorfer	
	sung in german	

0258/18-20 october 1942/musikvereinssaal/electrola sessions

mozart don giovanni overture; bizet carmen preludes acts 3 and 4	**böhm**	electrola unpublished
mozart symphony no 40; sinfonia concertante for wind	**fischer**	electrola unpublished

at the time of going to press tahra announces cd release of a wartime performance of mozart symphony no 40 conducted by böhm: it is not yet known if this is a newly-discovered version or the one from the above sessions actually directed by fischer

0259/20-24 october 1942/musikvereinssaal/electrola sessions

lully minuet and gavotte	**jerger**	electrola unpublished
mozart symphony no 8 k4b		electrola unpublished

0260/28 october 1942/staatsoper

puccini tosca excerpts (tosca e un buon falco; gia mi dicon venal!)	**reichwein** nemeth s.björling ettl *sung in german*	cd: koch 3-1454-2

0261/28 october 1942/musikvereinssaal/electrola sessions

mozart symphony no 35 "haffner"	**böhm**	78: electrola DB 7649-7651 cd: preiser 90922 cd: magic talent CD 48054
bach air/suite no 3		78: electrola DB 7651 cd: preiser 90922
mozart le nozze di figaro unspecified aria	**böhm** reining *sung in german*	electrola unpublished
haydn piano concerto in d	**fischer** conductor and soloist	78: electrola DB 7657-7658 lp: discocorp MLG 74 lp: emi EX 29 909913/137 2909913 cd: piano time (italy) PTC 2003 cd: appian APR 5525

0262/29 october 1942/staatsoper

gluck iphigenie in aulis fragments	**ludwig** vienna opera chorus h.konetzni braun svanholm schöffler	cd: koch 3-1469-2

0263/10 november 1942/staatsoper

wagner parsifal excerpts	**knappertsbusch** vienna opera chorus braun lorenz hotter	cd: koch 3-1472-2/3-1456-2

0264/21 november-4 december 1942/staatsoper

smetana	**ludwig**	cd: koch 3-1469-2
dalibor	vienna opera	
fragments	chorus	
	h.konetzni	
	rethy	
	mazaroff	
	jerger	
	franter	
	sung in german	

0265/november 1942/musikvereinssaal/electrola sessions

strauss	**moralt**	lp: preiser LV 1315
lieder:	reining	cd: preiser 89065
cäcilie;		*unpublished electrola 78rpm recordings*
meinem kinde;		
morgen;		
wiegenlied		

d'albert		lp: electrola E 60632
die toten		lp: preiser LV 1315
augen		cd: preiser 89065
excerpt		*unpublished electrola 78rpm recording*
(psyche wandelt)		

giordano	**moralt**	78: electrola DB 7648
andrea	reining	lp: electrola E 60632
chenier	*sung in german*	lp: preiser LV 1315
excerpt		cd: preiser 89065
(la mamma morta);		
puccini		
la bohème		
excerpt		
(si mi chiamano		
mimi)		

puccini	lp: preiser LV 1315
madama	cd: preiser 89065
butterfly	*unpublished electrola 78rpm recordings*
excerpt	
(che tua madre);	
manon lescaut	
excerpt	
(in quelle trine	
morbide)	

mozart arias recorded by reining and originally issued by electrola on DB 7665 and DA 4508 with attribution vpo/moralt were in fact recorded by this singer with berlin staatskapelle conducted by hans-udo müller

0266/2 january 1943/staatsoper

wagner	**furtwängler**	cd: koch 3-1461-2
tristan und	vienna opera	*excerpts*
isolde	chorus	lp: ed smith UORC 267
	a.konetzni	*recordings of acts 1 and 2 are*
	klose	*incomplete*
	lorenz	
	franter	
	monthy	
	schöffler	

0267/28 january 1943/staatsoper

wagner	**böhm**	cd: koch 3-1473-2
meistersinger	vienna opera	
von nürnberg	chorus	
excerpts	reining	
from acts	rohs	
2 and 3	lorenz	
including	klein	
guten abend	herrmann	
meister	kunz	
and quintet		

0268/31 january 1943/staatsoper

wagner	**böhm**	cd: koch 3-1469-2
meistersinger	vienna opera	
von nürnberg	chorus	
excerpts	reining	
including	rohs	
quintet	svanholm	
	klein	
	schöffler	
	böhme	
	kunz	

0269/16 march 1943/staatsoper

leoncavallo   **paulik**   cd: koch 3-1472-2
i pagliacci   hotter
excerpt   *sung in german*
(si puo!)

0270/28 march 1943/musikvereinssaal/reichsrundfunk

haydn   **krauss**   lp: nixa HLP 2005
die schöpfung   vienna opera   lp: haydn society HSLP 2005
     chorus   lp: saga 6213-6214
     eipperle   lp: erato LDE 3005-3006/
     patzak   ERM 160062
     hann
          lp: rrg 83917
          lp: victor (japan) ZL 30927
          cd: preiser 90104
          some issues incorrectly dated 1944;
          according to hc robbins landon the
          sections with adam and eve were
          recorded after the war under the
          conductor erwin baltzer with
          different soloists

0271/23 may 1943/stockholm konserthus

schubert symphony no 8 "unfinished", first movement	**furtwängler**	lp: french furtwängler society SWF 8403-8404 lp: tanaka (japan) AT 05-06 cd: dante LYS 109 cd: french furtwängler society SWF 973 cd: music and arts CD 802 *also issued in japan by seven seas*
schubert symphony no 9 "great"		lp: discocorp RR 405 lp: private issue (japan) JP 1190-1192 lp: french furtwängler society SWF 8403-8404 lp: nippon columbia OZ 7589 cd: french furtwängler society SWF 973 cd: dante LYS 109 cd: history 20.3090/20.3090 cd: music and arts CD 802 cd: tahra FURT 1040 *also issued in japan by seven seas*
j.strauss kaiserwalzer		lp: french furtwängler society SWF 8403-8404 cd: french furtwängler society SWF 973 cd: music and arts CD 802 *recording incomplete*

0272/31 may-1 june 1943/musikvereinssaal/reichsrundfunk

verdi macbeth	**böhm** vienna opera chorus höngen witt ahlersmayer alsen *sung in german*	lp: urania URLP 220 lp: acanta DE 23277-23278 cd: preiser 90175 *excerpts* lp: acanta KB 21488/72.221792/ 10.223205 cd: myto *these were concert performances of the opera*

0273/4-5 june 1943/musikvereinssaal/reichsrundfunk

bruckner	**böhm**	lp: vox PL 7192/PL 7190/VSPS 5
symphony		lp: discocorp IGI 365
no 7		lp: intercord INT 155.801
		cd: preiser 90192
		cd: grammofono AB 78812-78813
		cd: tahra TAH 335-336
		grammofono incorrectly dated 1949

0274/30 june 1943/staatsoper

wagner	**knappertsbusch**	cd: koch 3-1467-2
götter-	a.konetzni	cd: radio years RY 98
dämmerung	söderquist	
excerpts	svanholm	
including	alsen	
zu neuen taten		

0275/11 august 1943/salzburg mozarteum

strauss	**böhm**	cd: orfeo C376 941B
horn	freiberg	*incorrectly dated 1944*
concerto		
no 2		

0276/21 september 1943/staatsoper

schmidt	**moralt**	cd: koch 3-1457-2
notre dame	vienna opera	
excerpts	chorus	
	schulz	
	friedrich	
	witt	
	alsen	
	jerger	

0277/16 november 1943/staatsoper

strauss	**böhm**	unpublished metal foil discs
die frau ohne	schulz	*these fragments were taken down at the*
schatten	h.konetzni	*final dress rehearsal of a new production*
fragments	ralf	*of the opera*

0278/23 november 1943/staatsoper

strauss	**böhm**	cd: koch 3-1455-2
die frau ohne	vienna opera	*excerpts*
schatten	chorus	lp: ed smith UORC 345
extended	schulz	cd: koch 3-1450-2
excerpts	höngen	
	ralf	
	alsen	
	herrmann	

0278a/25 november 1943/staatsoper

verdi	**böhm**	cd: myto MCD 92260
otello	lorenz	cd: preiser 90230
excerpts	*sung in german*	
(dio mi potevi!;		
niun mi tema)		

0279/1 december 1943/staatsoper

wagner	**knappertsbusch**	cd: koch 3-1474-2
die walküre	braun	
excerpts	h.konetzni	
including	lorenz	
leb wohl, du	hotter	
kühnes		
herrliches kind!		

0280/18-23 december 1943/musikvereinssaal/electrola sessions

beethoven symphony no 6 "pastoral"	**furtwängler**	lp: turnabout TV 4408 lp: nippon columbia DXM 131 lp: vox (japan) H 5060 lp: emi ED 29 06661 cd: music and arts CD 954 cd: dante LYS 074 cd: preiser 90199 *unpublished electrola 78rpm recording;* *emi edition contains first movement* *repeat which was not sanctioned by* *the conductor*
brahms haydn variations		lp: french furtwängler society SWF 7602 lp: discocorp RR 456 lp: emi ED 29 06661 cd: music and arts CD 804/CD 954 cd: dante LYS 046/LYS 047 cd: preiser 90199 cd: tahra FURT 1012-1013 *unpublished electrola 78rpm recording;* *SWF 7602 and FURT 1012-1013 contain* *additional rejected 78rpm takes; CD 804* *incorrectly described as a recording by* *berlin philharmonic orchestra*

0281/19 january 1944/staatsoper

wagner meistersinger von nürnberg excerpts	**böhm** vienna opera chorus reining rohs ralf klein herrmann böhme kunz	cd: koch 3-1468-2

0282/7-9 february 1944/konzerthaus/reichsrundfunk

beethoven	**böhm**	lp: acanta DE 23116-23117
fidelio	vienna opera	cd: preiser 90195
	chorus	cd: grammofono AB 78807-78809
	h.konetzni	*excerpts*
	seefried	lp: vox OPL 370/SOPL 370
	ralf	lp: eterna 820 933
	klein	lp: emi EX 769 7411
	schöffler	cd: emi CHS 769 7412
	alsen	cd: preiser 90325

excerpts also on private lp edition by preiser; these were concert performances which followed a performance in the staatsoper on 6 february

0283/17 february 1944/funkhaus/reichsrundfunk

wagner	**böhm**	cd: dg 435 3212/435 3332
meistersinger		*incorrectly described by dg as a*
von nürnberg		*performance conducted by strauss:*
overture		*böhm conducted this opening work in a concert otherwise directed by strauss (information from gottfried kraus); an alternative suggestion that overture is taken from one of böhm's contemporaneous staatsoper performances of the opera cannot be entertained, as the concert ending of the work is used here*
strauss	**strauss**	lp: vox PL 7220/TV 4363
sinfonia		lp: intercord INT 120.929
domestica		cd: dg 435 3212/435 3332
		cd: preiser 90216
		cd: dante LYS 291

0284/1 march 1944/staatsoper

strauss			**böhm**			cd: koch 3-1471-2
capriccio		cebotari		*excerpts*
excerpts		noni			lp: acanta DE 23280-23281
			rohs			*first performance of the opera in vienna*
			dermota
			wenkoff
			jerger
			kunz
			schöffler

0285/28-29 march 1944/musikvereinssaal/reichsrundfunk

mozart			**böhm**			unpublished radio broadcast
violin			schneiderhan
concerto
no 3

mozart			**böhm**			45: vox VIP 5250
eine kleine					lp: vox PL 7760/PL 12230
nachtmusik					cd: orfeo C376 941B
						cd: magic talent CD 48054
						cd: wing (japan) WCD 9
						WCD 9 incorrectly dated 1952

mozart						lp: vox PL 7760/PL 12230
symphony					cd: orfeo C376 941B
no 41						cd: magic talent CD 48054
"jupiter"

the recordings in these sessions may alternatively have been the basis for electrola recording sessions but remained unpublished in that form

0286/12 april 1944/musikvereinssaal/reichsrundfunk

beethoven		**böhm**			cd: refrain (japan) MADR 206
piano			ney
concerto
no 3

0287/24 april 1944/musikvereinssaal/reichsrundfunk

j.strauss   **böhm**   45: urania UREP 60
die fledermaus   lp: urania URLP 7021/URLP 7096/
overture   URLP 7155
                                   cd: wing (japan) WCD 9

j.strauss   lp: vox VX 510
rosen aus
dem süden;
wiener blut
waltzes

0288/15-17 may 1944/musikvereinssaal/reichsrundfunk

strauss   **böhm**   cd: preiser 90237
daphne   vienna opera   *these were concert performances which*
                   chorus   *preceded a staatsoper performance on*
                   reining   *18 may*
                   loose
                   frutschnigg
                   friedrich
                   dermota
                   alsen

0289/2-3 june 1944/musikvereinssaal/reichsrundfunk

mozart symphony no 40	**furtwängler**	cd: music and arts CD 258 cd: as-disc AS 112 cd: history 20.3090/20.3091 cd: tahra FURT 1014-1015 *CD 258 and AS 112 incorrectly dated february 1949*
beethoven leonore no 3 overture		lp: french furtwängler society SWF 7101 lp: private issue (japan) JP 1190-1192 lp: discocorp RR 460 lp: nippon columbia OZ 7512 cd: rodolphe RPC 32522-32524 cd: dg 435 3242/435 3212 cd: french furtwängler society SWF 901 cd: dante LYS 063 cd: history 20.3090/20.3095 cd: preiser 90251 cd: music and arts CD 942/CD 4049 *many editions were incorrectly dated 2 may 1944 or 28 january 1945*
schubert rosamunde entr'acte no 3		cd: tahra FURT 1014-1015

0290/11 june 1944/staatsoper

strauss
ariadne auf
naxos
	böhm
	vienna opera
	chorus
	reining
	seefried
	noni
	lorenz
	witt
	schöffler
	kunz
	muzzarelli
		lp: dg LPM 18 850-18 852
		lp: discocorp IGI 378
		lp: acanta DE 23309-23310
		cd: preiser 90217
		cd: koch 3-1473-2
		cd: arlecchino ARL 14-16
		excerpts
		lp: dg LPEM 19 477/SLPEM 136 477/
		    2535 746/88 017
		lp: acanta DE 23280-23281/
		    22.221229
		lp: melodram MEL 084
		cd: dg 459 0072/459 0662
		cd: rca/bmg 74321 694272/74321 694782
		*this was a special performance to celebrate the
		composer's 80 th birthday*

0291/12-17 june 1944/funkhaus/reichsrundfunk
series of broadcasts to mark the composer's 80 th birthday

strauss der bürger als edelmann suite	**strauss**	lp: discocorp SID 710 lp: vanguard SRV 325 lp: eterna 826 205 cd: preiser 90216
strauss don juan		lp: discocorp SID 710 lp: intercord INT 120.927 cd: preiser 90216 cd: dante LYS 291
strauss also sprach zarathustra		lp: discocorp SID 710 lp: intercord INT 120.928 cd: preiser 90216
strauss divertimento after couperin; festliches präludium		unpublished radio broadcasts
strauss till eulenspiegels lustige streiche		lp: discocorp SID 710 cd: preiser 90216 cd: dg 435 3212/435 3332 cd: dante LYS 291
strauss ein heldenleben		lp: discocorp SID 710 cd: preiser 90216 cd: dante LYS 393
strauss tod und verklärung		lp: discocorp SID 710 lp: intercord INT 120.927 cd: preiser 90216

0292/24 june 1944/musikvereinssaal/reichsrundfunk

bach orchestral suite no 3	**knappertsbusch**	lp: private issue P 1017 cd: music and arts CD 897 cd: tahra TAH 320-322 *air only* lp: private issue P 1014
bach brandenburg concerto no 3		cd: tahra TAH 320-322

0293/1 july 1944/musikvereinssaal/reichsrundfunk

bach	**knappertsbusch**	lp: private issue P 1017
violin	schneiderhan	cd: music and arts CD 897
concerto		cd: tahta TAH 320-322
in a minor		
bwv 1041		

0294/july 1944/musikvereinssaal/telefunken session

tchaikovsky	**baltzer**	78: telefunken C 3006
waltz/		
serenade for		
strings;		
atterberg		
sic and gigue/		
baroque suite		

0295/4-6 september 1944/musikvereinssaal/reichsrundfunk

mozart	**moralt**	lp: melodram MEL 047
entführung	vienna opera	cd: gala GL 100.501
aus dem	chorus	cd: urania (italy) URN 22.134
serail	schwarzkopf	*excerpts*
	loose	lp: urania URLP 7036
	dermota	lp: rococo 5374
	klein	lp: saga XIG 8011/ST 7011/5911/
	alsen	FDY 2143/STFDY 2143
		lp: discoreale DR 10037
		lp: melodram MEL 082/MEL 088
		lp: historia H 677-678
		lp: acanta BB 23119
		cd: melodram MEL 16501
		cd: preiser 90345
		this was a concert performance of the opera; many early issues of martern aller arten from this recording were incorrectly described as a performance by maria cebotari (it was also misdated)

0296/23 september 1944/musikvereinssaal/reichsrundfunk

j.strauss	**böhm**	cd: dg 435 3352/459 7342
perpetuum		
mobile		

0297/24-29 september 1944/musikvereinssaal/telefunken sessions

wagner   **baltzer**   78: telefunken E 1008
meistersinger   h.konetzni
von nürnberg   höngen
excerpt   petrak
(selig wie   mohrwald
die sonne)   schöffler

strauss   **baltzer**   78: telefunken SK 3732
rosenkavalier   h.konetzni   cd: preiser 90246
excerpt   *also a private lp edition by preiser*
(da geht er hin)

mozart   **baltzer**   cd: preiser 90246
don giovanni   h.konetzni   *unpublished telefunken 78rpm recordings*
excerpts   a.konetzni
(taci ingiusto   loose
corel; solo   petrak
in buio loco)   welitsch
                           vogel
                           kunz
                           sung in german

wagner   **baltzer**   cd: preiser 90246
lohengrin   h.konetzni   *unpublished telefunken 78rpm recording;*
excerpt   a.konetzni   *recording incomplete due to overloading*
(euch lüften,
die mein klagen)

0297/concluded

bizet	**baltzer**	cd: preiser 90246
carmen	loose	*unpublished telefunken 78rpm recording*
excerpt	höngen	
(nous avons	hittroff	
en tete une	klein	
affaire!)	wernigk	
	sung in german	

strauss **baltzer** cd: preiser 90246
rosenkavalier loose *unpublished telefunken 78rpm recording*
excerpt höngen
(mir ist die ehre
widerfahren)

strauss **baltzer** 78: telefunken E 1008
rosenkavalier h.konetzni cd: preiser 90246
excerpt loose
(hab mir's höngen
gelobt)

verdi **baltzer** cd: preiser 90175/90345
don carlo höngen *unpublished telefunken 78rpm recording*
excerpt *sung in german*
(o don fatale!)

verdi **baltzer** cd: preiser 90175
don carlo h.konetzni *unpublished telefunken 78rpm recording*
excerpt höngen
(pieta perdon!) *sung in german*

0298/30 september-3 october 1944/staatsoper/reichsrundfunk

verdi	**böhm**	cd: myto MCD 92260
otello	vienna opera	cd: preiser 90230
	chorus	*excerpts*
	h.konetzni	lp: acanta 72.221792/BB 23058
	ralf	lp: eterna 820 933
	schöffler	*this was a concert performance of the*
	sung in german	*opera*
verdi	**böhm**	cd: melodram CDM 28044
requiem	vienna opera	*recording incomplete; recording was*
	chorus	*broadcast on 5 february 1945*
	seefried	
	höngen	
	dermota	
	alsen	

0299/12 october 1944/musikvereinssaal/reichsrundfunk

grieg	**böhm**	lp: urania URLP 7015
piano	wührer	
concerto		

0300/17 october 1944/musikvereinssaal/reichsrundfunk

bruckner	**furtwängler**	lp: unicorn UNI 109-110
symphony		lp: nippon columbia DXM 110-111
no 8		lp: dg 2740 201
		cd: dg 445 4152
		cd: music and arts CD 764
		cd: grammofono AB 78696-78697
		also issued in japan by dg and toshiba

telefunken recording sessions noted in the orchestra's archives for 17-19 october 1944, at which furtwängler was to have conducted schubert symphony no 8 "unfinished" and beethoven leonore no 2 overture, were presumably cancelled

0301/23 october-1 november 1944/musikvereinssaal/telefunken sessions

enescu	**krauss**	78: telefunken E 3836-3837
rumanian		cd: teldec 9031 764382
rhapsody		*9031 764382 incorrectly dated*
no 1		*18 august 1950*
debussy		telefunken unpublished
la cathédrale		
engloutie;		
j.strauss		
frühlingsstimmen		
waltz		

0302/3-4 november 1944/musikvereinssaal/reichsrundfunk

uhl	**krauss**	unpublished radio broadcast in
konzertante	wlach	clemens-krauss-archiv
sinfonie		
for clarinet		
and orchestra		

0303/7-9 november 1944/musikvereinssaal/reichsrundfunk

bruckner	**krauss**	unpublished radio broadcast in
te deum	vienna opera	clemens-krauss-archiv
	chorus	
	eipperle	
	nikolaidi	
	patzak	
	hann	
ravel	**krauss**	lp: melodiya M10 46981 001
rapsodie		
espagnole		
strauss	**krauss**	lp: acanta 10.220559
songs with	patzak	cd: acanta 40.2055
orchestra		

0304/14-16 november 1944/musikvereinssaal/reichsrundfunk

mozart	**böhm**	unpublished radio broadcast
zauberflöte	vienna opera	*excerpt (nur stille stille!)*
	chorus	cd: preiser 90249
	seefried	*these were concert performances*
	loose	*of the opera*
	h.konetzni	
	höngen	
	nikolaidi	
	dermota	
	kunz	
	schöffler	

0305/18-19 november 1944/musikvereinssaal/electrola sessions

brahms	**böhm**	78: electrola DB 7715-7719
symphony		lp: nippon columbia DXM 163
no 1		cd: preiser 90922
		cd: dante LYS 407
		nippon columbia incorrectly named
		conductor as furtwängler

0306/28 november-5 december 1944/musikvereinssaal/reichsrundfunk

wagner	**böhm**	cd: preiser 90234
meistersinger	vienna opera	*excerpts*
von nürnberg	chorus	cd: preiser 90325/90345
	seefried	*these were concert performances of the*
	schürhoff	*opera; opening of act 3 is missing from*
	seider	*tapes and has been replaced with the*
	klein	*corresponding section from 1943*
	schöffler	*bayreuth performance conducted by*
	poell	*abendroth*
	kunz	

0307/4-6 december 1944/musikvereinssaal/electrola sessions

vivaldi concerto grosso unspecified	**jerger**	electrola unpublished

0308/8-9 december 1944/musikvereinssaal/reichsrundfunk

schubert mass in e flat d950	**krauss** vienna opera chorus eipperle willer dermota friedrich hann	unpublished radio broadcast in clemens-krauss-archiv

0309/11-13 december 1944/musikvereinssaal/reichsrundfunk

pfitzner das käthchen von heilbronn overture	**pfitzner**	lp: urania URLP 7050 lp: varèse sarabande VC 81094

0310/19-20 december 1944/musikvereinssaal/reichsrundfunk

beethoven symphony no 3 "eroica"	**furtwängler**	lp: urania C 7095 lp: melodiya D06443-06444/M10 06443 lp: unicorn UNI 104 lp: turnabout THS 65020 lp:emi 2C05163332/3C153 53810-53816M lp: intercord INT 120.291 cd: priceless D 16395 cd: music and arts CD 814/CD 4049 cd: melodiya (japan) MEL 10.00710 cd: russian compact disc RCD 25001 cd: documents LV 919-920 cd: historical performers HP 2 cd: grammofono AB 78538 cd: preiser 90251 cd: bayer BR 200.002 cd: tahra FURT 1034-1039/FURT 1031/ FURT 1034-1035 cd: dante LYS 063 cd: urania URCD 7095 *some early issues incorrectly name orchestra* *as berlin philharmonic*

0311/29-30 december 1944/musikvereinssaal/reichsrundfunk
these may be the first extant recordings taken from a new year's concert or from the dress rehearsal performance

j.strauss klangfiguren waltz	**krauss**	lp: vox VL 3140 cd: wing (japan) WCD 8 cd: dg 459 7342
josef strauss mein lebenslauf ist lieb' und lust waltz		lp: vox VL 3140
j.strauss stadt und land polka		45: vox VIP 30040 lp: vox VL 3140 cd: wing (japan) WCD 8
j.strauss elyen a magyar polka		45: vox VIP 30040 lp: vox VL 3140 cd: wing (japan) WCD 8
josef strauss die libelle polka		lp: vox VL 3140 cd: wing (japan) WCD 8
josef strauss ohne sorgen polka		45: vox VIP 30040 lp: vox VL 3140
j.strauss vergnügungszug polka		45: vox VIP 30040 lp: vox VL 3140 cd: dg 435 3352/459 7342
j.strauss indigo und die 40 räuber overture		45: vox VIP 30040 cd: dg 459 7342

0312/1944/reichsrundfunk
the recordings in this section could not be dated precisely

beethoven symphony no 2	**böhm**	lp: discocorp IGI 384
schubert symphony no 8 "unfinished"		lp: urania URLP 7009
beethoven piano concerto no 5 "emperor"	**böhm** ney	lp: urania URLP 7150/URRS 7-10 cd: datum DAT 12305 cd: refrain (japan) MADR 206 cd: tahra TAH 335-336 *DAT 12305 incorrectly dated 1956*
reger mozart variations	**knappertsbusch**	cd: refrain (japan) DR 92 0029 *also issued in japan by seven seas*
bach matthäus- passion	**krauss** vienna opera chorus eipperle höngen patzak hann	unpublished radio broadcast in clemens-krauss-archiv
mozart don giovanni excerpt (dalla sua pace)	**moralt** dermota *sung in german*	cd: preiser 90345
j.strauss zigeunerbaron excerpt (wer uns getraut)	**schönherr** vienna opera chorus welitsch meyer-welfing	cd: polyhymnia 21212

0313/16-17 january 1945/musikvereinssaal/reichsrundfunk

pfitzner von deutscher seele	**krauss** vienna opera chorus eipperle willer patzak weber	cd: preiser 90255

0314/28-29 january 1945/musikvereinssaal/reichsrundfunk

franck symphony in d minor	**furtwängler**	lp: melodiya D 021903-021904 lp: vox PL 7230 lp: french furtwängler society SWF 7302 lp: discocorp RR 403 lp: private issue (japan) JP 1128-1129 cd: french furtwängler society SWF 902 cd: arlecchino ARL 140 *issued in japan by dg and seven seas*
brahms symphony no 2		lp: french furtwängler society SWF 7301 lp: discocorp SID 713/RR 418 lp: olympic OL 8141 lp: private issue (japan) JP 1128-1129 cd: nuova era NE 013.6322-013.6324 cd: french furtwängler society SWF 902 cd: dg 435 3242/435 3212 cd: music and arts CD 804/CD 4941 *issued in japan by toshiba, dg and* *nippon columbia*

0315/19-27 march 1945/musikvereinssaal/reichsrundfunk

respighi fontane di roma	**krauss**	lp: melodiya M10 46981 001 cd: refrain (japan) DR 92 0041 *refrain incorrectly dated 1948*
paganini moto perpetuo		unpublished radio broadcast in clemens-krauss-archiv
martucci notturno		unpublished radio broadcast in clemens-krauss-archiv
mancinelli fuga degli amanti a chioggia		unpublished radio broadcast in clemens-krauss-archiv
ravel miroirs		unpublished radio broadcast in clemens-krauss-archiv
ravel une barque sur l'océon		unpublished radio broadcast in clemens-krauss-archiv
ravel alborada del gracioso		unpublished radio broadcast in clemens-krauss-archiv
ravel daphnis et chloé 2 nd suite	**krauss** vienna opera chorus	cd: refrain (japan) DR 92 0041 *incorrectly dated 1948*
debussy rhapsodie pour clarinette et orchestre	**krauss** wlach	unpublished radio broadcast in clemens-krauss-archiv

0316/7 august 1946/salzburg mozarteum

mozart piano concerto no 25	**fischer** conductor and soloist	lp: discocorp IGI 290 cd: emi CDH 566 0852
mozart piano concerto no 22		cd: emi CDH 566 0852

0317/13-20 september 1946/musikvereinssaal/columbia sessions

beethoven   **karajan**   78: columbia LX 988-990/
symphony   LX 8557-8559 auto
no 8   78: columbia (france) LFX 824-826
                                  78: columbia (austria) LVX 48-50
                                  45: columbia (usa) EL 51
                                  lp: toshiba EAC 30102
                                  lp: emi RLS 7714/1C137 54370-54373M
                                  cd: emi CDM 566 3912/CMS 763 3262/
                                        CMS 566 4832
                                  cd: grammofono AB 78691

schubert   78: columbia LX 1138-1141/
symphony   LX 8644-8649 auto
no 9   78: columbia (france) LFX 818-823
"great"   78: columbia (italy) GQX 11130-11135/
                                  GQX 11271-11276
                                  lp: columbia (usa) ML 4631
                                  lp: toshiba EAC 30104
                                  lp: emi 2C153 03200-03205M
                                  cd: emi CDM 566 3892/CMS 566 4832
                                  cd: grammofono AB 78770

0318/18-23 october 1946/musikvereinssaal/columbia sessions

mozart
symphony
no 33
	karajan	78: columbia LX 1006-1008/
		    LX 8568-8570 auto
		78: columbia (france) LFX 781-783
		78: columbia (austria) LVX 84-86
		78: columbia (usa) M 778
		lp: columbia (france) 33FCX 145
		lp: columbia (italy) 33QCX 145
		lp: columbia (germany) C 90633
		lp: columbia (usa) ML 4370
		lp: toshiba EAC 30107
		cd: emi CMS 763 3262/CMS 566 4832/
		    CDM 566 3892
		cd: grammofono AB 78691
		cd: memoir classics CDMOIR 448

mozart eine kleine nachtmusik		78: columbia LX 1293-1294/LCX 134-135 78: columbia (france) LFX 832-833 78: columbia (italy) GQX 11157-11158 78: columbia (switzerland) LZX 215-216 lp: columbia (usa) ML 4370 lp: toshiba EAC 30108 lp: emi 2C153 03200-03205M cd: emi CDM 566 3882/CMS 566 4832
mozart le nozze di figaro overture		78: columbia LX 1008/LX 8568 78: columbia (france) LFX 783 78: columbia (italy) GQX 11169 78: columbia (austria) LVX 86 78: columbia (usa) M 778 lp: toshiba EAC 30107 lp: emi RLS 7714/1C137 54370-54373M/ 2C153 03200-03205M cd: emi CDM 566 3882/CMS 566 4832 cd: memoir classics CDMOIR 448
mozart adagio/ diverimento no 17		cd: emi CMS 763 3262/CDM 566 3912/ CMS 566 4832 *unpublished columbia 78rpm recording;* *recording completed on 13 december 1947*

0318/concluded

mozart german dances k600 no 5 and k605 no 3	**karajan**	cd: emi CMS 763 3262/CMS 566 4832/ CDM 566 3882 cd: grammofono AB 78691 *unpublished columbia 78 rpm recordings*

mozart
entführung
aus dem
serail
excerpt
(martern
aller arten)
	karajan
	schwarzkopf
		lp: emi RLS 763/RLS 7714/154 6133/
		    1C137 54370-54373M/
		    1C151 43160-43163M
		cd: emi CDH 763 7082/CDM 566 3942/
		    CMS 566 4832
		cd: notablu 935.0923
		unpublished columbia 78 rpm recording

0319/28-31 october 1946/musikvereinssaal/columbia sessions

tchaikovsky romeo and juliet fantasy overture	**karajan**	78:columbia LX1033-1035/LCX 105-107/ LX 8583-8585 auto 78: columbia (france) LFX 720-722 78: columbia (italy) GQX 11184-11186 lp: toshiba EAC 30112 cd: emi CDM 566 3922/CHS 764 8552/ CMS 566 4832/CMS 763 3262 cd: grammofono AB 78691
j.strauss zigeunerbaron overture		78: columbia LX 1009 78: columbia (france) LFX 773 78: columbia (italy) GQX 11139 78: columbia (austria) LVX 4 lp: toshiba EAC 30110 cd: emi CDH 764 2992/CDM 566 3952/ CHS 764 2942/CMS 566 4832 cd: iron needle IN 1408
j.strauss kaiserwalzer		78: columbia LX 1021/LCX 108 78: columbia (italy) GQX 11148 78: columbia (austria) LVX 2 78: columbia (usa) AL 28 lp: toshiba EAC 30111 cd: emi CDM 566 3952/CMS 763 3262/ CMS 566 4832 cd: iron needle IN 1408
j.strauss künstlerleben waltz		78: columbia LX 1013 78: columbia (italy) GQX 11173 78: columbia (switzerland) LZX 218 78: columbia (austria) LVX 3 45: columbia SEL 1503 45: columbia (germany) C 50142/ SELW 1503 45: columbia (france) ERBF 109 45: columbia (italy) SEBQ 101 lp: toshiba EAC 30111 cd: emi CDM 566 3952/CMS 566 4832 cd: iron needle IN 1408
j.strauss an der schönen blauen donau waltz		78: columbia LX 1118/LCX 123 78: columbia (france) LFX 840 78: columbia (switzerland) LZX 217 45: columbia SCD 2144 lp: toshiba EAC 30110 cd: emi CDM 566 3952/CMS 566 4832 cd: grammofono AB 78691

0319/concluded

j.strauss leichtes blut polka	**karajan**	cd: emi CDM 566 3962/CMS 566 4832 cd: iron needle IN 1408 *unpublished columbia 78rpm recording*
johann and josef strauss pizzicato polka		cd: emi CDM 566 3962/CMS 566 4832 *unpublished columbia 78rpm recording*
wagner meistersinger von nürnberg excerpts (wahn! wahn!; was duftet doch der flieder)	**karajan** hotter	columbia unpublished

0320/31 october-4 november 1946/musikvereinssaal/columbia sessions

mozart	**krips**	78: columbia LX 1249
entführung	schwarzkopf	78: columbia (switzerland) LZX 241
aus dem		lp: columbia (usa) ML 4649
serail		lp: emi RLS 763/154 6133/
excerpt		1C151 43160-43163M
(welcher kummer/		cd: emi CDH 763 7082
traurigkeit)		
j.strauss		lp: emi ALP 143 5501
frühlingsstimmen		*unpublished columbia 78rpm recording;*
waltz		*recording incomplete*
vocal version		
mozart		78: columbia LX 1096
il rè pastore		78: columbia (france) LFX 1018
excerpt		lp: emi RLS 763/1C151 43160-43163M
(l'amero saro		cd: emi CMS 763 7502
costante)		cd: grandi voci alla scala GVS 19
handel		78: columbia LX 1010
l'allegro		45: columbia SEL 1585
il pensieroso		lp: emi ALP 143 5501/154 6133
ed il moderato		cd: emi CDH 763 2012/CZS 479 9312
excerpt		cd: dutton CDLX 7029
(sweet bird)		
mozart	**krips**	columbia unpublished
le nozze di	seefried	
figaro		
excerpt		
(deh vieni		
non tardar);		
handel		
giulio cesare		
excerpt		
(v'adoro pupille)		
haydn		78: columbia LX 1011/LCX 114
die schöpfung		lp: emi EX 29 10563/EX 29 12363
excerpt		cd: toshiba shinseido SGR 8244
(nun beut die flur)		
haydn		78: columbia LX 1245
die schöpfung		lp: emi EX 29 10563/EX 29 12363
excerpt		cd: toshiba shinseido SGR 8244
(auf starkem		
fittiche)		

0321/5 november 1946/musikverein brahmssaal/columbia session

mozart zauberflöte excerpt (dies bildnis); don giovanni excerpt (dalla sua pace)	**moralt** meyer-welfing	78: columbia DX 1386
mozart don giovanni excerpt (il mio tesoro)		lp: emi EX 769 7411 cd: emi CHS 769 7412 *unpublished columbia 78rpm recording*

0322/6 november 1946/musikverein brahmssaal/columbia session

mozart exsultate jubilate	**krips** schwarzkopf	cd: testament SBT 2172 *unpublished columbia 78rpm recording*

0323/6 august 1947/salzburg festspielhaus

von einem dantons tod	**fricsay** vienna opera chorus cebotari patzak weber hann schöffler	lp: ed smith ANNA 1056 cd: stradivarius STR 10067 *world premiere performance*

0324/12 august 1947/salzburg festspielhaus

strauss arabella	**böhm** vienna opera chorus reining della casa anday taubmann patzak hotter hann	lp: discocorp RR 525 lp: melodram MEL 101 cd: melodram MEL 37077 cd: dg 445 3422/445 4912

0325/13 august 1947/salzburg festspielhaus

brahms symphony no 1	**furtwängler**	cd: refrain (japan) DR 92 0022
brahms violin concerto	**furtwängler** menuhin	unpublished newsreel recording *rehearsal extract only*

0326/20 august 1947/salzburg festspielhaus

weber euryanthe overture; delius walk to the paradise garden/ a village romeo and juliet   **barbirolli**   cd: dutton CDSJB 1999

0327/august-september 1947/edinburgh usher hall

mahler das lied von der erde	**walter** ferrier patzak	unpublished radio broadcast *this recording may be irretrievably lost*
schubert rosamunde excerpts	**walter**	cd: wing (japan) WCD 50
j.strauss die fledermaus overture; der zigeunerbaron overture; g'schichten aus dem wienerwald waltz		cd: wing (japan) WCD 3-4

0328/24 september 1947/london royal opera house

beethoven	**krauss**	unpublished radio broadcast
fidelio	vienna opera	*guest performance by vienna staatsoper*
	chorus	
	h.konetzni	
	schwarzkopf	
	friedrich	
	klein	
	weber	
	schöffler	
	alsen	

0329/27 september 1947/london royal opera house

mozart	**krips**	unpublished radio broadcast
don giovanni	vienna opera	*fragments*
	chorus	cd: eklipse EKRCD 5
	schwarzkopf	*guest performance by vienna staatsoper;*
	cebotari	*final public appearance of richard*
	güden	*tauber*
	tauber	
	hotter	
	kunz	
	sung in german	

0330/30 september 1947/london royal opera house

strauss	**krauss**	cd: legato LCD 211
salome	cebotari	cd: gebhardt JGCD 0011-2
	höngen	*guest performance by vienna staatsoper*
	friedrich	
	patzak	
	rothmüller	

0331/20 october-6 november 1947/musikvereinssaal/columbia sessions

brahms
ein deutsches
requiem
	karajan
	wiener singverein
	schwarzkopf
	hotter
		78: columbia LX 1055-1064/
		    LX 8595-8604 auto
		78: columbia (italy) GQX 11239-11248
		78: columbia (austria) LVX 68-77
		78: columbia (france) SL 157
		78: columbia (usa) M 755
		lp: toshiba EAC 30103
		lp: emi RLS 7714/1C137 54370-54373M/
		    2C153 03200-03205M
		cd: emi CDH 761 0102/CZS 479 9312
		cd: arkadia 78545
		cd: grammofono AB 78755
		excerpts
		78: columbia (usa) 72562D/72563D
		*first complete gramophone recording of
		the work*

beethoven
symphony
no 9
"choral"
	karajan
	wiener singverein
	schwarzkopf
	höngen
	patzak
	hotter
		78: columbia LX 1097-1105/
		    LX 8612-8620 auto
		78: columbia (france) LFX 846-854
		78: columbia (italy) GQX 11250-11258
		78: columbia (austria) LVX 32-40
		45: columbia (usa) EL 51
		lp: toshiba EAC 30101
		lp: emi RLS 7714/1C137 54370-54373M/
		    2C153 03200-03205M
		cd: emi CDH 761 0762/CZS 479 9312
		cd: arkadia 78544
		cd: grammofono AB 78736
		recording completed 10-14 december 1947

strauss
metamorphosen
	karajan	78: columbia LX 1082-1086/
		    LX 8606-8609 auto
		78: columbia (austria) LVX 64-67
		lp: toshiba EAC 30109
		lp: emi RLS 7714/1C137 54370-54373M/
		    2C153 03200-03205M
		cd: emi CDM 566 3902/CMS 763 3262/
		    CMS 566 4832
		cd: memoir classics CDMOIR 448
		first gramophone recording of the work

0332/10-17 november 1947/musikvereinssaal/hmv sessions

beethoven symphony no 3 "eroica"	**furtwängler**	78:hmv DB6741-6747/DB9296-9302 auto lp: discocorp RR 456 lp: private issue (japan) JP 1190-1192 lp: french furtwängler society SWF 7903 lp: emi 3C153 53800-53805M cd: toshiba shinseido SGR 8221 cd: dante LYS 197 cd: tahra FURT 1027 *also issued in japan by toshiba; first side* *of second movement was re-recorded on* *15 february 1949: both takes were used* *at different times*

0333/11 november-3 december 1947/musikverein brahmssaal/hmv sessions

mozart serenade for 13 wind instruments	**furtwängler**	78:hmv DB6707-6711/DB9226-9230 auto lp: electrola E 91175/WALP 579 lp: unicorn WFS 10 lp: emi 1C047 01244M cd: emi CDH 763 8182 cd: dante LYS 250 cd: french furtwängler society SWF 991 cd: gebhardt JGCD 0010-3 *first complete gramophone recording of* *the work; also issued in japan by toshiba*

0334/21 november 1947/musikverein brahmssaal/columbia session

mozart zauberflöte excerpt (der vogelfänger bin ich ja!)	**moralt** kunz	lp: emi EX 769 7411 cd: emi CHS 769 7412 cd: testament SBT 1059 *unpublished columbia 78 rpm recording*

mozart
zauberflöte
excerpt
(ein mädchen
oder weibchen)
		78: columbia LX 1123
		45: columbia SEL 1575
		lp: columbia (germany) C 70407
		lp: columbia (austria) 33VS 811
		lp: emi RLS 764/EX 29 05983/
		    1C147 03580-03581M/
		    1C137 43187-43189M
		cd: emi CMS 763 7502
		cd: testament SBT 1059
		cd: toshiba shinseido SGR 8244
		also private lp edition by preiser

0335/22-24 november 1947/musikverein brahmssaal/hmv sessions

mozart symphony no 25	**böhm**	78: hmv C 4086-4088/C 7843-7845 auto

0336/25 november 1947/musikvereinssaal/hmv session

beethoven   **furtwängler**   78: hmv DB 6625
coriolan   78: victor 11-8036
overture   lp: hmv (france) FBLP 25113
     lp: unicorn WFS 9
     lp: emi 1C149 53432-53439M/
         2C153 52540-52551/
         1C047 00843M
     cd: emi CHS 565 5132
     cd: dante LYS 249
     also issued in japan by toshiba

0337/1-2 december 1947/musikverein brahmssaal/hmv sessions

mozart   **böhm**   hmv unpublished
symphony
no 26

mozart   hmv unpublished
serenata
notturna
k239

mozart   78: hmv C 3990
posthorn   cd: emi CZS 569 7432
serenade,
3 rd movement

mozart   hmv unpublished
posthorn
serenade,
4 th movement

mozart   78: hmv C 4088/C 7843
divertimento
k251,
1 st movement

0338/3-8 december 1947/musikverein brahmssaal/columbia sessions

mozart adagio and fugue in c minor	**karajan**	78: columbia LX 1076 lp: columbia (usa) ML 4370 lp: toshiba EAC 30108 lp: emi RLS 7714/1C137 54370-54373M/ 2C153 03200-03205M cd: emi CDM 566 3912/CMS 566 4832 cd: grammofono AB 78770 cd: memoir classics CDMOIR 448
mozart le nozze di figaro excerpt (se vuol ballare)	**karajan** kunz	columbia unpublished
mozart le nozze di figaro excerpt (non piu andrai)		78: columbia LX 1123 45: columbia SEL 1574 lp: columbia (germany) C 70407 lp: emi RLS 764/1C137 43187-43189M/ 1C147 03580-03581M cd: emi CDM 566 3932/CMS 566 4832 cd: testament SBT 1059 cd: preiser 90345 *also private lp edition by preiser*
mozart don giovanni excerpt (la ci darem la mano)	**karajan** seefried kunz	lp: emi RLS 764/EX 29 12363/ 1C137 43187-43189M cd: emi CDM 566 3932/CMS 566 4832 cd: testament SBT 1059 *unpublished columbia 78 rpm recording;* *also private lp edition by preiser*
mozart zauberflöte excerpt (bei männern, welche liebe fühlen)	**karajan** schwarzkopf kunz	cd: emi CDM 566 3942/CMS 566 4832 *unpublished columbia 78 rpm recording*

0339/8-12 december 1947/musikvereinssaal/columbia sessions

reznicek donna diana overture	**karajan**	78: columbia LX 1402/LCX 145 78: columbia (france) LFX 1013 78: columbia (italy) GQX 11437 78: columbia (germany) LWX 403 45: columbia SCB 112/SCD 2075 45: columbia (italy) SCBQ 3017 45: columbia (germany) SCBW 107 lp: columbia (usa) ML 5141 lp: toshiba EAC 30111 lp: emi RLS 7714/1C137 54370-54373M cd: emi CDH 764 2992/CDM 566 3962/ CHS 764 2942/CMS 566 4832 cd: iron needle IN 1408
puccini manon lescaut intermezzo		columbia unpublished *published recording taken from later november 1948 session*

strauss
rosenkavalier
excerpt
(mir ist die
ehre widerfahren)
	karajan
	schwarzkopf
	seefried
		78: columbia LX 1225-1226
		lp: columbia (usa) ML 2126
		lp: world records SH 286
		lp: emi RLS 763/RLS 7714/154 6133/
		    1C151 43160-43163M/
		    1C137 54370-54373M
		cd: emi CDH 769 7932/CDM 566 3942/
		    CMS 566 4832
		cd: grandi voci alla scala GVS 19

0340/11-13 december 1947/musikverein brahmssaal/columbia sessions

mozart maurerische trauermusik	**karajan**	78: columbia LX 1155 78: columbia (france) LFX 950 78: columbia (usa) 72846D lp: columbia (usa) 3-288 lp: toshiba EAC 30108 lp: emi 2C153 03200-03205M cd: emi CDM 566 3902/CMS 763 3262/ CMS 566 4832 cd: memoir classics CDMOIR 448

0340/concluded

mozart	**karajan**	78: columbia LB 76
le nozze di	seefried	78: columbia (australia) LO 82
figaro		lp: emi RLS 764/1C137 43187-43189M/
excerpt		EX 29 12363
(voi che sapete)		cd: emi CDM 566 3932/CMS 566 4832
		also private lp edition by preiser

mozart
le nozze di
figaro
excerpt
(deh vieni
non tardar)

78: columbia LX 1145
lp: emi RLS 764/1C137 43187-43189M/
   EX 29 12363
cd: emi CDM 566 3932/CMS 566 4832
cd: preiser 90345
also private lp edition by preiser

mozart
don giovanni
excerpt
(batti batti)

78: columbia LB 76
lp: emi RLS 764/1C137 43187-43189M/
   EX 29 12363
cd: emi CDM 566 3932/CMS 566 4832
also private lp edition by preiser

0341/15-16 december 1947/musikvereinssaal/columbia and hmv sessions

    chabrier   **karajan**   cd: emi CDM 566 3922/CMS 566 4832
espana   cd: iron needle IN 1408
                                                     unpublished columbia 78rpm recording

strauss   **karajan**   78: columbia LX 1168
rosenkavalier   h.konetzni   78: columbia (austria) LVX 45
excerpt   cd: preiser 90078/90345
(kann mich auch   cd: emi CDM 566 3942/CMS 566 4832
an ein mädel   cd: dutton CDLX 7034
erinnern)   cd: rca/bmg 74321 694272/74321 694282

strauss   78: columbia LX 1168
rosenkavalier   78: columbia (austria) LVX 45
excerpt   cd: preiser 90078
(quinquin, er   cd: emi CDM 566 3942/CMS 566 4832
soll jetzt geh'n!)   cd: dutton CDLX 7034

smetana   **karajan**   78: columbia LX 1074
the bartered   h.konetzni   78: columbia (austria) LVX 54
bride   *sung in german*   lp: emi RLS 764/1C137 43187-43189M
excerpt   cd: preiser 90078
(sweet dream   cd: emi CDM 566 3942/CMS 566 4832
of love)   *also private lp edition by preiser*

mozart   **karajan**   78: hmv DB 7638
don giovanni   cebotari   45: hmv 7ER 5126
excerpt   lp: electrola E 60050/WDLP 563
(non mi dir)   lp: emi RLS 764/1C147 29118-29119M/
                                                        1C137 43187-43189M
                                                        lp: preiser PR 9860
                                                         cd: preiser 90034
                                                        cd: emi CDM 566 3932/CMS 566 4832
                                                        cd: toshiba shinseido SGR 8244
                                                        also private lp edition by preiser; lp
                                                        editions incorrectly named conductor
                                                        as prohaska

mozart   lp: electrola E 60050/WDLP 563
don giovanni   lp: emi RLS 764/1C147 29118-29119M/
excerpt   1C137 43187-43189M
(or sai chi   lp: preiser PR 9860
l'onore!)   cd: preiser 90034/90345
                                                        cd: emi CDM 566 3932/CMS 566 4832
                                                        unpublished hmv 78rpm recording;
                                                        lp editions incorrectly named conductor
                                                        as prohaska

0342/17-18 april 1948/musikvereinssaal

beethoven	**karajan**	unpublished radio broadcast
violin	neveu	*recording probably incomplete*
concerto		

0343/15 may 1948/musikvereinssaal

mahler	**walter**	lp: discocorp BWS 367
symphony	wiener singverein	cd: grammofono AB 78787-78788
no 2	cebotari	cd: nuova era NE 2314-2315
"resurrection"	anday	

0344/28 july 1948/salzburg felsenreitschule

gluck	**karajan**	unpublished video recording
orfeo ed	vienna opera	*newsreel extract from rehearsal only*
euridice,	ballet	
fragment from		
ballet music		

0345/31 july 1948/salzburg felsenreitschule

beethoven	**furtwängler**	cd: orfeo C525 991B
leonore no 3		*taken from complete performance of*
overture		*the opera fidelio*

0346/3 august 1948/salzburg felsenreitschule

beethoven	**furtwängler**	lp: rococo 1012
fidelio	vienna opera	cd: melodram CDM 25009
	chorus	cd:french furtwängler societySWF 992-993
	schlüter	cd: tahra FURT 1047-1048
	della casa	*excerpts*
	patzak	lp: tanaka (japan) AT 07-08
	schock	cd:german furtwängler societyTMK 10670
	frantz	*recording has nos. 5-8 missing*
	edelmann	
	poell	

0347/8 august 1948/salzburg mozarteum

mozart piano concerto no 26 "coronation"	**fischer** conductor and soloist	unpublished video recording *newsreel extract from rehearsal only*

0348/15 august 1948/salzburg festspielhaus

martin le vin herbé	**fricsay** vienna opera chorus cebotari zadek ilosvay patzak koreh	unpublished radio broadcast

0349/3 october 1948/london royal albert hall

beethoven symphony no 2	**furtwängler**	lp: emi 1C149 53432-53439M/ 2C051 03649/3C153 53432-53439M cd: emi CDH 763 1922/CHS 763 6062 cd: music and arts CD 942

0350/4-8 november 1948/musikvereinssaal/columbia sessions

tchaikovsky   **karajan**   78: columbia LX 1234-1239/
symphony   LX 8699-8704 auto
no 6   78: columbia (austria) LVX 87-92
"pathétique"   lp: columbia 33CX 1026
                                          lp: columbia (france) 33FCX 105
                                          lp: columbia (germany) C 90302/
                                               33WCX 1026
                                          lp: columbia (usa) ML 4299
                                          lp: toshiba EAC 30105
                                          lp: emi 2C153 03200-03205M
                                          cd: emi CDM 566 3922/CMS 566 4832
                                          cd: grammofono AB 78792
                                          recording completed on 15 january 1949;
                                          this recording was also published
                                          unofficially in a number of lp and cd
                                          editions with incorrect attribution 1950

0351/6 november 1948/musikverein brahmssaal/columbia session

puccini	**karajan**	lp: emi ALP 143 5501/154 6133
la bohème	schwarzkopf	cd: emi CDM 763 5572/CDM 566 3932/
excerpt		CMS 566 4832
(si mi chiamano		*unpublished columbia 78rpm recording*
mimi)		

puccini
gianni schicchi
excerpt
(o mio babbino
caro)

78: columbia LB 85
78: columbia (austria) LV 7
78: columbia (poland) LM 4
78: columbia (italy) GQ 7240
45: columbia SEL 1575
lp: toshiba EAC 30112
lp: emi RLS 763/154 6133/
   1C151 43160-43163M
cd: emi CDM 566 3932/CMS 566 4832

puccini
la bohème
excerpt
(donde lieta usci);
turandot
excerpt
(tu che di gel
sei cinta)

columbia unpublished

0352/11-17 november 1948/musikvereinssaal/columbia sessions

beethoven	**karajan**	78:columbia LX1330-1333/LCX 140-143/
symphony		LX 8752-8755 auto
no 5		78: columbia (austria) LVX 79-82
		lp: columbia 33CX 1004
		lp: columbia (france) 33FCX 107
		lp: columbia (italy) 33QCX 107
		lp: columbia (austria) 33VCX 506
		lp: columbia (usa) RL 3063
		lp: toshiba EAC 30111
		cd: emi CDM 566 3912/CMS 566 4832
		cd: javelin HADCD 134
		cd: grammofono AB 78792

0353/16 november 1948/musikverein brahmssaal/hmv session

strauss	**karajan**	78: hmv DB 6914
ariadne auf	cebotari	45: hmv 7ER 5141
naxos		lp: world records SH 286
excerpt		lp: emi RLS 764/1C137 43187-43189M/
(es gibt		1C147 29150-29151M/
ein reich)		1C147 29118-29119M
		lp: preiser PR 9860
		cd: preiser 90034
		cd: emi CDM 566 3942/CMS 566 4832/
		CZS 569 7432
		also in a private lp edition by preiser
j.strauss		78: hmv DB 6947
zigeunerbaron		lp: columbia (usa) RL 3068
excerpt		lp: preiser PR 9860
(so elend		lp: emi RLS 764/1C137 43187-43189M/
und treu)		1C147 29118-29119M/
		1C147 30226-30227M
		cd: emi CDM 566 3942/CMS 566 4832
		cd: preiser 90034

0354/19 november 1948/musikvereinssaal/columbia session

wagner	**karajan**	78: columbia LX 1440
der fliegende	wiener singverein	lp: toshiba EAC 30109
holländer	schuster	cd: emi CMS 566 4832
excerpt		
(summ und brumm)		
wagner	**karajan**	columbia unpublished
lohengrin	wiener singverein	
excerpt		
(treulich geführt)		
puccini	**karajan**	78: columbia LB 82
la bohème	welitsch	lp: emi HLM 7002/1C047 01267M
excerpt		lp: world records SH 289
(quando m'en vo)		lp: angel 60202
		cd: polyhymnia 21212
		cd: melodram CD 1204 004
		cd: emi CDH 761 0072/CDM 566 3932/
		CMS 566 4832
		melodram incorrectly dated 1952
mozart		columbia unpublished
don giovanni		
excerpt		
(or sai chi l'onore)		

0355/22-24 november 1948/musikvereinssaal/columbia sessions

strauss	**karajan**	lp: world records SH 286
salome	welitsch	cd: emi CDM 566 3942/CMS 566 5832
excerpt	schuster	*excerpts*
(closing scene)	witt	cd: polyhymnia 21212
		cd: emi CZS 569 7432
		cd: rca/bmg 74321 694272/74321 694282
		unpublished columbia 78rpm recording:
		recording omits the section "öffne deine
		augen....geheimnisvolle musik" as matrix
		of this 78rpm side was damaged; rca/bmg
		issue incorrectly dated december 1948
j.strauss	**karajan**	78: columbia LX 1274
g'schichten		78: columbia (france) LFX 1014
aus dem		78: columbia (austria) LVX 137
wienerwald		78: columbia (denmark) LDX 12
waltz		lp: toshiba EAC 30110
		lp: emi RLS 7714/1C137 54370-54373M
		cd: emi CDM 566 3962/CMS 763 3262/
		CMS 566 4832
		cd: iron needle IN 1408

0356/26 november 1948/musikverein brahmssaal/columbia session

mozart	**prohaska**	78: columbia LX 1260
don giovanni	w.ludwig	
excerpts	*sung in german*	
(il mio tesoro;		
dalla sua pace)		
mozart		columbia unpublished
cosi fan tutte		
excerpt		
(un aura		
amorosa)		

0357/27 november 1948/musikvereinssaal/columbia session

j.strauss   **karajan**   78: columbia LX 1546
die fledermaus   78: columbia (france) LFX 989
overture   78: columbia (austria) LVX 152
                                        78: columbia (italy) GQX 11435
                                        78: columbia (denmark) LDX 11
                                        45: columbia SCD 2101
                                        lp: toshiba EAC 30110
                                        cd: emi CDM 566 3952/CMS 566 4832
                                        cd: iron needle IN 1408

puccini   78: columbia LX 1208
manon lescaut   78: columbia (italy) GQX 11322
intermezzo   45: columbia SCB 109/SCD 2084
                                        45: columbia (germany) SCBW 108
                                        45: columbia (italy) SCBQ 3013
                                        lp: toshiba EAC 30112
                                        cd: emi CDM 566 3932/CMS 566 4832

0358/november 1948/film soundtrack recording

bach   **karajan**   private video issue in japan
matthäus-   wiener singverein   *heavily abridged soundtrack recording*
passion   schwarzkopf   *for film depicting the passion story*
                       höngen   *illustrated with 15 th-17 th century*
                       w.ludwig   *paintings; spoken commentary super-*
                       schmitt-walter   *imposed over the music*
                       braun

0359/7-8 december 1948/musikvereinssaal/hmv sessions

mendelssohn hebrides overture	**furtwängler**	hmv unpublished
mozart symphony no 40		78: hmv DB 6997-6999/ DB 9441-9443 auto 45: victor WHMV 1010 lp: victor LHMV 1010 lp: hmv ALP 1498 lp: electrola E 90152/E 91075/E 70361/ STE 91075/SME 91075/WALP 1498/ WALP 502/WBLP 547 lp: hmv (france) FALP 117/FALP 50033 lp: hmv (italy) QALP 117 lp: emi XLP 30104/1C027 00906M cd: emi CDH 763 1932/CHS 566 7702 cd: dante LYS 246 *recording completed on 17 february 1949;* *also private lp edition by preiser*

0360/9-10 december 1948/musikvereinssaal/columbia sessions

wagner meistersinger von nürnberg excerpt (was duftet doch der flieder)	**zallinger** hotter	lp: emi RLS 764/1C137 43187-43189M cd: emi CMS 566 4832/CZS 569 7432 *unpublished columbia 78 rpm recording;* *only second half of fliedermonolog has* *been published; also private lp edition* *by preiser*
wagner meistersinger von nürnberg excerpt (wahn! wahn!)		lp: emi RLS 764/1C137 43187-43189M *unpublished columbia 78 rpm recording;* *only second half of wahnmonolog has* *been published; also private lp edition* *by preiser*
wagner die walküre excerpt (leb wohl, du kühnes herrliches kind!)		lp: emi RLS 764/1C137 43187-43189M *unpublished columbia 78 rpm recording; also* *private lp edition by preiser*

0361/10-13 december 1948/musikvereinssaal/hmv and columbia sessions

puccini madama butterfly excerpt (un bel di)	**prohaska** cebotari	78: hmv DB 6940 lp: electrola E 60050/WDLP 563 lp: emi 1C147 29118-29119M lp: preiser PR 9860 cd: preiser 90034 cd: toshiba shinseido SGR 8244
puccini madama butterfly excerpt (con onor muore)		78: hmv DB 6940 lp: electrola E 60050/WDLP 563 lp: emi 1C147 29118-29119M lp: preiser PR 9860 cd: preiser 90034
mozart entführung aus dem serail excerpt (o wie will ich triumphieren!)	**prohaska** weber	78: columbia LB 87 lp: emi RLS 764/1C137 43187-43189M/ 1C177 00933-00934M cd: testament SBT 1171 *also private lp edition by preiser*
mozart entführung aus dem serail excerpts (wer ein liebchen hat gefunden; solche hergelauf'ne laffen!); beethoven fidelio excerpt (hat man nicht auch gold beineben)		columbia unpublished

0362/1948/music films produced by eugen sharin

	krips	krips is seen rehearsing carmen with cebotari and rothmüller, and in 4 titles in a series "ambassador masterworks" (unspecified works)

0363/30 december 1948-2 january 1949/milan teatro alla scala

mozart	**karajan**	lp:melodramMEL087/MEL088/MEL 089
le nozze di	schwarzkopf	*each lp contains different brief excerpts*
figaro	cebotari	*from two separate performances: these*
fragments	seefried	*guest performances by vienna staatsoper*
	jurinac	
	taddei	
	höfermeyer	

0364/21 january 1949/musikvereinssaal/columbia session

j.strauss	**karajan**	78: columbia LB 128
perpetuum		78: columbia (germany) LW 62
mobile		78: columbia (italy) GQ 7251
		45: columbia SCD 2111
		lp: toshiba EAC 30110
		lp: emi RLS 7714/1C137 54370-54373M
		cd: emi CDM 566 3952/CMS 763 3262/
		CMS 566 4832
mascagni		78: columbia LX 1208
cavalleria		78: columbia (italy) GQX 11322
rusticana		45: columbia SCB 109/SCD 2084
intermezzo		45: columbia (germany) SCBW 108
		45: columbia (italy) SCBQ 3013
		cd: emi CDM 566 3932/CMS 566 4832

0365/28 january 1949/musikvereinssaal/hmv session

nicolai	**prohaska**	78: hmv DB 6939
die lustigen	cebotari	45: hmv 7ER 5141
weiber von		lp: emi RLS 764/1C137 43187-43189M/
windsor		1C147 29118-29119M
excerpt		lp: preiser PR 9860
(nun eilt herbei)		cd: preiser 90034
		also private lp edition by preiser
gounod		78: hmv DB 6947
faust		lp: emi 1C147 29118-29119M
excerpt		lp: preiser PR 9860
(ah que de bijoux!/		cd: preiser 90034
ah je ris!)		

0366/2 february 1949/musikverein brahmssaal/columbia session

mozart	**ackermann**	78: columbia LB 81
don giovanni	kunz	78: columbia (germany) LW 48
excerpt		45: columbia SEL 1574
(madamina!)		lp: emi RLS 764/1C137 43187-43189M/
		1C147 03580-03581M
		cd: testament SBT 1059
		cd: toshiba shinseido SGR 8244
		also private lp edition by preiser

mozart	**ackermann**	lp: emi EX 769 7411
zauberflöte	w.ludwig	cd: emi CHS 769 7412
excerpt		*unpublished columbia 78 rpm recording*
(dies bildnis)		

0367/3 february 1949/musikverein brahmssaal/columbia session

mozart	**prohaska**	columbia unpublished
entführung	weber	
aus dem		
serail		
excerpt		
(o wie will ich		
triumphieren!)		

beethoven		78: columbia LB 87
fidelio		lp: emi RLS 764/1C137 43187-43189M/
excerpt		1C177 00933-00934M
(hat man auch nicht		cd: testament SBT 1171
gold beineben)		*also private lp edition by preiser*

weber		78: columbia LX 1310
der freischütz		78: columbia (austria) LVX 148
excerpt		lp: emi RLS 764/1C137 43187-43189M/
(schweig, damit dich		1C177 00933-00934M
niemand warnt!)		cd: testament SBT 1171
		cd: toshiba shinseido SGR 8244
		also private lp edition by preiser

weber		78: columbia LB 87
der freischütz		lp: emi RLS 764/1C137 43187-43189M/
excerpt		1C177 00933-00934M
(hier im ird'schen		cd: testament SBT 1171
jammertal!)		cd: toshiba shinseido SGR 8244
		also private lp edition by preiser

0368/4-9 february 1949/musikverein brahmssaal/columbia sessions

mussorgsky	**ackermann**	lp: emi 1C177 00933-00934M
boris godunov	weber	cd: testament SBT 1171
excerpt	*sung in german*	*unpublished columbia 78 rpm recording*
(varlaam's song)		

verdi
i vespri
siciliani
excerpt
(o tu palermo!)
78: columbia LX 1310
78: columbia (austria) LVX 148
lp: emi 1C177 00933-00934M
cd: testament SBT 1171

mozart	**ackermann**	78: columbia LB 96
entführung	weber	lp: emi RLS 764/1C137 43187-43189M/
aus dem		1C177 00933-00934M
serail		cd: testament SBT 1171
(wer ein liebchen		*also private lp edition by preiser, which*
hat gefunden)		*incorrectly names conductor as prohaska*

strauss	**ackermann**	78: columbia LX 1226-1227
rosenkavalier	d.herrmann	lp: columbia (usa) ML 2126
excerpt	weber	lp: world records SH 286
(da lieg' ich!)		lp: emi RLS 764/1C137 43187-43189M/
		1C177 00933-00934M
		cd: testament SBT 1171
		cd: toshiba shinseido SGR 8244
		also private lp edition by preiser

0369/8 february 1949/musikvereinssaal

mozart	**furtwängler**	unpublished private recording
concerto	bella	*although a recording of this performance*
for 2	badura-skoda	*was arranged by paul badura-skoda, it*
pianos		*seems that the one published by discocorp,*
		nippon columbia, music and arts and
		french furtwängler society does not
		contain the named furtwängler performance

0370/15-23 february 1949/musikvereinssaal/hmv sessions

mendelssohn hebrides overture	**furtwängler**	78: hmv DB 6941 78: victor 66-6024 45: hmv 7R 102 45: hmv (france) 7RF 102 45: hmv (italy) 7RQ 102 lp: hmv ALP 1526/XLP 30097 lp: hmv (france) FALP 617 lp: hmv (italy) QALP 10298 lp: electrola E 60655/WDLP 662 lp: emi 1C149 03584-03586M lp: french furtwängler society SWF 8001 cd: emi CHS 566 7702
wagner siegfried idyll		78: hmv DB 6916-6917 lp: hmv (france) FALP 110/FALP 546 lp: hmv (italy) QALP 10216 lp: unicorn WFS 2-3 lp: angel 1B-6024 lp: emi 1C149 01197-01199M/29 12343 cd: emi CZS 252 3282 cd: testament SBT 1141
wagner götter- dämmerung excerpt (siegfrried's rhine journey)		78: hmv DB 6949-6950 lp: hmv (france) FALP 110/FALP 194/ COLH 307 lp: electrola SME 91399 lp: victor LHMV 1049 lp: french furtwängler society SWF 7803 lp: emi 2C051 03855 cd: testament SBT 1141 *catalogue number FALP 194 was also used for later 1954 version with same artists*
wagner tannhäuser overture		cd: testament SBT 1141 *unpublished hmv 78rpm recording*
wagner götter- dämmerung excerpt (siegfried's funeral march)		cd: testament SBT 1141 *unpublished hmv 78rpm recording, incorrectly dated by testament as 31 january 1950 (information about this misdating comes from samy habra of french furtwängler society)*

*0371/3 march 1949/musikvereinssaal/columbia session

gruber stille nacht	unnamed conductor vienna opera chorus schwarzkopf	78: columbia LC 32 lp: emi ALP 143 5501
o tannenbaum		78: columbia LC 32
es ist ein ros' entsprungen; o du fröhliche!		78: columbia LC 33

0372/14-17 march 1949/musikvereinssal/hmv and columbia sessions

mozart symphony no 41 "jupiter"	**böhm**	78: hmv C 3884-3887/DB 11532-11535/ C 7759-7762 auto 78: hmv (austria) GB 31-34 45: victor WBC 1018 lp: victor LBC 1018 lp: vox (japan) H 5062 cd: emi CDH 764 2952/CHS 764 2942 *H 5062 incorrectly dated 1952*
mozart schauspiel- direktor overture		78: hmv C 3887/C 7759/DB 11535 78: hmv (austria) GB 34 cd: wing (japan) WCD 9
schmidt notre dame intermezzo		78: hmv C 3975/DB 20400 78: hmv (switzerland) FKX 226 45: hmv 7P 575 45: electrola E 30039 cd: toshiba shinseido SGR 8243
josef strauss frauenherz polka		hmv unpublished

0372/concluded

josef strauss sphärenklänge waltz	**böhm**	78: hmv C 4070 78: hmv (austria) GB 49 78: electrola EH 1360 45: victor WBC 1008 lp: victor LBC 1008 lp: turnabout THS 65066 cd: emi CDH 764 2992/CHS 764 2942 cd: wing (japan) WCD 9
j.strauss rosen aus dem süden waltz		78: hmv C 3919 78: hmv (austria) GB 19 78: electrola EH 1374 45: hmv (france) 7BF 1005 45: victor WBC 1008 lp: victor LBC 1008 cd: wing (japan) WCD 9
j.strauss morgenblätter waltz		78: hmv C 3938 78: hmv (austria) GB 29 45: victor WBC 1008 lp: victor LBC 1008 cd: wing (japan) WCD 9 cd: dg 459 7342
j.strauss neue pizzicato polka		78: hmv C 3975/DB 11521 78: hmv (switzerland) FKX 226 78: hmv (austria) GB 35 45: electrola E 30039 lp: emi 1C147 30226-30227M cd: wing (japan) WCD 9 cd: toshiba shinseido SGR 8243
puccini turandot excerpt (tu che di gel sei cinta)	**böhm** schwarzkopf	78: columbia LB 85 78: columbia (poland) LM 4 78: columbia (japan) GO 7240 45: columbia SEL 1575 lp: emi RLS 763/1C151 43160-43163M cd: toshiba shinseido SGR 8244

0373/30 march-4 april 1949/musikvereinssaal/hmv sessions

wagner
der fliegende
holländer
overture
	furtwängler	78: hmv DB 6975-6976/
		    DB 9727-9728 auto
		78: hmv (australia) ED 1233-1234
		lp: hmv (france) FALP 289/FALP 30039
		lp: electrola E 90023/E 91074/
		    WALP 534/WALP 561
		lp: columbia (austria) VALP 538
		lp: unicorn WFS 2-3
		lp: angel 1B-6024
		lp: melodiya D 0132137-0132138
		lp: emi 1C149 01197-01199M/29 12343
		cd: historical performers HP 4
		cd: emi CZS 252 3282/CHS 764 9352

brahms
haydn
variations
		78: hmv DB 6932-6934/
		    DB 9402-9404 auto
		45: victor WHMV 1010
		lp: hmv ALP 1011
		lp: hmv (france) FALP 188
		lp: hmv (italy) QALP 188
		lp: electrola E 90025/E 70420/
		    WALP 1011/WBLP 558
		lp: columbia (austria) VALP 505
		lp: victor LHMV 1010
		lp: emi 3C153 53661-53669M/
		    1C047 01415M
		cd: flowers (japan) BL 024
		cd: dante LYS 206
		cd: emi CZS 252 3212/CHS 566 5132
		also private lp edition by preiser; BL 024 and CZS 252 3212 incorrectly dated 27 january 1952

berlioz marche hongroise/ la damnation de faust		lp: emi 1C149 03584-03586M cd: emi CHS 566 7702 *unpublished hmv 78rpm recording*

0373/continued

wagner walkürenritt/ die walküre	**furtwängler**	78: hmv DB 6950 45: hmv 7R 141/7P 206 45: hmv (france) 7RF 203 45: hmv (italy) 7RQ 3004 45: electrola 7RW 125 45: victor EHA 17 lp: hmv (france) FBLP 25057 lp: victor LHMV 1049 lp: unicorn WFS 2-3 lp: angel 1B 6024 lp: emi 1C149 01197-01199M/29 12343 cd: emi CZS 252 3282/CHS 764 9352 *CZS 252 3282 incorrectly dated 1954*

mozart
eine kleine
nachtmusik
		78: hmv DB 6911-6912
		45: hmv 7R 122-123
		45: hmv (france) ERF 17013
		45: electrola E 50063/7ERW 5315
		45: victor 11-7965-7966/WHMV 1018
		lp: hmv ALP 1498/XLP 30104
		lp: hmv (france) FALP 117/FALP 30033
		lp: hmv (italy) QALP 117
		lp: electrola E 90152/WALP 1498/
		    E 60543/WDLP 601/E 80801/
		    SME 90801/WCLP 854/
		    HZE 105/SHZE 105
		lp: victor LHMV 1018
		lp: emi 1C149 03584-03586M
		cd: emi CDH 763 8182

wagner
meistersinger
von nürnberg
overture
		78: hmv DB 6942-6943
		lp: hmv (france) FALP 289/FALP 546/
		    FALP 30039/FALP 30213
		lp: hmv (italy) QALP 10216
		lp: electrola E 90023/WALP 534/
		    E 80801/WCLP 854/E 91074/
		    WALP 561/SME 80801/E 83388/
		    WCLP 820/HZE 105/SHZE 105
		lp: columbia (austria) VALP 538
		lp: victor LHMV 1049
		lp: unicorn WFS 2-3
		lp: angel 1B 6024
		lp: emi 1C149 01197-01199M/29 12343
		cd: historical performers HP 4
		cd: emi CZS 252 3282/CHS 764 9352

0373/concluded

brahms
hungarian
dance
no 1
	furtwängler	78: hmv DB 6976/DB 9729
		78: hmv (australia) ED 1233
		45: victor EHA 17
		lp: unicorn WFS 1
		lp: emi 1C149 03584-03586M/
		    1C149 53420-53426/
		    2C153 53420-53426/
		    3C153 53661-53669M
		cd: dante LYS 204
		cd: emi CZS 252 3212/CHS 566 5132
		also private lp edition by preiser

brahms
hungarian
dance
no 3
		78: hmv DB 6943/DB 9402
		lp: unicorn WFS 1
		lp: emi 1C149 03584-03586M/
		    1C149 53420-53426/
		    2C153 53420-53426/
		    3C153 53661-53669M
		cd: dante LYS 204
		cd: emi CZS 252 3212/CHS 566 5132
		also private lp edition by preiser

brahms
hungarian
dance
no 10
		78: hmv DB 6943/DB 9402
		45: victor EHA 17
		lp: unicorn WFS 1
		lp: emi 1C149 03584-03586M/
		    1C149 53420-53426/
		    2C153 53420-53426/
		    3C153 53661-53669M
		cd: dante LYS 204
		cd: emi CZS 252 3212/CHS 566 5132
		also private lp edition by preiser

wagner tanz der lehrbuben/ meistersinger von nürnberg		78: hmv DB 6943 45: hmv 7R 141/7P 206 45: hmv (france) 7RF 203 45: hmv (italy) 7RQ 3004 45: electrola 7RW 125 45: victor EHA 17 lp: victor LHMV 1049 lp: unicorn WFS 2-3 lp: emi 1C149 01197-01199M/29 12343 cd: emi CZS 252 3282/CHS 764 9352

0374/27 july 1949/salzburg felsenreitschule

mozart	**furtwängler**	lp: ed smith EJS 572
zauberflöte	vienna opera	lp: discocorp IGI 337
	chorus	lp: nippon columbia OZ 7572-7574
	seefried	cd: arlecchino ARL 78-80
	lipp	cd: music and arts CD 882
	oravez	cd: gebhardt JGCD 0010-3
	w.ludwig	*excerpts*
	schmitt-walter	cd: di stefano GDS 1201
	greindl	*complete opera also issued in japan*
	schöffler	*by cetra*

0375/3 august 1949/salzburg felsenreitschule

beethoven	**furtwängler**	unpublished radio broadcast
fidelio	vienna opera	
	chorus	
	flagstad	
	seefried	
	patzak	
	holm	
	greindl	
	schöffler	
	braun	

0376/7 august 1949/salzburg festspielhaus

pfitzner	**furtwängler**	lp: rococo 2109
symphony		lp: discocorp RR 437
in c		lp: cetra FE 26
		lp: nippon columbia OZ 7593
		cd: as-disc AS 370
		cd: dante LYS 212
		cd: theatre (japan) 400.3531
		cd:german furtwängler societyTMK 10670
		cd: urania URN 22.125
		cd: orfeo C525 911B

0377/9 august 1949/salzburg felsenreitschule

orff	**fricsay**	cd: stradivarius STR 10060
antigonae	vienna opera	
	chorus	
	zadek	
	krebs	
	haefliger	
	kusche	
	greindl	

0378/12 august 1949/salzburg festspielhaus

strauss	**szell**	lp: cetra LO 69
rosenkavalier	vienna opera chorus	cd: arlecchino ARL 46-48
	reining	*excerpts*
	güden	lp: longanesi GML 45
	novotna	
	rosvaenge	
	hann	
	prohaska	

0379/14 august 1949/salzburg festspielhaus

verdi	**karajan**	lp: cetra LO 524
requiem	wiener singverein	lp: discocorp RR 391
	zadek	lp: rodolphe RP 12403-12404
	klose	lp: dei della musica DMV 34-35
	rosvaenge	cd: datum DAT 12323
	christoff	

0380/30 august 1949/salzburg festspielhaus

wagner siegfried idyll	**knappertsbusch**	lp: melodram MEL 711
bruckner symphony no 7		lp: discocorp RR 209
		lp: melodram MEL 711
		cd: arkadia CD 712/CDGI 712
		cd: music and arts CD 209/CD 1028
		cd: instituto discografico italiano IDI5-316
		cd: preiser 90408

0381/1 october 1949/london bbc maida vale studio

beethoven coriolan; schubert unfinished; brahms haydn variations; j.strauss kaiserwalzer	**furtwängler**	unpublished radio broadcast *recordings were broadcast on 25 december 1949*

0382/4 october 1949/london kingsway hall/columbia session

mahler	**walter**	78: columbia LX 8939-8941
kindertoten-	ferrier	lp: columbia 33C 1009
lieder		lp: columbia (france) 33FC 1033
		lp: columbia (germany) C 70086/33WC 1009
		lp: columbia (usa) ML 2187/ML 4980/
		3226 0016
		lp: emi HLM 7002/2C061 01209/
		1C147 01402-01403M
		lp: angel 60203
		cd: gala GL 307
		cd: emi CDH 761 0032/CDM 566 9112

0383/18-20 october 1949/musikvereinssaal/columbia sessions

josef strauss	**karajan**	78: columbia LX 1250
sphärenklänge		78: columbia (france) LFX 1027
waltz		78: columbia (usa) M 15175
		78: electrola EW 53
		45: columbia SEL 1505
		45: columbia (italy) SEBQ 107
		45: columbia (germany) C 50143/SELW 1505
		cd: emi CDM 566 3952/CMS 566 4832/
		CMS 763 3262
		cd: dg 435 3352

josef strauss		78: columbia LX 1257
transaktionen		78: columbia (france) LFX 1022
waltz		45: columbia SEL 1505
		45: columbia (italy) SEBQ 107
		45: columbia (germany)C50143/SELW1505
		cd: emi CDM 566 3962/CMS 566 4832/
		CMS 763 3262

0383/concluded

j.strauss	**karajan**	78: columbia LX 1402/LCX 145
wein weib		78: columbia (france) LFX 1013
und gesang		78: columbia (italy) GQX 11437
waltz		78: columbia (germany) LWX 403
		78: columbia (usa) M 15141
		45: columbia SCB 112/SCD 2075
		45: columbia (italy) SCBQ 3017
		lp: toshiba EAC 30111
		cd: emi CDM 566 3952/CMS 566 4832/ CMS 763 3262

j.strauss
tritsch-tratsch
polka

78: columbia LB 128
78: columbia (italy) GQ 7251
78: columbia (germany) LW 62
45: columbia SCD 2111
lp: toshiba EAC 30110
lp: emi RLS 7714/1C137 54370-54373M
cd: emi CDM 566 3962/CMS 566 4832/ CDM 567 1772/CMS 763 3262

j.strauss
unter donner
und blitz
polka

lp: preiser LV 15
cd: emi CDH 764 2992/CDM 566 3952/ CHS 764 2942/CMS 566 4832/ CMS 763 3262/CDM 567 1772
cd: dg 459 7342
unpublished columbia 78rpm recording

0384/18-27 october 1949/musikvereinssaal/columbia sessions

brahms symphony no 2	**karajan**	78: columbia (austria) LVX 125-129 78: columbia (italy) GQX 11441-11445 lp: columbia (france) 33FCX 285 lp: angel 35007 lp: toshiba EAC 30106 cd: emi CDM 566 3902/CMS 763 3262/ CMS 566 4832 *recording completed 8-10 november 1949*
mozart symphony no 39		78: columbia LX 1375-1377/ LX 8785-8787 auto 78: columbia (italy) GQX 11405-11407 78: columbia (germany) LWX 398-400 lp: columbia (france) 33FCX 145 lp: columbia (italy) 33QCX 145 lp: columbia (usa) RL 3068 lp: toshiba EAC 30107 cd: emi CDM 566 3882/CMS 566 4832 *recording completed on 10 november 1949*
josef strauss delirien waltz		78: columbia LX 1303 78: columbia (austria) LVX 142 lp: toshiba EAC 30111 lp: emi RLS 7714/1C137 54370-54373M cd: emi CDM 566 3962/CMS 566 4832/ CMS 763 3262
j.strauss wiener blut waltz		78: columbia LX 1321 78: columbia (france) LFX 1023 78: columbia (italy) GQX 11436 78: columbia (austria) LVX 167 78: electrola EW 22 45: columbia SEL 1503 45: columbia (france) ESBF 109 45: columbia (italy) SEBQ 101 lp: toshiba EAC 30111 cd: emi CDM 566 3962/CMS 566 4832/ CMS 763 3262/CDM 567 1772 cd: dg 459 7342 *recording completed on 10 november 1949*

0385/2-3 november 1949/musikvereinssaal/columbia sessions

wagner	**karajan**	78: columbia LX 1347
tannhäuser	vienna	78: columbia (france) LFX 1021
excerpt	opera chorus	78: columbia (italy) GQX 11463
(freudig		78: columbia (austria) LVX 154
begrüssen		78: columbia (usa) M 15154
wir die		lp: toshiba EAC 30109
edle halle)		cd: emi CMS 566 4832

wagner
meistersinger
von nürnberg
excerpt
(da zu dir der
heiland kam)

78: columbia LX 1258
lp: toshiba EAC 30109
cd: emi CMS 566 4832

wagner
meistersinger
von nürnberg
excerpt (wach auf!)

78: columbia LX 1258
cd: emi CMS 566 4832

wagner
der fliegende
holländer
excerpt
(mit gewitter
und sturm)

78: columbia LX 1440
lp: toshiba EAC 30109
cd: emi CMS 566 4832

wagner
lohengrin
excerpt
(treulich geführt)

78: columbia LX 1360
lp: toshiba EAC 30109
cd: emi CMS 566 4832

wagner **karajan**
lohengrin
act 3
prelude

78: columbia LX 1360
cd: emi CMS 566 4832

0386/7-8 november 1949/musikverein brahmssaal/columbia sessions

mozart	**karajan**	78: columbia (germany) LWX 445-448
clarinet	wlach	78: columbia (italy) GQX 11484-11487
concerto		lp: toshiba EAC 30108
		cd: emi CDH 764 2952/CDM 566 3882/
		CHS 764 2942/CMS 566 4832

0387/9 november 1949/musikverein brahmssaal/columbia and hmv sessions

mozart zauberflöte excerpt (dies bildnis)	**loibner** w.ludwig	columbia unpublished
mozart entführung aus dem serail exscerpts (o wie ängstlich!; wenn der freude tränen fliessen)		lp: emi RLS 764/1C137 43187-43189M *also private lp edition by preiser;* *unpublished columbia 78 rpm recordings*
tchaikovsky pique dame excerpt (i love you dearly)	**loibner** braun *sung in german*	78: hmv C 3982 78: hmv (austria) GB 38 78: electrola EH 1355 *also private lp edition by preiser*
offenbach les contes d'hoffmann excerpt (scintille diamant)		78: hmv C 3982 78: hmv (austria) GB 38 78: electrola EH 1355

0388/12 november 1949/musikverein brahmssaal/columbia session

j.strauss eine nacht in venedig excerpt (komm' in gondel!)	**paulik** kunz	78: columbia LX 1544 45: columbia SEB 3507 lp: emi 1C147 03580-03581M lp: world records SH 284 cd: testament SBT 1059
j.strauss eine nacht in venedig excerpt (ach wie so herrlich!)		78: columbia LB 86 45: columbia SEB 3507 lp: emi 1C147 03580-03581M/ 1C147 30226-30227M lp: world records SH 284 cd: testament SBT 1059
j.strauss zigeunerbaron excerpt (ja das schreiben und das lesen!)		78: columbia LB 86 45: columbia SEB 3507 lp: emi 1C147 03580-03581M/ 1C147 30226-30227M lp: world records SH 284 cd: testament SBT 1059

188
0389/23 december 1949/theater an der wien

puccini	**krips**	cd: polyhymnia 21212
tosca	welitsch	
excerpts	rosvaenge	
(ah frascigia	*sung in german*	
a floria tosca!;		
senti l'ore		
e vicina!)		

0390/18-24 january 1950/musikvereinssaal/hmv sessions

beethoven	**furtwängler**	78: hmv DB 21106-21110/
symphony		DB 9516-9520 auto
no 7		45: victor WHMV 1008
		lp: hmv (france) FALP 115/
		FALP 30031/UVT 3031
		lp: hmv (italy) QALP 115
		lp: electrola E 90016/WALP 527/
		SME 90016/SMVP 8048
		lp: victor LHMV 1008
		lp: angel 1C 6018
		lp: emi 1C149 53432-53439M/
		1C027 00809M/2C051 03089/
		2C153 52540-52551
		cd: emi CHS 763 6062/CDH 769 8032
schubert		78: hmv DB 21131-21133/
symphony		DB 9538-9540 auto
no 8		45: victor WHMV 1020
"unfinished"		lp: hmv (france) FALP 317/
		FALP 30043/FBLP 1005
		lp: electrola E 90153/WALP 1500/
		E 60550/WDLP 603/SME 91486/
		SMVP 8040
		lp: victor LHMV 1020
		lp: emi XLP 30104/1C047 00907M/
		2C051 03614
		cd: emi CDC 747 1202/CDH 763 1932/
		CDM 565 9172/CMS 565 9152/
		CHS 566 7702
		also private lp edition by preiser

0390/concluded

strauss tod und verklärung	**furtwängler**	78: hmv DB 21169-21171/ DB 9592-9594 auto 45: victor WHMV 1023 lp: hmv (france) FALP 546 lp: hmv (italy) QALP 10216 lp: electrola HZEL 71 lp: victor LHMV 1023 lp: angel 60094 lp: emi HQM 1137/10 1151/ 1C049 01155M cd: emi CDH 565 1972
j.strauss kaiserwalzer		78: hmv DB 21174 45: hmv (france) 7RF 104 45: hmv (italy) 7RQ 104 lp: hmv ALP 1526/XLP 30106 lp: hmv (france) FALP 617 lp: electrola SMVP 8016 lp: french furtwängler society SWF 8001 cd: dg 435 3352/459 7342 cd: emi CHS 566 7702/CDM 567 1772 *also private lp edition by preiser*

0391/25-30 january 1950/musikvereinssaal/hmv sessions

beethoven symphony no 4	**furtwängler**	78: hmv DB 21099-21103/ DB 9524-9528 auto lp: hmv (france) FALP 116 lp: discocorp RR 437 lp: french furtwängler society SWF 7904 lp: emi 3C153 53800-53805M *issued on cd in japan by toshiba;* *catalogue number FALP 116* *also used for 1952 hmv version* *of this symphony conducted by* *furtwangler*

0392/31 january-1 february 1950/musikvereinssaal/hmv sessions

wagner	**furtwängler**	78: hmv DB 6946
götter-		45: hmv 7R 151
dämmerung		45: hmv (france) 7RF 149
excerpt		45: hmv (italy) 7RQ 3011
(siegfried's		45: electrola 7RW 124
funeral march)		45: victor EHB 2
		lp: hmv (france) FALP 194
		lp: victor LHMV 1049
		lp: french furtwängler society SWF 7803
		lp: emi 2C051 03855
		issued on cd by toshiba in japan; catalogue number FALP 194 also used for 1954 recording of the piece by furtwängler
weber		78: hmv DB 21104
oberon		78: hmv (australia) ED 1246
overture		45: hmv (france) 7RF 258
		45: hmv (italy) 7RQ 258
		lp: hmv ALP 1526/XLP 30090
		lp: hmv (france) FALP 617
		lp: hmv (italy) QALP 10298
		lp: electrola E 60655/WDLP 662/ SMVP 8016
		lp: melodiya M10 41233-41234
		lp: emi 1C149 03584-03586M/ F666.699
		cd: palladio PD 4124
		cd: historical performers HP 8
		cd: emi CHS 566 7702
wagner		lp: unicorn WFS 2-3
meistersinger		lp: private issue (japan) JP 1114
von nürnberg		lp: emi 1C149 01197-01199M/ 29 12343
act 3		
prelude		cd: historical performers HP 4
		cd: emi CHS 764 9352
		unpublished hmv 78rpm recording

0393/2-3 february 1950/musikverein brahmssaal/hmv sessions

tchaikovsky waltz/ serenade for strings	**furtwängler**	78: hmv DB 21173 45: hmv 7R 134/7ER 5001 45: hmv (france) 7RF 148/7ERF 131 45: hmv (italy) 7RQ 3032/7ERQ 110 45: electrola E 50033/7ERW 5001/ 7RW 101 lp: hmv ALP 1526 lp: hmv (france) FALP 617 lp: electrola SMVP 8016 lp: unicorn WFS 7 lp: emi 1C149 03584-03586M cd: emi CHS 764 8552
tchaikovsky finale/ serenade for strings		78: hmv DB 21172 78: hmv (australia) ED 1227 45: hmv 7R 140/7ER 5001 45: hmv (france) 7RF 146/7ERF 131 45: hmv (italy) 7RQ 3002/7ERQ 110 45: electrola E 50033/7ERW 5001/ 7RW 123 45: victor EHA 9 lp: hmv ALP 1526 lp: hmv (france) FALP 617 lp: electrola SMVP 8016 lp: unicorn WFS 7 lp: emi 1C149 03584-03586M cd: emi CHS 764 8552

schubert
rosamunde
ballet music
no 2
		78: hmv DB 21192/DB 11530
		45: hmv 7R 121
		45: hmv (france) 7RF 145
		45: hmv (italy) 7RQ 3012
		45: electrola 7RW 122
		45: victor WHMV 1020
		lp: hmv (france) FALP 317/FALP 30043
		lp: electrola E 90153/WALP 1500/
		    E 70420/WBLP 558
		lp: victor LHMV 1020
		lp: emi XLP 30106/2C051 03614/
		    1C149 03584-03586M
		cd: emi CDH 763 1932/CHS 566 7702

0393/concluded

schubert
rosamunde
entr'acte
no 3
	furtwängler	78: hmv DB 21192/DB 11530
		45: hmv 7R 121
		    45: hmv (france) 7RF 145
		45: hmv (italy) 7RQ 3012
		45: electrola 7RW 122
		45: victor WHMV 1020
		lp: hmv (france) FALP 317/FALP 30043
		lp: electrola E 90153/WALP 1500/
		    E 70420/WBLP 558
		lp: victor LHMV 1020
		lp: emi XLP 30106/2C051 03514/
		    1C149 03584-03586M
		cd: emi CDH 763 1932/CHS 566 7702

johann and
josef strauss
pizzicato
polka
		78: hmv DB 21173
		45: hmv 7R 134/7ER 5001
		45: hmv (france) 7RF 148/7ERF 131
		45: hmv (italy) 7RQ 3032/7ERQ 110
		45: electrola E 50033/7RW 101/
		    7ERW 5001
		lp: emi 1C149 03584-03586M/
		    XLP 30106
		cd: emi CHS 566 7702/CDM 567 1772
		*2 different takes of the 78rpm
		recording seem to have circulated,
		one with standard triangle part
		and the other without*

mozart
zauberflöte
excerpts
(zum leiden
bin ich
auserkoren;
der hölle
rache)
	furtwängler
	lipp
		lp: emi 1C137 43187-43189M/
		    RLS 764
		lp: french furtwängler society
		    SWF 8601
		lp: tanaka (japan) AT 13-14
		cd: emi CHS 566 7702
		*unpublished hmv 78rpm
		recordings; also private lp edition
		by preiser*

0394/3-9 june 1950/musikvereinssaal/decca sessions

mozart	**krips**	78: decca (switzerland) KX 28341-28353
entführung	vienna	lp: decca LXT 2536-2538/ECM 730-731/
aus dem	opera chorus	411 6741
serail	lipp	lp: london (usa) LLPA 3/A 4301/
	loose	RS 63015
	w.ludwig	cd: decca 443 5302
	klein	*excerpts*
	koreh	lp: decca LXT 2635
		lp: london (usa) XLL 458
		cd: decca 444 8792

mozart	**krips**	78: decca (switzerland) KX 28353
rondo alla turca		
arranged by		
herbeck		

0395/12 june 1950/musikvereinssaal/decca session

mozart	**krips**	lp: decca LXT 2685
le nozze	reining	cd: preiser 90083
di figaro	*sung in german*	
excerpts		
(porgi amor;		
dove sono)		

0396/14-16 june 1950/musikvereinssaal/decca sessions

strauss	**krauss**	78: decca K 23099-23100
also sprach		lp: decca LXT 2548/ECM 572/ECS 572
zarathustra		lp: london (usa) LLP 232/B 23208
		cd: decca 425 9742
		cd: testament awaiting publication
		also private lp edition by preiser

strauss		78: decca K 28364-28365
till eulenspiegels		lp: decca LXT 2549/ACL 16/
lustige streiche		ECM 572/ECS 572
		lp: london (usa) LLP 233/B 19043/B 23208
		cd: testament awaiting publication
		issued on cd by polygram in japan

strauss		78: decca K 28366-28367
don juan		lp: decca LXT 2549/ACL 16/
		ECM 608/ECS 608
		lp: london (usa) LLP 233/B 19043/
		STS 15504
		cd: decca 425 9932/433 3302/433 3312
		cd: testament awaiting publication

0397/17-21 june 1950/musikvereinssaal/columbia sessions

mozart	**karajan**	78: columbia (germany) LWX 410-425
le nozze	vienna	lp: columbia 33CX 1007-1009
di figaro	opera chorus	lp: columbia (france) 33FCX 174-176
	schwarzkopf	lp: columbia (germany) C 90292-90294/
	seefried	33WCX 1007-1009
	jurinac	lp: columbia (italy) 33QCX 10002-10004
	kunz	lp: columbia (austria) 33VCX 503-505
	london	lp: columbia (usa) SL 114
		lp: emi 1C147 01751-01753M/
		1C19754200-54208M/2C16501751-01753
		cd: emi CMS 769 6392/CMS 567 0682
		excerpts
		78: columbia LX 1575
		lp: columbia 33CX 1558
		lp: columbia (france) 33FCX 30170
		lp: columbia (germany) C 80531/
		C 70373/33WSX 548/33WC 518
		lp: columbia (usa) RL 3050
		lp: angel 35326
		lp: emi RLS 764/1C047 01444M/
		1C187 29225-29226M/EX 29 10563/
		1C063 00839/1C137 43187-43189M
		cd: emi CDH 763 5572/CDM 763 6572/
		CMS 763 7902
		recording made without recitatives; recording completed 23-31 october 1950; excerpts also on private lp edition by preiser

0398/22 june 1950/musikvereinssaal/decca session

j.strauss	**krauss**	78: decca K 23037/KX 28373
künstlerleben		lp: decca LXT 2634/LXT 2965/
waltz		ACL 24/ECS 2058
		lp: london (usa) LLP 454
		lp: preiser PR 135033/PR 135040
		cd: preiser 90336
		cd: arlecchino ARL 83-85
		also private lp edition by preiser
j.strauss		78: decca K 23226/KX 28374
frühlings-		78: telefunken E 1075/E 3861
stimmen		lp: decca LXT 2634/LXT 2965/
waltz		ACL 24/ECS 2058
		lp: london (usa) LLP 454
		lp: preiser PR 135032/PR 135040
		cd: preiser 90336
		cd: dg 435 3352/459 7342
		this recording also included in complete recording of fledermaus conducted by krauss

0399/23-24 june 1950/musikvereinssaal/decca sessions

wagner	**knappertsbusch**	78: decca K 28359-28360
parsifal		lp: decca LX 3036
prelude		lp: london (usa) LLP 451/LS 287
		cd: decca 440 0622

wagner 78: decca K 28361-28362
rienzi lp: decca LX 3034
overture lp: london (usa) LLP 451/LS 290
cd: decca 440 0622

wagner **knappertsbusch** 78: decca K 28442
siegfried lechleitner lp: decca LX 3034/LXT 2644
excerpt lp: london (usa) LS 290
(dass der cd: decca 440 0622
mein vater
nicht ist)

wagner **knappertsbusch** 78: decca K 28359-28360
parsifal vienna lp: decca LX 3036
excerpt opera chorus lp: london (usa) LLP 451/LS 287
(transformation treptow *issued on cd by polygram in japan*
scene act 1)

0400/june 1950/musikvereinssaal/decca sessions

beethoven **böhm** 78: decca AX 373-376
piano backhaus lp: decca LXT 2553/LXT 5353/
concerto ACL 148/ECM 524/ECS 524
no 3 lp: london (usa) LLP 289

*0401/june 1950/musikvereinssaal/decca sessions

verdi	**moralt**	78: decca K 28378
un ballo in	welitsch	lp: decca LXT 2567/LW 5050/BR 3035
maschera		lp: london (usa) LLP 69/R 23188
excerpts		cd: decca 448 1532
(ma dall'		cd: myto MCD 954 135
arrido stelo		
divulsa;		
morro ma prima		
in grazia)		

millöcker		78: decca K 28377
die dubarry		lp: decca LXT 2567/BR 3053
excerpt		lp: london (usa) LLP 69/R 23188
(ich schenk'		cd: decca 448 1532
mein herz)		cd: myto MCD 954 135

lehar		78: decca K 28377
zarewitsch		lp: decca LXT 2567/BR 3053
excerpt		lp: london (usa) LLP 69/R 23188
(einer wird		cd: decca 448 1532
kommen)		cd: polyhymnia 21212
		cd: myto MCD 954 135

lehar		78: decca X 534/K 28375
zigeunerliebe		lp: decca LXT 2567/BR 3035
excerpt		lp: london (usa) LLP 69/R 23188
(lied und		cd: decca 448 1532
czardas)		cd: myto MCD 954 135

lehar		78: decca X 534/K 28375
lustige witwe		lp: decca LXT 2567/BR 3053
excerpt		lp: london (usa) LLP 69/R 23188
(vilja-lied)		cd: decca 448 1532
		cd: myto MCD 954 135

tchaikovsky	**moralt**	78: decca X 523/K 28376
pique dame	welitsch	lp: decca LXT 2567/LW 5050/
excerpts	*sung in german*	BR 3035/ECS 812
('tis evening;		lp: london (usa) LLP 69/R 23188
it is close on		cd: decca 448 1532
midnight)		cd: myto MCD 954 135

0402/27 july 1950/salzburg festspielhaus

mozart	**furtwängler**	lp: ed smith EJS 419
don giovanni	vienna	lp: olympic 9109
	opera chorus	lp: discocorp RR 407
	schwarzkopf	lp: turnabout THS 65154–65156
	welitsch	lp: melodram MEL 713
	seefried	cd: priceless D 16581
	dermota	cd: laudis LCD 34001
	gobbi	cd: emi CHS 566 5672
	kunz	*excerpts*
	greindl	lp: discoreale DR 10037
	poell	lp: melodram MEL 082/MEL 088/MEL 095
		cd: melodram MEL 16501/MEL 26511

side 3 of olympic edition derived from 1953 performance also conducted by furtwängler

0403/5 august 1950/salzburg festspielhaus

beethoven	**furtwängler**	lp: morgan MOR 5001
fidelio	vienna	lp: mrf records MRF 50
	opera chorus	lp: bjr records BJR 112
	flagstad	lp: discocorp IGI 328
	schwarzkopf	lp: cetra FE 44
	patzak	lp: cls records AMDRL 32819
	dermota	cd: arkadia CDWFE 304/CDWFE 354
	braun	cd: verona 27044-27045
	schöffler	cd: emi CHS 764 9012
	greindl	*excerpts*
		cd: priceless D 16395
		cd: bayer BR 200 002

many editions were dated 22 august 1950, the date on which the recording was broadcast by austrian radio

0404/9 august 1950/salzburg festspielhaus

blacher romeo und julia	**krips** vienna opera chorus güden wagner holm witt uhde böhme	unpublished radio broadcast *the two chamber operas were played* *as a double bill*
britten the rape of lucretia	**krips** kupper güden höngen patzak uhde poell	

0405/15 august 1950/salzburg festspielhaus

stravinsky symphony in three movements	**furtwängler**	lp: cetra FE 14 cd: varese srabande VCD 47259 cd: cetra CDE 1043 cd: virtuoso 269.7322
brahms symphony no 4		cd: music and arts CD 258 cd: nuova era 013.6332-6334 cd: orfeo C525 991B

0406/16 august 1950/salzburg felsenreitschule

mozart zauberflöte	**furtwängler** vienna opera chorus seefried lipp heusser dermota kunz greindl schöffler	unpublished radio broadcast *no. 21-end missing from recording;* *newsreel film fragments also survive*

0407/23 august 1950/salzburg festspielhaus

mahler	**walter**	cd: varese sarabande VCD 47228
symphony	seefried	cd: mca classics MCAD 42337
no 4		cd: originals SH 836
		final movement
		cd: orfeo/salzburg festival SF 001

0408/31 august 1950/salzburg festspielhaus

bach	**furtwängler**	lp: discocorp RR 515
brandenburg		lp: nippon columbia OZ 7594
concerto		cd: refrain (japan) DR 92 0018
no 3		

bach	**furtwängler**	lp: discocorp RR 515
brandenburg	boskovsky	lp: nippon columbia OZ 7594
concerto	niedermayer	cd: refrain (japan) DR 92 0018
no 5	furtwängler	

beethoven	**furtwängler**	unpublished radio broadcast
symphony		*tape stored in private archive*
no 3		*in berlin*
"eroica"		

0409/2-9 september 1950/musikvereinssaal/decca sessions

wagner	**knappertsbusch**	78: decca K 28385-28392/
meistersinger	vienna	KX 53046-53053
von nürnberg	opera chorus	lp: decca LXT 2560-2561
act 2	güden	lp: london (usa) LLP 284-285
	schürhoff	*recording of acts 1 and 3 took*
	treptow	*place in september 1951:*
	dermota	*issue details of complete*
	schöffler	*opera can be found under that*
	edelmann	*entry*

0410/11 september 1950/musikvereinssaal/decca session

wagner	**knappertsbusch**	78: decca K 28443
parsifal	vienna	lp: decca LXT 2644/LX 3036
excerpt	opera chorus	lp: london (usa) LLP 287/LL 447
(flower maidens'	treptow	*issued on cd in japan by polygram*
scene)		

0411/12-13 september 1950/musikvereinssaal/decca sessions

mozart	**böhm**	78: decca X 53069-53071
symphony		lp: decca LXT 2558/LXT 2562/ACL 147
no 36		lp: london (usa) LLP 286

0412/14 september 1950/musikvereinssaal/decca session

mozart	**böhm**	45: decca 45-71116
zauberflöte	dermota	lp: decca LXT 2592/LXT 2685/ECS 812
excerpt		lp: london (usa) LLP 345
(dies bildnis)		
strauss		45: decca 45-71116
capriccio		lp: decca LXT 2592
excerpt		lp: london (usa) LLP 345
(kein andres		lp: everest SDBR 3202
das mir so		lp: emi EX 769 7411
im herzen)		cd: emi CMS 769 7412
mozart	**böhm**	78: decca K 28393
don giovanni	dermota	lp: decca LXT 2592/LXT 2685
excerpt	*sung in german*	lp: london (usa) LLP 345
(dalla sua pace)		lp: everest SDBR 3202
mozart		78: decca K 28393
don giovanni		lp: decca LXT 2592/LXT 2685
excerpt		lp: london (usa) LLP 345
(il mio tesoro)		lp: everest SDBR 3202
		also private lp edition by preiser

0413/15 september 1950/musikvereinssaal/decca sessions

wagner die walkure excerpt (wotan's farewell and magic fire music)	**moralt** schöffler	lp: decca LXT 2554/414 4531 lp: london (usa) LL 447 cd: decca 448 1532
mozart don giovanni excerpt (madamina!)	**böhm** schöffler	lp: decca LXT 2554/LXT 2685/ ECS 811/414 4531 lp: london (usa) LLP 288/LL 457
mozart le nozze di figaro (non piu andrai)		78: decca K 23305/KX 28443 lp: decca LXT 2554/LXT 2685/ ECS 811/414 4531 lp: london (usa) LLP 288/LL 457 cd: decca 448 1532
verdi otello excerpt (credo in un dio crudel!)		lp: decca LXT 2554/414 4531 lp: london (usa) LLP 288
verdi otello excerpt (era la notte)		78: decca K 23145/KX 28395 lp: decca LXT 2554/414 4531 lp: london (usa) LLP 288
beethoven fidelio excerpt (gott! welch' dunkel hier!)	**böhm** patzak	78: decca X 489/K 23076 45: decca 45-71016 lp: decca LXT 2672/BR 3062/ ECS 812/414 1781 lp: london (usa) LLP 427 cd: decca 448 1522 *also private lp edition by preiser, which* *incorrectly names conductor as moralt*

0414/16-22 september 1950/konzerthaus/decca sessions

j.strauss	**krauss**	78: decca X 470-481/K 23112-23122
die fledermaus	vienna	lp: decca LXT 2550-2551/ACL 145-146/
	opera chorus	DPA 585-586
	güden	lp: london (usa) LLP 281-282/A 4207
	lipp	lp: preiser PR 135035-135036
	wagner	cd: decca 425 9902
	patzak	*excerpts*
	dermota	45: decca CEP 552
	poell	lp: decca LXT 2576/LXT 2634/LXT 2965/
		LW 5005/LW 5020/LW 5138/
		ACL 24/ACL 73/BR 3062/ECS 2058
		lp: london (usa) LLP 305/LL 454/LD 9008/
		5023
		lp: preiser PR 135031
		cd: decca 444 8802
		cd: preiser 90336
		cd: arlecchino ARL 83-85
		krauss replaced krips as conductor

0415/25 september 1950/stockholm konserthuset

austrian national anthem	**furtwängler**	lp: private issue (japan) GC 570234-570235 lp: tanaka (japan) AT 13-14
swedish national anthem		lp: private issue (japan) GC 570234-570235 lp: tanaka (japan) AT 13-14 cd: theatre (japan) 400.3531
haydn symphony no 94 "surprise"		lp: discocorp RR 399 lp: private issue (japan) GC 570234-570235 lp: nippon columbia OS 7075 cd: music bridge (japan) cd: music and arts CD 802 *also issued in japan by seven seas*
sibelius en saga		lp: private issue (japan) GC 570234-570235 lp: discocorp RR 403/RR 507 cd: theatre (japan) 400.3531 cd: music and arts CD 799 *also issued in japan by seven seas*
strauss don juan		lp: private issue (japan) GC 570234-570235 lp: discocorp RR 460 cd: music and arts CD 802 *also issued in japan by seven seas*
beethoven symphony no 5		lp: private issues (japan) JP 1190-1192/ GC 570234-570235 lp: discocorp RR 507 lp: nippon columbia OZ 7585 cd: music and arts CD 802 *also issued in japan by seven seas and palette*

0416/1 october 1950/copenhagen odd fellow palaet

schubert **furtwängler** unpublished radio broadcast
symphony *danish radio archive*
no 8
"unfinished"

beethoven lp: danacord DACO 114
symphony cd: danacord DACOCD 301
no 5

0417/21 october 1950/theater an der wien

tchaikovsky **zallinger** unpublished radio broadcast
evgeny vienna opera *recording incomplete*
onegin chorus
welitsch
rohs
wagner
dermota
london
sung in german

0418/2-21 november 1950/musikvereinssaal/columbia sessions

mozart	**karajan**	78: columbia (germany) LWX 426-444
zauberflöte	wiener	lp: columbia 33CX 1013-1015
	singverein	lp: columbia (germany) C 90296-90298/
	seefried	33WCX 1013-1015
	lipp	lp: columbia (france) 33FCX 150-152
	loose	lp: columbia (italy) 33QCX 150-152
	dermota	lp: columbia (austria) 33VCX 508-510
	kunz	lp: columbia (usa) SL 115
	london	lp: emi 1C147 01663-01665M/SLS 5052/
	weber	1C197 54200-54208M/
		2C163 01663-01665/
		3C153 01663-01665
		cd: emi CMS 769 6312/CMS 567 0712
		excerpts
		lp: columbia 33CX 1572
		lp: columbia (germany) C 80532/
		33WSX 549
		lp: columbia (france) 33FCX 30172
		lp: emi RLS 764/EX 29 10563/
		1C147 03580-03581M/
		1C187 29225-29226M
		lp: toshiba EAC 30112
		cd: emi CDM 763 5572
		excerpts also on private lp edition by preiser

0419/1950/private session

wagner	**loibner**	78: masterseal MW 51
der fliegende	schöffler	cd: preiser 90325
holländer		
excerpt		
(die frist ist um)		

wagner		78: masterseal MW 43
tannhäuser		cd: preiser 90325
excerpt		
(o du mein		
holder		
abendstern)		

*0420/1950/decca sessions

operetta   schönherr   lp: decca LXT 5033
potpourri   vienna   lp: london (usa) LL 477/LS 47
               opera chorus   cd: decca/belart 461 6232
               güden

recording of a 1950 performance of le nozze di figaro conducted by busch from theater an der wien may also survive

0421/3 january 1951/musikvereinssaal/hmv session

smetana   furtwängler   78: hmv DB 9787-9789
vltava/   45: hmv (france) 7ERF 153/ERF 17023
ma vlast   45: electrola E 41130/7EGW 8596
                                     45: victor WHMV 1023
                                     lp: hmv BLP 1009/XLP 30106
                                     lp: hmv (france) FBLP 1046/FBLP 25024
                                     lp: hmv (italy) QBLP 5006/QALP 10298
                                     lp: electrola E 70023/WBLP 1009/
                                            E 60543/WDLP 601/E 80801/
                                            WCLP 854/SME 80801/
                                            HZE 105/SHZE 105
                                     lp: columbia (austria) VBLP 802
                                     lp: victor LHMV 1023
                                     lp: emi 1C149 03584-03586M/
                                          2C053 01193/F666.702
                                     cd: palladio PD 4122
                                     cd: historical performers HP 14
                                     cd: emi CDH 764 2982/CDH 565 1972/
                                          CHS 764 2942
                                     recording completed on 24 january 1951

0422/4-10 january 1951/musikvereinssaal/hmv sessions

tchaikovsky   furtwängler   78: hmv DB 21376-21381
symphony   45: victor WHMV 1005
no 4   lp: hmv ALP 1025/ENC 109
                                     lp: hmv (france) FALP 120
                                     lp: electrola E 90030/WALP 1025
                                     lp: columbia (austria) VALP 515
                                     lp: victor LHMV 1005/LVT 1018
                                     lp: melodiya D 078793-078794
                                     lp: unicorn WFS 7
                                     cd: palladio PD 4124
                                     cd: historical performers HP 8
                                     cd: emi CHS 764 8552
                                     DB 21376-21381 was not actually published

0423/7 january 1951/musikvereinssaal

beethoven	**furtwängler**	lp: cetra FE 33
symphony	wiener	cd: cetra CDC 1
no 9	singakademie	cd: bellaphon 689.22005
"choral"	seefried	*also issued in japan by seven seas*
	anday	
	patzak	
	edelmann	

0424/11-17 january 1951/musikvereinssaal/hmv sessions

cherubini   **furtwängler**   78: hmv DB 21493
anacreon   78: hmv (argentina) 266601
overture   lp: hmv ALP 1498
                                                                   lp: electrola E 90152/WALP 1498/
                                                                         E 70361/WBLP 547
                                                                   lp: emi 1C149 03584-03586M
                                                                   cd: emi CHS 566 7702

haydn   78: hmv DB 21506-21508
symphony   45: victor WHMV 1018
no 94   lp: hmv ALP 1011
"surprise"   lp: hmv (france) FALP 188/FBLP 25034
                                                                   lp: hmv (italy) QALP 188
                                                                   lp: electrola E 90025/WALP 1011/
                                                                        E 91075/WALP 562/STE 91075/
                                                                        SME 91075/SMVP 8053
                                                                   lp: columbia (austria) VALP 505
                                                                   lp: victor LHMV 1018
                                                                   lp: unicorn WFS 11
                                                                   lp: emi 1C027 00906M
                                                                   cd: emi CHS 566 7702
                                                                   also private lp edition by preiser

schubert   lp: hmv (france) FALP 317/FALP 30043
rosamunde   lp: electrola E 90153/WALP 1500/
overture   E 70420/WBLP 558
                                                                   lp: emi XLP 30097/2C051 03614/
                                                                      1C149 03584-03586M/F666.699
                                                                   cd: emi CDH 763 1932/CHS 566 7702
                                                                   also private lp edition by preiser

0425/24 january 1951/musikvereinssaal/hmv session

nicolai	**furtwängler**	78: hmv DB 21502
die lustigen		45: victor WHMV 1020/EHA 9
weiber von		lp: hmv ALP 1526/XLP 30097
windsor		lp: hmv (france) FALP 617
overture		lp: hmv (italy) QALP 10298
		lp: electrola E 60655/WALP 662/ SMVP 8016
		lp: victor LHMV 1020
		lp: emi 1C149 03584-03586M
		cd: emi CDH 764 2982/CHS 764 2942/ CHS 566 7702
schumann		78: hmv DB 9787-9789
manfred		45: victor WHMV 1023
overture		lp: hmv BLP 1009/XLP 30097
		lp: hmv (france) FBLP 1046
		lp: hmv (italy) QBLP 5006
		lp: electrola E 70023/WBLP 1009/ E 70362/WBLP 546/E 60661/ WDLP 667
		lp: columbia (austria) VBLP 802
		lp: victor LHMV 1023
		lp: emi 1C047 01415M
		cd: emi CDH 764 2982/CHS 764 2942/ CHS 566 7702
		also private lp edition by preiser

0426/24 january 1951/musikvereinssaal/columbia session

j.strauss	**moralt**	78: columbia LX 1544
der lustige	kunz	78: columbia (australia) LOX 816
krieg		45: columbia SEB 3507
excerpt		45: columbia (france) ESBF 184
(nur fur natur)		lp: world records SH 284
		lp: emi 1C147 03580-03581M
		cd: testament SBT 1059

j.strauss
eine nacht in
venedig
excerpt
(treu sein, das
liegt mir nicht)

78: columbia LB 117
78: columbia (germany) LW 60
lp: world records SH 284
cd: testament SBT 1059

zeller
vogelhändler
excerpt
(wie mein ahn'l
20 jahr')

78: columbia LB 117
78: columbia (germany) LW 60
lp: world records SH 284
lp: emi 1C147 03580-03581M
cd: testament SBT 1059

millöcker
gasparone
excerpt
(dunkelrote rosen);
bettelstudent
excerpt
(ich hab' sie ja nur!)

columbia unpublished

0427/25 january 1951/musikvereinssaal

brahms	**furtwängler**	lp: tanaka (japan) AT 01-02
ein deutsches	wiener	cd: refrain (japan) DR 92 0021
requiem	singakademie	*section of 6th movement taken from a*
	seefried	*performance with a different*
	fischer-dieskau	*orchestra and conductor*

0428/29 january 1951/musikvereinssaal/columbia session

wagner	**moralt**	78: columbia (germany) LWX 449
götter-	weber	lp: emi RLS 764/1C137 43187-43189M
dämmerung		cd: testament SBT 1171
excerpt		*also private lp edition by preiser*
(hier sitz' ich		
zur wacht)		

wagner	**moralt**	78: columbia LX 1394
parsifal	ralf	lp: emi 1C177 00933-00934M
excerpt	weber	cd: testament SBT 1171
(karfreitags-		
zauber)		

0429/april 1951/musikvereinssaal/decca sessions

beethoven piano concerto no 2	krauss backhaus	lp: decca LX 3083/ACL 148/ ECM 524/ECS 524 lp: london (usa) LS 630 lp: turnabout THS 65004-65006 *issued on cd in japan by polygram*

j.strauss
der zigeunerbaron
	krauss
	vienna opera
	chorus
	loose
	zadek
	anday
	patzak
	poell
	dönch
		78: decca K 28526-28537
		lp: decca LXT 2612-2613/ACL 166-167/
		    ECM 2148-2149
		lp: london (usa) LLP 418-419/A 4208
		excerpts
		45: decca CEP 585
		lp: decca LXT 2634/LXT 2991/ACL 24/
		    BR 3033/BR 3062/ECS 2058
		lp: london (usa) LLP 454/LD 9008/5075
		lp: preiser PR 135032
		cd: preiser 90336
		cd: decca 452 6902
		cd: dg 459 7342
		cd: arlecchino ARL 83-85

0430/april 1951/musikvereinssaal/decca sessions

weber der freischütz	ackermann vienna opera chorus cunitz loose hopf bierbach rus edelmann poell	lp: decca LXT 2597-2599 lp: london (usa) LLA 5/A 4303 *excerpts* lp: london (usa) LLP 646/5074

0431/30 april 1951/theater an der wien

verdi il trovatore excerpts (anima mia!/di geloso amor sprezzato....to end of act 1)	rossi welitsch rosvaenge baylé *sung in german*	cd: polyhymnia 21212

0432/3-4 may 1951/musikvereinssaal/decca sessions

weber	**böhm**	lp: decca LXT 2633/LW 5002/ACL 28
euryanthe;		lp: london (usa) LLP 354/LD 9002
oberon		*issued on cd in japan by polygram*
overtures		

weber		lp: decca LXT 2633/LW 5032/ACL 28
preciosa;		lp: london (usa) LLP 354/LD 9034
peter schmoll		*issued on cd in japan by polygram*
overtures		

0433/22 may 1951/musikvereinssaal/decca session

beethoven	**böhm**	lp: decca LXT 2627/ACL 84
piano	gulda	lp: london (usa) LLP 421
concerto		cd: philips 456 8202
no 1		

0434/23 may 1951/musikvereinssaal/decca sessions

wagner	**moralt**	lp: decca LXT 2672
tannhäuser	edelmann	lp: london (usa) LLP 427
excerpt		
(gar viel und schön!);		
beethoven		
fidelio		
excerpt		
(ha welch ein augenblick!)		

verdi		lp: decca LXT 2672
falstaff		lp: london (usa) LLP 427
excerpt		*also private lp edition by preiser*
(ehi! taverniere!)		

cornelius	**moralt**	lp: decca LXT 2672
barbier von bagdad	edelmann	lp: london (usa) LLP 427
excerpt	vienna	
(salamaleikum!)	opera chorus	

offenbach	**moralt**	lp: decca LXT 2672/414 1781
les contes	patzak	lp: london (usa) LLP 427
d'hoffmann	*sung in german*	cd: decca 448 1522
excerpts		
(ah! vivre deux!;		
legende de		
kleinzach)		

0435/31 may 1951/musikvereinssaal/decca sessions
beethoven	**krauss**	78: decca AKX 28542-28545
piano	backhaus	lp: decca LXT 2629/LXT 5354/ACL 36
concerto		lp: london LLP 419/B 19017
no 4		lp: turnabout THS 65004-65006
		cd: decca 425 9622

0436/30 july 1951/salzburg mozarteum
mozart	**fischer**	unpublished private recording
piano concerto	conductor	
no 24;	and soloist	
haydn		
symphony		
no 104		
"london";		
beethoven		
piano concerto		
no 1		

0437/6 august 1951/salzburg felsenreitschule
mozart	**furtwängler**	lp: cetra LO 9/FE 19
zauberflöte	vienna	lp: foyer FO 1028
	opera chorus	cd: foyer 3CF-2003
	seefried	cd: priceless D 16603
	lipp	cd: rodolphe RPC 32527-32530
	oravez	cd: virtuoso 269.9192
	dermota	cd: emi CHS 565 3562
	kunz	*excerpts*
	greindl	cd: virtuoso 269.7352
	schöffler	cd: music and arts CD 882
		cd: verona 28013

0438/7 august 1951/salzburg festspielhaus
verdi	**furtwängler**	lp: mrf records MRF 45
otello	vienna	lp: discocorp IGI 342
	opera chorus	lp: cetra LO 6/FE 28
	martinis	lp: turnabout THS 65120-65122
	wagner	lp: foyer FO 1018
	vinay	cd: foyer 2CF-2002
	dermota	cd: arkadia CDWFE 303/CDWFE 353
	schöffler	cd: rodolphe RPC 32561-32562
		cd: virtuoso 269.7382
		cd: emi CHS 565 7512

0439/19 august 1951/salzburg festspielhaus

mendelssohn hebrides overture	**furtwängler**	lp: german furtwängler society F667.497-F667.498 lp: discocorp RR 314 lp: cetra FE 35 lp: nippon columbia OZ 7590 cd: salzburg festival/orfeo SF 001 *also issued in japan by seven seas*
mahler lieder eines fahrenden gesellen	**furtwängler** fischer-dieskau	lp: cetra LO 510/FE 29 lp: rococo 2105 lp: discocorp IGI 382/RR 314 lp: nippon columbia OZ 7603 lp: german furtwängler society F667.497-F667.498 cd: priceless D 18355 cd: cetra CDE 1045 cd: virtuoso 269.7392 cd: orfeo C336 931B *also issued in japan by seven seas*
bruckner symphony no 5	**furtwängler**	lp: rococo 2034 lp: discocorp RR 314/RR 508 lp: german furtwängler society F667.497-F667.498 lp: cetra FE 42 cd: virtuoso 269.7342 cd: arkadia CDWFE 360 cd: emi CDH 565 7502 *also issued in japan by seven seas*

0440/31 august 1951/salzburg festspielhaus

beethoven symphony no 9 "choral"	**furtwängler** vienna opera chorus seefried wagner dermota greindl	unpublished radio broadcast *also unpublished newsreel film fragment*

0441/11-20 september 1951/musikvereinssaal/decca sessions

wagner	**knappertsbusch**	*act one*
meistersinger	vienna	lp: decca LXT 2646-2647
von nürnberg	opera chorus	lp: london (usa) LLP 478-479
acts 1	güden	*act three*
and 3	schürhoff	lp: decca LXT 2648-2649
	treptow	lp: london (usa) LLP 480-482
	dermota	*complete opera*
	schöffler	lp: decca LXT 2659-2664/GOM 535-539
	edelmann	lp: london LLA 9/A 4601
		cd: decca 440 0572
		excerpts
		78: decca K 1731/K 28573-28574
		lp: decca LXT 5544/LW 5082/LW 5083/ LW 5101/LW 5103/BR 3089/ ECS 812/414 4531
		lp: london (usa) LD 9026
		act two recorded in september 1950

0442/september 1951

strauss	**kempe**	unpublished video recording
salome	welitsch	*promotional film soundtrack*
excerpt		
(closing scene)		

0443/21 october 1951/frankfurt-am-main

brahms	**furtwängler**	unpublished radio broadcast
symphony		*reported by henning smidth olsen to*
no 4		*be stored in private archive in munich*

0444/22 october 1951/stuttgart

haydn symphony no 88	**furtwängler**	lp: french furtwängler society SWF 8501 lp: victor/jvc (japan) RCL 3337 cd: virtuoso 269.7332 cd: french furtwängler society SWF 931 cd: evangel (japan) FRL 1002
ravel rapsodie espagnole		lp: cetra FE 15 lp: french furtwängler society SWF 8501 cd: cetra CDE 1044 cd: virtuoso 269.7332 cd: french furtwängler society SWF 931 cd: evangel (japan) FRL 1002 cd: music and arts CD 719 *also issued in japan by dg*
bruckner symphony no 4 "romantic"		lp: dg 2740 201 lp: discocorp RR 557 cd: dg 415 6642/427 4032/445 4152

0445/29 october 1951/munich deutsches museum

beethoven coriolan overture	**furtwängler**	lp: decca ECM 684/592.110 cd: nuova era 013.6313/013.6300 cd: elaborations (japan) ELA 906 cd: french furtwängler society SWF 892
schumann symphony no 1 "spring"		lp: mrf records MRF 45/MRF 64 lp: decca ECM 684/592.110/417 2871 lp: nippon columbia DXM 170 cd: decca 417 2872 cd: virtuoso 269.7402 cd: arlecchino ARL 151-152 *also issued in japan by seven seas*
bruckner symphony no 4 "romantic"		lp: decca ECM 685 cd: priceless D 14228 cd: virtuoso 269.7372 cd: music and arts CD 796 *also issued in japan by seven seas and palette*

0446/17 november 1951/musikvereinssaal

strauss	**krauss**	unpublished radio broadcast in
tod und		clemens-krauss-archiv
verklärung		

*0447/1951/musikvereinssaal/decca session

operetta	**loibner**	lp: decca LX 3071
potpourri	güden	lp: london (usa) 5360
	friedrich	cd: preiser 90176

0448/1 january 1952/musikvereinssaal

j.strauss	**krauss**	unpublished radio broadcast in
an der		clemens-krauss-archiv
schönen		
blauen donau		
waltz		

0449/27 january 1952/musikvereinssaal

brahms	**furtwängler**	lp: emi 1C149 53420-53426M/
haydn		2C153 53420-53426/
variations		3C153 53661-53669M
		cd: testament SBT 1142

brahms	**furtwängler**	lp: emi 1C149 53420-53426M/
double	boskovsky	2C153 53420-53426/
concerto	brabec	3C153 53661-53669M
		lp: cetra FE 16
		cd: curcio CON 05
		cd: emi CZS 252 3212/CDH 763 4962

brahms	**furtwängler**	lp: emi ED 27 01241
symphony		cd: history 20.3090/20.3094
no 1		cd: emi CZS 252 3212/CHS 565 5132
		also issued in japan by palette and flowers;
		CZS 252 3212 and 20.3090/20.3094
		incorrectly dated november 1947

0450/27 january 1952/schönbrunn schlosstheater

mozart	**furtwängler**	lp: discocorp AUDAX 765
piano	badura-skoda	lp: nippon columbia OW 7826/OZ 7602
concerto		lp:french furtwängler societySWF8401-8402
no 22		cd: music and arts CD 895

also issued in japan by seven seas; lp editions have edits with sections from a performance probably not conducted by furtwängler

0451/3 february 1952/musikvereinssaal

beethoven	**furtwängler**	lp: rococo 2109
symphony	wiener	cd: refrain (japan) DR 91 0003
no 9	singakademie	
"choral"	güden	
	anday	
	patzak	
	poell	

0452/2 march 1952/musikvereinssaal

verdi	**krauss**	unpublished radio broadcast in
4 pezzi	vienna	clemens-krauss-archiv
sacri	opera chorus	

0453/9 march 1952/musikvereinssaal

stravinsky **krauss** cd: dg 435 3292/435 3212
pulcinella

beethoven   unpublished radio broadcast in
leonore no 1   clemens-krauss-archiv
overture;
respighi
pini di roma

0454/29 march 1952/musikvereinssaal

beethoven **krauss** unpublished radio broadecast in
egmont   clemens-krauss-archiv
overture;
symphony
no 6
"pastorale";
enescu
rumanian
rhapsody
no 1

0455/9 april 1952/konzerthaus

bach **furtwängler** lp: private issue (japan) GCL 5003
matthäus- wiener cd: refrain (japan)
passion singakademie *recording incomplete*
part one seefried
  rössl-majdan
  patzak
  braun
  wiener

0456/may 1952/musikvereinssaal/decca sessions

strauss sinfonia domestica	**krauss**	78: decca AKX 28576-28580 lp: decca LXT 2643/ECM 606/ECS 606 lp: london (usa) LLP 483/B 23239 cd: testament awaiting publication
mozart le nozze di figaro excerpt (voi che sapete)	**krauss** güden	78: decca K 28575 lp: decca LXT 5242/LX 3067/ ECM 557/ECS 557 lp: london (usa) LL 1508/LS 485 cd: preiser 90227
mozart le nozze di figaro excerpt (deh vieni non tardar)		lp: decca LXT 5242/LX 3067/ ECM 557/ECS 557 lp: london (usa) LL 1508/LS 485 cd: preiser 90227
mozart idomeneo excerpt (se il padre perdei)		78: decca K 23292 lp: decca LXT 5242/LX 3067/ ECM 557/ECS 557 lp: london (usa) LL 1508/LS 485 cd: preiser 90227
mozart idomeneo excerpt (non temer amato bene)		78: decca K 28570 lp: decca LXT 5242/LX 3067/ ECM 557/ECS 557 lp: london (usa) LL 1508/LS 485 cd: preiser 90227
verdi rigoletto excerpt (caro nome)		78: decca K 23277/K 28571 lp: decca LX 3067 lp: london (usa) LS 485 cd: preiser 90227
verdi rigoletto excerpt (tutte le feste)		78: decca K 23277/K 28571 lp: decca LX 3067 lp: london (usa) LS 485 cd: preiser 90227

0457/14-16 may 1952/musikvereinssaal

mozart **walter** lp: sony (japan) SOC 0110/15AC-1497
symphony
no 40

0458/14-20 may 1952/musikvereinssaal/decca sessions

mahler **walter** lp: decca LXT 2721-2722/LXT 5575-5576/
das lied von ferrier LXT 6278/ACL 305/AKF 1-7/414 1941
der erde patzak lp: london (usa) LLP 625-626/5069-5070/
  A 4212/R 23182/STS 15200
 cd: decca 414 1942

mahler **walter** lp: decca LXT 2722/LW 5123/LW 5225/
um mitternacht/ ferrier ACL 318/AKF 1-7/PA 172
rückert-lieder lp: london (usa) LLP 626/LD 9137/5069/
  A 4212/STS 15202
 cd: decca 421 2992/430 0962/433 4772/
  433 8022/448 1502/448 2952/
  448 1502/458 8702

mahler lp: decca LXT 2722/LW 5123/ACL 318/
ich bin der AKF 1-7
der welt lp: london (usa) LLP 626/LD 9137/5069/
abhanden A 4212/STS 15202
gekommen/ cd: decca 421 2992/433 4772/433 8022/
rückert-lieder 448 1502/455 2952

mahler lp: decca LXT 2722/LW 5123/ACL 318/
ich atmet' einen AKF 1-7
linden duft/ lp: london (usa) LLP 626/LD 9137/5069/
rückert-lieder A 4212/STS 15202
 cd: decca 421 2992/433 4772/433 8022/
  448 1502/455 2952

0459/19-20 may 1952/musikvereinssaal/decca sessions

mozart	**erede**	lp: decca LXT 5242/LX 3103/
exsultate	güden	ECM 557/ECS 557
jubilate		lp: london (usa) LS 681
		cd: preiser 90227
		cd: decca 448 1522

strauss   **moralt**   lp: decca LXT 2865/LW 5029
arabella   della casa   lp: london (usa) LLP 856/LD 9027/CM 5093
excerpt   poell   cd: decca 425 9592
(das war sehr   *also private lp edition by preiser*
gut, mandryka!)

strauss   **moralt**   lp: decca LXT 2865/LW 5029
arabella   della casa   lp: london (usa) LLP 856/LD 9027/CM 5093
excerpt   güden   cd: decca 425 9592
(aber der
richtige)

0460/22 may 1952/musikvereinssaal/decca session

josef strauss   **krauss**   lp: decca LXT 2755/LXT 2991/
dorfschwalben   LW 5019/ACL 80
aus österreich   lp: london LLP 683
                                           lp: preiser PR 135032
                                           cd: preiser 90336
                                           cd: dg 435 3352
                                           cd: arlecchino ARL 83-85

j.strauss   lp: decca LXT 2755/LW 5053/ACL 80
moulinet   lp: london LLP 683
polka   lp: preiser PR 135032
                                           cd: preiser 90336
                                           cd: arlecchino ARL 83-85

j.strauss   lp: decca LXT 2755/LXT 2991/
morgenblätter   LW 5020/ACL 80
waltz   lp: london LLP 683
                                           lp: preiser PR 135032
                                           cd: preiser 90336
                                           cd: arlecchino ARL 83-85

0461/25-30 may 1952/musikvereinssaal/decca sessions

brahms piano concerto no 2	**schuricht** backhaus	lp: decca LXT 2723/LXT 5365 lp: london (usa) LLP 628 lp: turnabout TV 34419 lp: everest SDBR 3279 cd: philips 456 7182 *philips has added applause in order to simulate a live performance*
beethoven symphony no 2	**schuricht**	lp: decca LXT 2724/ACL 116 lp: london (usa) LLP 629 *issued on cd in japan by polygram*
beethoven symphony no 1		lp: decca LXT 2824/LXT 5362/ LX 3084/ACL 147 lp: london (usa) LLP 825/LLP 631 *issued on cd in japan by polygram*

0462/may 1952/musikvereinssaal/decca sessions

j.strauss   **krauss**   78: decca K 28581-28582
g'schichten   lp: decca LXT 2645/LXT 2965/LW 5040/
aus dem   ACL 49/ECS 2058
wienerwald   lp: london (usa) CMA 7206/LLP 484
waltz   lp: preiser PR 135031/PR 135040
                                              cd: preiser 90336
                                              cd: decca 425 9902
                                              cd: dg 459 7342
                                              cd: arlecchino ARL 83-85

josef strauss   78: decca K 28582
die libelle   45: decca 45-71079
polka   lp: decca LXT 2645/LW 5053/ACL 49
                                              lp: london (usa) CMA 7206/LLP 484
                                              lp: preiser PR 135031
                                              cd: preiser 90336
                                              cd: decca 425 9902
                                              cd: arlecchino ARL 83-85

josef strauss   78: decca K 28583
mein lebenslauf   lp: decca LXT 2645/LXT 2991/LW 5019
ist lieb' und   lp: london (usa) CMA 7206/LLP 484
lust   lp: preiser PR 135031
                                              cd: preiser 90336
                                              cd: decca 425 9902
                                              cd: arlecchino ARL 83-85

josef strauss   78: decca (switzerland) M 38127
jockey   lp: decca LXT 2645/LW 5053/ACL 49
polka   lp: london (usa) CMA 7206/LLP 484
                                              lp: preiser PR 135031
                                              cd: preiser 90336
                                              cd: decca 425 9902
                                              cd: arlecchino ARL 83-85

j.strauss   78: decca (switzerland) M 38127
elyen a magyar   lp: decca LXT 2645/ACL 49/ECS 2058
polka   lp: london (usa) CMA 7206/LLP 484
                                              lp: preiser PR 135031
                                              cd: preiser 90336
                                              cd: decca 425 9902
                                              cd: arlecchino ARL 83-85
                                              cd: dg 459 7472/459 7462

0462/concluded

j.strauss	**krauss**	78: decca K 23210/K 28584
ägyptischer		lp: decca LXT 2645/ACL 49/ECS 2058
marsch		lp: london (usa) CMA 7206/LLP 484
		lp: preiser PR 135031
		cd: preiser 90336
		cd: decca 425 9902
		cd: arlecchino ARL 83-85

j.strauss 　　　　　　　　　　78: decca K 23210/K 28584
im krapfenwald'l 　　　　　　45: decca 45-71119
polka 　　　　　　　　　　　lp: decca LXT 2645/LW 5052/ACL 49
　　　　　　　　　　　　　　lp: london (usa) CMA 7206/LLP 484
　　　　　　　　　　　　　　lp: preiser PR 135031
　　　　　　　　　　　　　　cd: preiser 90336
　　　　　　　　　　　　　　cd: decca 425 9902
　　　　　　　　　　　　　　cd: arlecchino ARL 83-85
　　　　　　　　　　　　　　cd: dg 459 7522/459 7462

j.strauss 　　　　　　　　　　78: decca (switzerland) M 38128
vergnügungszug 　　　　　　lp: decca LXT 2645/LW 5052/
polka 　　　　　　　　　　　　　ACL 49/ECS 2058
　　　　　　　　　　　　　　lp: london (usa) CMA 7206/LLP 484
　　　　　　　　　　　　　　lp: preiser PR 135031
　　　　　　　　　　　　　　cd: decca 425 9902
　　　　　　　　　　　　　　cd: arlecchino ARL 83-85

josef and johann 　　　　　　78: decca (switzerland) M 38128
strauss 　　　　　　　　　　lp: decca LXT 2645/LW 5052/
pizzicato 　　　　　　　　　　　ACL 49/ECS 2058
polka 　　　　　　　　　　　lp: london (usa) CMA 7206/LLP 484
　　　　　　　　　　　　　　lp: preiser PR 135031
　　　　　　　　　　　　　　cd: preiser 90336
　　　　　　　　　　　　　　cd: decca 425 9902
　　　　　　　　　　　　　　cd: dg 435 3352

josef strauss 　　　　　　　　lp: decca LXT 2755/LW 5053/ACL 80
feuerfest 　　　　　　　　　　lp: london (usa) CMA 7206/LLP 683
polka 　　　　　　　　　　　lp: preiser PR 135032
　　　　　　　　　　　　　　cd: arlecchino ARL 83-85

0463/1-5 june 1952/musikvereinssaal/decca sessions

beethoven	**kleiber**	lp: decca LXT 2725-2726/LXT 5362-5363/
symphony	vienna	LXT 5645/LXT 6277-6280/
no 9	opera chorus	SXL 6277-6280/ECM 501/ECS 501
"choral"	güden	lp: london (usa) LLP 632-633/CMA 7203
	wagner	LLA 10032-10033/B 19083
	dermota	cd: decca 425 9552
	weber	

0464/13 august 1952/salzburg festspielhaus

strauss	**krauss**	unpublished radio broadcast in
don juan		clemens-krauss-archiv

0465/14 august 1952/salzburg festspielhaus

strauss	**krauss**	lp: ed smith EJS 314/P 4
die liebe	vienna	lp: discocorp IGI 464
der danae	opera chorus	lp: melodram MEL 111
	kupper	cd: melodram MEL 37061
	rethy	cd: orfeo C292 923D
	milinkovic	
	gostic	
	traxel	
	schöffler	

0466/september 1952/musikvereinssaal/decca sessions

strauss   **krauss**   lp: decca LXT 2729/ACL 241/
ein heldenleben   ECM 584/ECS 584
                                     lp: london (usa) LLP 659/B 19108/
                                     R 23209
                                     cd: decca 425 9932
                                     cd: testament awaiting publication
                                     also private lp edition by preiser

strauss   lp: decca LXT 2726/ECM 608/ECS 608
der bürger   lp: london (usa) LLP 684/STS 15504
als edelmann   cd: testament awaiting publication
suite

mozart   **krauss**   lp: decca LXT 5242/LX 3103/
le nozze di   güden   ECM 557/ECS 557
figaro   lp: london (usa) LS 681/LL 1508
excerpt   cd: preiser 90227
(venite   *preiser incorrectly describes*
inginocchiatevi)   *conductor as erede*

mozart   lp: decca LXT 5242/LX 3103/
zauberflöte   ECM 557/ECS 557
excerpt   lp: london (usa) LS 681/LL 1508
(ach ich   cd: preiser 90227
fühl's)   *preiser incorrectly describes conductor as erede;*
                                     also private lp edition by preiser

mozart   lp: decca LXT 5242/LX 3103/
il re pastore   ECM 557/ECS 557
excerpt   lp: london (usa) LS 681/LL 1508
(l'amero saro   cd: preiser 90227
costante)   cd: decca 448 1522
                                     preiser incorrectly describes
                                     conductor as erede

0466/concluded

j.strauss czardas aus ritter pasman	**krauss**	lp: decca LXT 2755/ACL 80 lp: london (usa) CMA 7206/LLP 683 lp: preiser PR 135032 cd: preiser 90336 cd: arlecchino ARL 83-85 cd: dg 459 7472/459 7462
josef strauss auf der jagd polka		lp: decca LXT 2755/LW 5052/ACL 80 lp: london (usa) CMA 7206/LLP 683 lp: preiser PR 135032/PR 135040 cd: preiser 90336
josef strauss ohne sorgen polka		lp: decca LXT 2755/LXT 2913/ LW 5053/ACL 80 lp: london (usa) CMA 7206/LLP 683 lp: preiser PR 135032 cd: arlecchino ARL 83-85
j.strauss stadt und land polka		lp: decca LXT 2755/LW 5052/ACL 80 lp: london (usa) CMA 7206/LLP 683 lp: preiser PR 135032 cd: preiser 90336 cd: arlecchino ARL 83-85 cd: dg 459 7492/459 7462
j.strauss perpetuum mobile		lp: decca LXT 2755/LW 5052/ACL 80 lp: london (usa) CMA 7206/LLP 683 lp: preiser PR 135032 cd: preiser 90336

0467/27 september 1952/musikvereinssaal

strauss don juan; debussy childrens' corner; haydn symphony no 100 "military"	**krauss**	unpublished radio broadcast in clemens-krauss-archiv

0468/4 october 1952/musikvereinssaal

weber oberon overture; ravel boléro; haydn symphony no 93	**krauss**	unpublished radio broadcast in clemens-krauss-archiv

0469/4-5 november 1952/klagenfurt

reznicek donna diana overture; strauss till eulenspiegel; mozart zauberflöte overture; wagner meistersinger von nürnberg overture; beethoven symphony no 6 "pastoral"; haydn symphony no 88; brahms symphony no 1;	**krauss**	unpublished radio broadcasts in clemens-krauss-archiv
mozart violin concerto no 4	**krauss** boskovsky	unpublished radio broadcast in clemens-krauss-archiv

0470/24-27 november 1952/musikvereinssaal/hmv sessions

beethoven
symphony
no 6
"pastoral"
	furtwängler	lp: hmv ALP 1041
		lp: hmv (france) FALP 288/FALP 30038/
		    UVT 3038
		lp: hmv (italy) QALP 10034
		lp: electrola E 90040/WALP 1041/
		    SME 90040/SMVP 8038
		lp: columbia (austria) VALP 535
		lp: victor LHMV 1066
		lp: angel (argentina) LPC 11526
		lp: eterna 820 045
		lp: unicorn WFS 9
		lp: emi 1C149 53432-53439M/
		    1C027 00807M/100 8071/
		    2C153 52540-52551
		cd: emi CDC 747 1212/CDH 763 0342/
		    CHS 763 6062

beethoven
symphony
no 1
		lp: hmv ALP 1324
		lp: hmv (france) FALP 30124/
		    FBLP 25023/UVT 3124
		lp: electrola E 90132/WALP 1324/
		    E 60657/WDLP 663/SME 91412
		lp: victor LHMV 700
		lp: melodiya D 03375-03376
		lp: RLS 727/1C149 53432-53439M/
		    1C027 00806M/
		    2C153 52540-52551/
		    2C153 53678-53679
		cd: emi CDC 747 4092/CDH 763 0332/
		    CHS 763 6062

beethoven
symphony
no 3
"eroica"
		lp: hmv ALP 1060
		lp: hmv (france) FALP 287/
		    FALP 50037/UVT 3037
		lp: hmv (italy) QALP 10030
		lp: electrola E 90050/WALP 1060/
		    EBE 600 000/STE 90050/
		    SME 90050/SMVP 8041
		lp: columbia (austria) VALP 530
		lp: victor LHMV 1044
		lp: angel 1C-6018
		lp: world records SH 375
		lp: emi 1C149 53432-53439M/
		    1C027 00810M/3C053 00810/
		    2C153 52540-52551
		cd: emi CDC 747 4102/CDH 763 0332/
		    CHS 763 6062
		also private lp edition by preiser

0471/30 november 1952/musikvereinssaal/hmv sessions

beethoven symphony no 1	**furtwängler**	lp: cetra FE 33 lp: german furtwangler society F669.056-F669.057 cd: arkadia CD 504/CDHP 504 cd: curcio CON 02 cd: cetra CDE 1013 cd: nuova era 013.6305/013.6300 cd: virtuoso 269.7162 cd: classical collection CD3-CLC 4006 cd: music and arts CD 711/CD 942 cd: emblem (japan) EF 4003 *some editions incorrectly dated* *29 november 1952*
mahler lieder eines fahrenden gesellen	**furtwängler** poell	lp: harold moores HMRJ 1240 lp: cetra FE 29
beethoven symphony no 3 "eroica"	**furtwängler**	cd: nuova era 013.6314/013.6300 cd: virtuoso 269.7182

0472/1-3 december 1952/musikvereinssaal/hmv sessions

beethoven	**furtwängler**	lp: hmv ALP 1059
symphony		lp: hmv (france) FALP 116/
no 4		FALP 30032/FALP 30124/UVT 3124
		lp: hmv (italy) QALP 10025
		lp: electrola E 90059/WALP 1059/
		SME 91412
		lp: columbia (austria) VALP 518
		lp: victor LHMV 1059
		lp: emi MFP 2072/1C027 00806M/
		1C149 53432-53439M/
		2C153 52540-52551
		cd: emi CDC 747 4092/CDH 763 1922/
		CHS 763 6062
		catalogue number FALP 116 also used
		for 1950 recording with same conductor
		and orchestra
wagner		45: hmv (france) 7ERF 154/ERF 17024
tannhäuser		lp: hmv ALP 1220/XLP 30082
overture		lp: hmv (france) FALP 289/FALP 362/
		FALP 30039/FALP 30215/FBLP 25057
		lp: hmv (italy) QALP 10088
		lp: electrola E 90023/WALP 1220/
		E 90097/WALP 534/E 91074/
		WALP 561
		lp: columbia (austria) VALP 538
		lp: angel 1B-6024
		lp: melodiya D 032137-032138
		lp: emi 1C149 01197-01199M/29 12343
		lp: french furtwängler society SWF 8001
		lp: acanta 40.23520
		lp: discocorp RR 229
		cd: acanta 43.121/44.1055
		cd: historical performers HP 4
		cd: magic talent MT 48090
		cd: dante LYS 115
		cd: grammofono AB 78515
		cd: iron needle IN 1364-1365
		cd: emi CZS 252 3282/CHS 764 9352
		SWF 8001 and 29 12343 incorrectly dated
		february 1949; discocorp, acanta, magic
		talent, grammofono and iron needle
		incorrectly described as staatskapelle
		berlin 1940

0473/3-4 january 1953/musikvereinssaal

brahms   **krauss**   unpublished radio broadcast in
piano   backhaus   clemens-krauss-archiv
concerto
no 2

dukas   **krauss**   cd: dg 435 3292/435 3212
l'apprenti
sorcier

0474/22 february 1953/musikvereinssaal

gluck   **furtwängler**   lp: private issue (japan) GMV 10S
iphigenie   lp: tanaka (japan) AT 09-10
in aulis   cd: refrain (japan) DR 92 0022
overture   cd: theatre (japan) 400.3531
                                                cd: german furtwängler society TMK 10670

furtwängler   cd: theatre (japan) 400.3531
symphony   cd: orfeo C375 941B
no 2

0475/march 1953/musikvereinssaal

strauss   **krauss**   unpublished radio broadcast in
till eulenspiegels   clemens-krauss-archiv
lustige streiche

0476/6-7 may 1953/musikvereinssaal/decca sessions

wagner tannhäuser overture and venusberg music	**knappertsbusch**	lp: decca LXT 2882/ACL 22/ 　　ECM 672/ECS 672/220.032 lp: london (usa) LLP 800/CM 9069/ 　　B 19099 cd: decca 440 0622
wagner der fliegende holländer overture		lp: decca LXT 2882/LW 5106/ACL 22/ 　　ECM 672/ECS 672/220.032 lp: london (usa) LLP 800/LD 9064/ 　　CM 9069/B 19099 cd: decca 440 0622
wagner walkürenritt/ die walküre		lp: decca LXT 2882/LW 5106/ACL 22/ 　　ECM 672/ECS 672/220.032 lp: london (usa) LLP 800/LD 9064/ 　　CM 9069/B 19099 cd: decca 440 0622

0477/27 may 1953/musikvereinssaal/decca session

beethoven symphony no 8	**böhm**	lp: decca LXT 2824/LXT 5361/ACL 86/ 　　ECM 558/ECS 558 lp: london (usa) LLP 825

0478/31 may 1953/musikvereinssaal

beethoven symphony no 9 "choral"	**furtwängler** wiener singakademie seefried anday dermota schöffler	lp: discocorp RR 460 lp: nippon columbia OZ 7588 lp: german furtwängler society 　　F669.056-F669.057 cd: rodolphe RPC 32465 cd: arkadia CD 532/CDHP 532 cd: nuova era 013.6301/013.6300 cd: virtuoso 269.7202 cd: dg 435 3252/435 3212 cd: music and arts CD 942 *some editions incorrecyly dated* *and with soprano soloist* *incorrectly named*

0479/may 1953/musikvereinssaal/decca sessions

beethoven	**krauss**	lp: decca LXT 2839/LXT 5355/ACL 98
piano	backhaus	lp: london (usa) LLP 789/B 19072
concerto		lp: turnabout THS 65004-65006
no 5		cd: decca 425 9622
"emperor"		

0480/11-14 june 1953/konzerthaus

strauss	**böhm**	unpublished radio broadcast
die frau ohne	vienna opera	*excerpts from acts 2 and 3*
schatten	chorus	cd: vai audio VAIA 1012
	steber	*incorrectly described by vai audio as munich*
	goltz	*4 june 1953; these were concert performances*
	höngen	*of the opera*
	svanholm	
	kamann	
	schöffler	

0481/june 1953/musikvereinssaal/decca sessions

strauss	**krauss**	lp: decca LXT 2842/ECM 609/ECS 609
don quixote	fournier	lp: london (usa) LLP 855/B 23241
		cd: decca 425 9742
		cd: testament awaiting publication

0482/june 1953/musikvereinssaal/decca sessions

brahms	**schuricht**	lp: decca LXT 2859/ACL 256
symphony		lp: london (usa) LLP 867
no 2		*issued on cd in japan by polygram*

0483/june 1953/musikvereinssaal/decca sessions

brahms symphony no 3	**böhm**	lp: decca LXT 2843/ACL 14 lp: london (usa) LLP 857 lp: vox STPL 13 *issued on cd in japan by polygram*
brahms piano concerto no 1	**böhm** backhaus	lp: decca LXT 2866/LXT 5364/592.135 lp: london (usa) LLP 911/CM 9079 lp: turnabout TV 34549 cd: decca 433 8952/433 9032
strauss 4 letzte lieder	**böhm** della casa	lp: decca LXT 2865/LXT 5403-5406/ LW 5056/BR 3100/ACL 318/ ECM 778/411 6601 lp: london LLP 856/LD 9072/ A 4412/RS 23215 cd: decca 425 9592/458 1502

0484/june 1953/graz

strauss till eulenspiegels lustige streiche	**krauss**	unpublished radio broadcast in clemens-krauss-archiv

0485/27 july 1953/salzburg felsenreitschule

mozart don giovanni	**furtwängler** vienna opera chorus schwarzkopf grümmer berger dermota edelmann siepi arié	cd: rodolphe RPC 32527-32530 cd: virtuoso 269.9052 cd: gala GL 100.602

0486/28 july 1953/salzburg festspielhaus

strauss	**krauss**	unpublished radio broadcast
rosenkavalier	vienna opera	
	chorus	
	reining	
	güden	
	della casa	
	terkal	
	böhme	
	poell	

0487/1 august 1953/salzburg festspielhaus

strauss	**de sabata**	lp: melodram MEL 706
tod und		cd: nuova era NE 2210
verklärung		
berlioz		lp: melodram MEL 706
le carnaval		lp: discocorp RR 202
romain		cd: nuova era NE 2319
overture		
verdi		lp: melodram MEL 706
i vespri		lp: discocorp RR 202
siciliani		cd: nuova era NE 2319
overture		
ravel		lp: cetra DOC 59
la valse		cd: nuova era NE 2219

0488/7 august 1953/salzburg festspielhaus

mozart	**furtwängler**	lp: ed smith GMR 999
le nozze di	vienna opera	lp: discocorp IGI 343
figaro	chorus	lp: cetra LO 8/FE 27
	schwarzkopf	cd: rodolphe RPC 32527-32530
	seefried	cd: emi CHS 566 0802
	güden	cd: eklipse EKRCD 59
	schöffler	*excerpts*
	kunz	lp: melodram MEL 082
	sung in german	cd: melodram MEL 16501
		GMR 999 appeared to contain a different performance of porgi amor

0489/17 august 1953/salzburg festspielhaus

von einem	**böhm**	cd: orfeo C393 952I
der prozess	della casa	*world premiere performance*
	lorenz	
	hofmann	
	berry	
	poell	

0490/19-20 august 1953/salzburg festspielhaus

bruckner **walter** lp: movimento musica 01.053
symphony
no 9

0491/30 august 1953/salzburg festspielhaus

hindemith **furtwängler** lp: cetra FE 22
die harmonie cd: cetra CDE 1049
der welt cd: emi CHS 565 3532

schubert lp: victor/jvc (japan) RCL 3336
symphony cd: virtuoso 269.7362
no 9 cd: emi CHS 565 3532
"great" *virtuoso incorrectly dated 1952*

0492/4 september 1953/munich deutsches museum

beethoven **furtwängler** lp: cetra FE 50
egmont lp: tanaka (japan) AT 04/AT 07-08
overture cd: rodolphe RPC 32522-32524
  cd: french furtwängler society
    SWF 892
  cd: melodram CDM 25009
  cd: elaborations (japan) ELA 906
  cd: music and arts CD 792
  *AT 04 and CDM 25009 incorrectly
  described as vienna 24 september
  1948*

beethoven lp: cetra FE 49
symphony lp: victor/jvc (japan) RCL 3333
no 4 cd: nuova era 013.6310/013.6300
  cd: rodolphe RPC 32522-32524
  cd: virtuoso 269.7192
  cd: french furtwängler society
    SWF 892
  cd: emblem EF 4005-4006
  cd: music and arts CD 792/CD 942
  also issued in japan by seven seas

0493/8-10 september 1953/edinburgh usher hall

brahms	**walter**	cd: wing (japan) WCD 3-4
tragic overture;	edinburgh	
ein deutsches	choral union	
requiem	seefried	
	fischer-dieskau	

0494/12 october 1953/theater an der wien

beethoven	**furtwängler**	lp: replica RPL 2439-2441
fidelio	vienna	lp: cetra FE 8-10
	opera chorus	cd: cetra CDC 12
	mödl	cd: priceless D 20902
	jurinac	cd: rodolphe RPC 32494
	windgassen	cd: virtuoso 269.7272
	schock	*excerpts*
	poell	cd: nuova era 013.6300
	frick	cd: virtuoso 269.7182
	edelmann	

0495/13-17 october 1953/musikvereinssaal/hmv sessions

beethoven	**furtwängler**	lp: hmv ALP 1130-1132/
fidelio	vienna	HQM 1109-1110
	opera chorus	lp: hmv (france) FALP 323-325
	mödl	lp: hmv (italy) QALP 10061-10063
	jurinac	lp: electrola E 90071-90073/
	windgassen	WALP 1130-1132
	schock	lp: victor LHMV 700
	poell	lp: angel 1C-6022
	frick	lp: emi 1C147 01105-01107M/
	edelmann	2C153 01105-01107
		cd: emi CHS 764 4962
		excerpts
		45: hmv 7ER 5036/7ER 5065/7ER 5137
		45: hmv (italy) 7ERQ 123
		45: electrola E 50042/E 50048/
		7ERW 5036/7ERW 5393
		lp: hmv (france) FBLP 25113
		lp: hmv (italy) QALP 10298
		lp: electrola E 80038/WCLP 600/
		E 60655/WDLP 662/SMVP 8029
		lp: melodiya D 033275-033276
		lp: world records SH 375
		lp: emi XLP 30090/1C047 00832M/
		1C047 00843M/1C14903584-03586M/
		1C149 53432-53439M/
		3C153 53800-53805M
		cd: emi CDM 565 9172/CMS 565 9152

this recording omitted spoken dialogue;
HQM 1109-1110 omitted leonore 3 overture;
excerpts also in private lp edition by preiser

0496/14-15 december 1953/musikvereinssaal/decca sessions

franck
symphony
in d minor
	furtwängler	lp: decca LXT 2905/ACL 179/ECM 563/
		    ECS 563/220.037/592.107/
		    417 2871
		lp: london (usa) LLP 967/CM 9091/
		    R 23027
		lp: eurodisc KK 70368
		lp: melodiya D 021093-021094
		lp: nippon columbia DXM 113
		cd: decca 417 2872
		cd: arlecchino ARL 140
		also issued in japan by toshiba and
		seven seas; melodiya catalogue
		number D 021093-021094 also
		used for 1945 recording with same
		orchestra and conductor, but both
		issues were dated 1945; nippon
		columbia and seven seas were
		incorrectly described as vienna 1945

0497/december 1953/musikvereinssaal/decca sessions

strauss aus italien	**krauss**	lp: decca LXT 2917/ACL 249/ ECM 610/ECS 610 lp: london (usa) LLP 969/R 23210 cd: testament awaiting publication *also private lp edition by preiser;* *issued on cd in japan by polygram*
j.strauss bei uns z' haus waltz		lp: decca LXT 2913/LXT 2991/ACL 99 lp: london (usa) LLP 970 lp: preiser PR 135033/PR 135040 cd: preiser 90336 cd: arlecchino ARL 83-85 cd: dg 459 7492/459 7462
josef strauss sphärenklänge waltz		lp: decca LXT 2913/LXT 2991/ACL 99 lp: london (usa) LLP 970 lp: preiser PR 135033 cd: preiser 90336 cd: arlecchino ARL 83-85

0497/concluded

j.strauss an der schönen blauen donau waltz	**krauss**	lp: decca LXT 2913/LXT 2965/ACL 99 lp: london (usa) LLP 970 lp: preiser PR 135033/PR 135040 cd: preiser 90336 cd: arlecchino ARL 83-85 *also private lp edition by preiser*
josef strauss plapper- mäulchen polka		lp: decca LXT 2913/ACL 80/ACL 99 lp: london (usa) LLP 970 lp: preiser PR 135033 cd: preiser 90336 cd: arlecchino ARL 83-85
j.strauss auf ferienreisen polka		lp: decca LXT 2913/ACL 99 lp: london (usa) LLP 970 lp: preiser PR 135033 cd: preiser 90336 cd: arlecchino ARL 83-85
j.strauss annen polka		lp: decca LXT 2913/ACL 99 lp: london (usa) LLP 970 lp: preiser PR 135033/PR 135040 cd: preiser 90336 cd: arlecchino ARL 83-85 cd: dg 459 7342
j.strauss father radetzky march		lp: decca LXT 2913/ACL 99 lp: london (usa) LLP 970 lp: preiser PR 135033 cd: preiser 90336 cd: arlecchino ARL 83-85 cd: dg 435 3352/459 7342

0498/1953/theater an der wien

wagner der fliegende holländer	**knappertsbusch** vienna opera chorus goltz schürhoff lorenz edelmann frick	unpublished radio broadcast

0499/1 january 1954/musikvereinssaal

complete new year's day concert	**krauss**	unpublished radio broadcast in clemens-krauss-archiv *final new year's concert conducted by krauss*

0500/17 january 1954/musikvereinssaal

beethoven coriolan overture	**krauss**	cd: refrain (japan) DR 92 0030
beethoven symphony no 7		cd: refrain (japan) DR 92 0030 cd: chaconne CHCD 1007
beethoven piano concerto no 4	**krauss** backhaus	cd: stradivarius STR 10002

0501/24 january 1954/musikvereinssaal

strauss sinfonia domestica	**krauss**	unpublished radio broadcasts in clemens-krauss-archiv
strauss die liebe der danae, symphonic fragments		
strauss duett- concertino	**krauss** wlach öhlberger	unpublished radio broadcast in clemens-krauss-archiv

0502/15 february 1954/theater an der wien

strauss   **moralt**   unpublished radio broadcast
intermezzo   zadek
                   felbermayer
                   christ
                   meyer-welfing
                   poell
                   czerwenka

0503/28 february-1 march 1954/musikvereinssaal/hmv sessions

beethoven   **furtwängler**   lp: hmv ALP 1195
symphony   lp: hmv (france) FALP 260/
no 5   FALP 30128/UVT 3128
                                       lp: hmv (italy) QALP 10086
                                       lp: electrola E 90088/WALP 1195/
                                             EBE 600 000/STE 90088/
                                             SME 90088/SMVP 8049
                                       lp: victor LHMV 9
                                       lp: eterna 820 053
                                       lp: angel 1C-6018
                                       lp: emi 1C149 53432-53439M/
                                             1C027 00771M/
                                             2C153 52540-52551
                                       cd: emi CDC 747 8032/CDH 769 8032/
                                             CHS 763 6062

0504/2-4 march 1954/musikvereinssaal/hmv sessions

wagner	**furtwängler**	lp: hmv ALP 1016/XLP 30082
siegfried's		lp: hmv (france) FALP 194/
funeral		FALP 30295/FBLP 25057
march/		lp: hmv (italy) QALP 10079
götter-		lp: electrola E 90026/WALP 1016
dämmerung		lp: angel 60003
		lp: french furtwängler society SWF 8001
		lp: emi F666.701/29 12343/
		1C149 01197-01199M
		cd: emi CZS 252 3582/CHS 764 9352
		SWF 8001 incorrectly dated february
		1949; catalogue number FALP 194
		also used for 1950 recording by same
		orchestra and conductor
strauss		lp: hmv ALP 1208/HQM 1137
don juan		lp: hmv (france) FBLP 25082
		lp: hmv (italy) QALP 10085
		lp: electrola E 90093/WALP 1208/
		E 70429/WBLP 561/HZEL 71
		lp: victor LHMV 19
		lp: angel 60094
		lp: emi 1C149 01155M/10 11551/
		F666.702
		cd: emi CDH 764 2982/CDH 565 1972/
		CHS 764 2942/CHS 565 3532
		also private lp edition by preiser
liszt		lp: hmv ALP 1220/XLP 30106
les préludes		lp: hmv (france) FALP 363/FBLP 25024
		lp: hmv (italy) QALP 10088
		lp: electrola E 90097/WALP 1220/
		E 60661/WDLP 667/E 80801/
		WCLP 854/SME 80801/
		HZE 105/SHZE 105
		lp: emi F666.702/2C053 01193/
		1C149 03584-03586M
		cd: palladio PD 4122
		cd: historical performers HP 14
		cd: emi CHS 566 7702

0504/concluded

strauss
till eulenspiegels
lustige streiche
	furtwängler	lp: hmv ALP 1208/HQM 1137
		lp: hmv (france) FBLP 25082
		lp: hmv (italy) QALP 10085
		lp: electrola E 90093/WALP 1208/
		   E 70429/WBLP 561/HZEL 71
		lp: victor LHMV 19
		lp: angel 60094
		lp: emi 1C049 01155M/10 11551/
		   F666.702
		cd: emi CDH 565 1972

wagner
lohengrin
prelude
		lp: hmv ALP 1220/XLP 30082
		lp: hmv (france) FALP 362/FALP 30213
		lp: hmv (italy) QALP 10088
		lp: electrola E 90097/WALP 1220/
		   E 91074/WALP 561
		lp: angel 1B-6024
		lp: melodiya D 032137-032138
		lp: emi 1C149 01197-01199M/
		   29 12343
		cd: historical performers HP 4
		cd: emi CZS 252 3282/CHS 764 9352

0505/5-8 march 1954/musikvereinssaal/hmv sessions

weber der freischütz overture	**furtwängler**	lp: victor LHMV 19 lp: emi 1C149 03584-03586M/ XLP 30090 cd: palladio PD 4124 cd: historical performers HP 8 cd: emi CHS 566 7702
weber euryanthe overture		lp: victor LHMV 19 lp: emi 1C149 03584-03586M/ XLP 30090/F666.699 cd: palladio PD 4124 cd: historical performers HP 8 cd: emi CHS 566 7702
gluck iphigenie in aulis overture		lp: emi 1C149 03584-03586M/ XLP 30090 lp: french furtwängler society XPMX 2273 lp: private issue (japan) NA 96 cd: emi CHS 566 7702
gluck alceste overture		lp: emi 1C149 03584-03586M/ XLP 30090 lp: french furtwängler society XPMX 2273 lp: private issue (japan) NA 96 cd: emi CHS 566 7702
wagner götter- dämmerung excerpt (siegfried's rhine journey)		lp: hmv ALP 1016/XLP 30082 lp: hmv (france) FALP 194/FALP 30295 lp: hmv (italy) QALP 10079 lp: electrola E 90026/WALP 1016 lp: angel 60003 lp: melodiya D 033213-033214 lp: emi 1C149 01197-01199M/ 29 12343/F666.701 cd: emi CZS 252 3282/CHS 764 9352 *29 12343 and 1C149 01197-01199M incorrectly dated february 1949; catalogue number FALP 194 also used for 1949 recording with same conductor and orchestra*

0506/15-20 march 1954/musikvereinssaal/decca sessions

strauss	**krauss**	lp: decca LXT 2863-2864/GOM 549-550
salome	goltz	lp: london (usa) LLP 11038-11039/
	kenney	A 4217/RS 62007
	patzak	*excerpts*
	dermota	lp: decca BR 3021
	braun	

0507/22-23 march 1954/musikvereinssaal/decca sessions

beethoven   **krauss**   lp: decca LW 5165/ECM 558/ECS 558
fidelio   lp: london (usa) LLP 1319/LD 9186
overture   *issued on cd in japan by polygram*

beethoven   lp: decca LW 5164/ECM 558/ECS 558
leonore   lp: london (usa) LLP 1319/LD 9185
no 1
overture

beethoven   lp: decca LW 5164/ACL 116/
leonore   ECM 558/ECS 558
no 2   lp: london (usa) LLP 1319/LD 9185
overture   *issued on cd in japan by polygram*

beethoven   lp: decca LW 5165
leonore   lp: london (usa) LLP 1319/LD 9186
no 3   *issued on cd in japan by polygram;*
overture   *also private lp edition by preiser*

0508/march 1954/musikvereinssaal

beethoven   **krauss**   unpublished radio broadcast in
leonore   clemens-krauss-archiv
no 3
overture

0509/1-5 april 1954/musikvereinssaal/decca sessions

bruckner symphony no 3	**knappertsbusch**	lp: decca LXT 2967/ECM 553/ECS 553 lp: london (usa) LLP 1044/CM 9107 cd: palladio PD 4111 cd: andromeda ANR 2511 *also issued in japan by seven seas*
beethoven piano concerto no 4	**knappertsbusch** curzon	lp: decca LXT 2948/ECM 572/ECS 572 lp: london (usa) LLP 1045/CM 9108

0510/10 april 1954/musikvereinssaal

bruckner symphony no 8	**furtwängler**	lp: cetra FE 17 cd: arkadia CDWFE 355 cd: emblem EF 4005-4006

0511/14-17 april 1954/musikvereinssaal

bach matthäus-passion	**furtwängler** wiener singakademie grümmer höffgen dermota edelmann fischer-dieskau	lp: cetra LO 508/FE 34 lp: movimento musica 03.008 cd: movimento musica 013.005 cd: priceless D 20899 cd: virtuoso 269.9212 cd: emi CHS 565 5092 *the performance included cuts* *and emi further omits the bass arias*

0512/19-20 april 1954/musikvereinssaal/decca sessions

brahms violin concerto	**schuricht** ferras	lp: decca LXT 2949/ACL 17/ ECM 704/ECS 704 lp: london (usa) LLP 1046/B 19018

0513/21-23 april 1954/musikvereinssaal/decca sessions

strauss	**hollreiser**	lp: decca LXT 5017/BR 3100/ECM 778/
capriccio	della casa	ECS 778/ECS 812/411 6601
excerpt	bierbach	lp: london (usa) LLP 1047/R 23215
(closing		cd: decca 425 9592
scene)		

strauss	**hollreiser**	45: decca CEP 571
ariadne	della casa	lp: decca LXT 5017/ECM 778/ECS 778/
auf naxos		ECS 812/411 6601
excerpt		lp: london (usa) LLP 1047/R 23215
(es gibt		cd: decca 425 9592
reich)		

0514/26-27 april 1954/musikvereinssaal/decca sessions

brahms	**schuricht**	decca unpublished
ein deutsches	wiener	*recording incomplete*
requiem	singakademie	
	della casa	
	rehfuss	

mendelssohn	**schuricht**	lp: decca LXT 2961/LW 5193/ACL 33/
hebrides		ECM 664/ECS 664
overture		lp: london (usa) LLP 1048/CM 9109
		issued on cd in japan by polygram

mendelssohn		lp: decca LXT 2961/ACL 33/
meeresstille		ECM 664/ECS 664
glückliche fahrt		lp: london (usa) LLP 1048/CM 9109
overture		*issued on cd in japan by polygram*

mendelssohn		lp: decca LXT 2961/ACL 33/
die schöne		ECM 664/ECS 664
melusine		lp: london (usa) LLP 1048/CM 9109
overture		*issued on cd in japan by polygram*

mendelssohn		lp: decca LXT 2961/LW 5193/ACL 33/
ruy blas		ECM 664/ECS 664
overture		lp: london (usa) LLP 1048/CM 9109
		issued on cd in japan by polygram

0515/april 1954/musikvereinssaal

strauss   **krauss**   unpublished radio broadcast in
sinfonia   clemens-krauss-archiv
domestica

0516/29 may-28 june 1954/musikvereinssaal/decca sessions

strauss   **kleiber**   lp: decca LXT 2954-2957/GOM 512-515/
rosenkavalier   vienna   4BB 115-118
                        opera chorus   lp: london (usa) XLLA 22/A 4404/
                        reining   RS 64001
                        jurinac   cd: decca 425 9502
                        güden   *excerpts*
                        dermota   lp: decca LXT 5623/LW 5336
                        weber
                        poell

0517/30 may 1954/musikvereinssaal

schubert   **furtwängler**   unpublished radio broadcast
symphony   *private archive in vienna*
no 8
"unfinished"

0518/june 1954/musikvereinssaal/decca sessions

mahler   **kubelik**   lp: decca LXT 2973/ACL 188/
symphony   ECM 503/ECS 503
no 1   lp: london (usa) LLP 1107/CM 9115/
                                          B 19109
                                          issued on cd in japan by polygram

dvorak   **kubelik**   lp: decca LXT 2999/ECM 512/ECS 512
cello   fournier   lp: london (usa) LLP 1106/CM 9114
concerto

0519/june 1954/musikvereinssaal/decca sessions

schubert symphony no 8 "unfinished"	**böhm**	lp: decca LXT 2824/LXT 2998/LXT 5381/ LW 5257/ACL 86/ECM 536/ECS 536 lp: london (usa) LLP 1105/CM 9113 *issued on cd in japan by polygram*
schubert symphony no 5		lp: decca LXT 2998/LXT 5381/ ECM 536/ECS 536 lp: london (usa) LLP 1105/CM 9113 *issued on cd in japan by polygram*

0520/26 july 1954/salzburg festspielhaus

weber der freischütz	**furtwängler** vienna opera chorus grümmer streich hopf edelmann böhme poell	lp: discocorp IGS 008-010/IGI 338 lp: cetra LO 21/FE 24 lp: turnabout THS 65148-65150 lp: robin hood RHR 522 lp: nippon columbia OZ 7575-7577 cd: rodolphe RPC 32519-32520 cd: nuova era 013.6324-013.6326 cd: arkadia CDWFE 302/CDWFE 352 cd: virtuoso 269.7222 cd: gala GL 100.510 *excerpts* cd: foyer CDS 16007 cd: german furtwängler society TMK 10670 *virtuoso edition omits spoken dialogue;* *some editions described as stereophonic recording*

0521/2 august 1954/salzburg residenzhof

mozart cosi fan tutte	**böhm** vienna opera chorus seefried hermann otto dermota kunz schöffler	cd: orfeo C357 942I

0522/3 august 1954/salzburg felsenreitschule

mozart	**furtwängler**	lp: morgan MOR 5302
don giovanni	vienna	lp: discocorp MORG 003
	opera chorus	lp: cetra LO 7
	schwarzkopf	lp: foyer FO 1017
	grümmer	lp: nippon columbia OZ 7568-7571
	berger	lp: emi EX 29 06673
	dermota	cd: music and arts CD 003
	edelmann	cd: cetra CDE 1050
	siepi	cd: arkadia CD 509/CDHP 509
	ernster	cd: emi CHS 763 8602
	berry	*excerpts*
		lp: gioielli della lirica GML 05
		also issued in japan by cetra and toshiba; final scene of opera is missing from this recording and replacement is spliced in from the 1953 salzburg recording; CD 509/ CDHP 509 is incorrectly dated 1953 throughout

0523/7 august 1954/salzburg festspielhaus

strauss	**böhm**	lp: melodram MEL 104
ariadne	della casa	cd: gala GL 100.513
auf naxos	seefried	cd: dg 445 3322/445 4912
	güden	
	schock	
	schöffler	

0524/17 august 1954/salzburg festspielhaus

liebermann	**szell**	cd: orfeo C328 931I
penelope	vienna	*world premiere performance*
	opera chorus	
	goltz	
	rothenberger	
	schock	
	klein	
	dönch	
	berry	

0525/august 1954/salzburg felsenreitschule

mozart	**furtwängler**	unused soundtrack recording for paul czinner film
don giovanni	vienna	
	opera chorus	*recording may not have been*
	schwarzkopf	*completed, as schwarzkopf did*
	grümmer	*not in the event participate in*
	berger	*the film*
	dermota	
	edelmann	
	siepi	
	ernster	
	berry	

0526/august 1954/salzburg felsenreitschule

mozart	**furtwängler**	vhs video: dg 072 4403
don giovanni	vienna	*final scene*
	opera chorus	lp: private issue (japan) W 28-29
	della casa	
	grümmer	
	berger	
	dermota	
	edelmann	
	siepi	
	ernster	
	berry	

0527/30 august 1954/salzburg festspielhaus

beethoven symphony no 8	**furtwängler**	lp: cetra LO 530 lp: discocorp RR 522 cd: nuova era 013.6310/013.6300 cd: virtuoso 269.7172 cd: as-disc AS 115 cd: orfeo C293 921B *also issued in japan by seven seas*
beethoven grosse fuge		lp: discocorp RR 522 lp: nippon columbia OZ 7584 lp: cetra FE 40 cd: virtuoso 269.7322 cd: arkadia CDWFE 363 cd: as-disc AS 373 cd: music and arts CD 520/CDHP 520 cd: dg 435 3242/435 3212
beethoven symphony no 7		lp: movimento musica 01.029 cd: nuova era 013.6313/013.6300 cd: foyer CDS 16007 cd: virtuoso 269.7172 cd: classical collection CD3-CLC 4006 cd: orfeo C293 921B *also issued in japan by seven seas*

0528/28 september-6 october 1954/musikvereinssaal/hmv sessions

wagner
die walküre
	furtwängler
	mödl
	rysanek
	klose
	suthaus
	frantz
	frick
		lp: hmv ALP 1257-1261/HQM 1019-1023
		lp: hmv (france) FALP 383-387
		lp: hmv (italy) QALP 10098-10102
		lp: electrola E 90100-90104/
		    WALP 1257-1261/SME 90100-90104
		lp: victor LHMV 900
		lp: angel 1E-6012
		cd: emi CHS 763 0452
		excerpts
		lp: electrola E 80039/WCLP 901/
		    SME 80039
		lp: eterna 820 510
		lp: emi 1C063 00830

0529/4 october 1954/theater an der wien

wagner	**böhm**	unpublished radio broadcast
meistersinger	vienna opera	
von nürnberg	chorus	
	seefried	
	milinkovic	
	svanholm	
	dermota	
	schöffler	
	weber	
	kunz	

0530/15-18 november 1954/musikvereinssaal/decca sessions

mozart **böhm** lp: decca LXT 5111/LXT 6277-6280/
symphony   SXL 6277-6280/LW 5316
no 38 lp: london (usa) LLP 1198
"prague"

mozart   lp: decca LXT 5111/LXT 6277-6280/
symphony   SXL 6277-6280/LW 5299
no 34   lp: london (usa) LLP 1198

0531/19-23 november 1954/musikvereinssaal/decca sessions

haydn **münchinger** lp: decca LXT 5040
symphony   lp: london (usa) LLP 1199/CM 9130
no 101
"clock"

haydn   lp: decca LXT 5040/LW 5280
symphony   lp: london (usa) LLP 1199/CM 9130
no 88

OESTERR. COLUMBIA GRAPHOPHON GES. M.B.H. – MADE IN AUSTRIA

Magic ♪ Notes
TRADE MARK

SYMPHONIE Nr. 6 IN H-MOLL, op. 74
„Pathétique"
(Tschaikowsky)

COLUMBIA
Langspiel – Mikrorillen

1. 33⅓ TOUREN
(XHAX 38)

Unzerbrechlich 1.
33 VCX 511

1. SATZ: Adagio—Allegro non troppo—Andante
2. SATZ: Allegro con grazia

WIENER PHILHARMONIKER
Dir.: Herbert KARAJAN

Alle Rechte d. Erzeuger u. Urheber vorbehalten. Jede Art Vervielfältigung, öffentlicher Aufführung u. Radiosendung etc. verboten

index of conductors
this refers to session numbers, not page numbers

abbado claudio

0812	0822	0836	0892
0897	0914	0958	0970
0976	0986	0990	0998
1002	1023	1024	1034
1045	1049	1055	1062
1097	1182	1190	1214
1260	1273	1288	1289
1303	1312	1314	1319
1325	1327	1328	1329
1338	1339	1340	1342
1343	1345	1349	1362
1369	1376		

abbado roberto
1028

ackermann otto

0366	0368	0430

albrecht gerd
1076

alwin karl

0012	0013	0015	0017
0019	0022	0024	0031
0033	0034	˙0040	0042
0073	0076	0101	0140
0145	0146	0169	0170

andreae volkmar
0572

ansermet ernest
0559

baltzer erwin

0294	0297

barbirolli sir john

0326	0869	0870

bareza niksa
1263   1344

baudo serge
0953

bernstein leonard
0830   0831   0833   0834
0874   0917   0923   0939
0940   0941   0942   0943
0954   0960   0961   0962
1026   1051   1052   1077
1092   1104   1113   1114
1115   1132   1137   1145
1147   1154   1185   1194
1207   1222   1249   1255
1256   1257   1277   1278
1281   1296   1297   1318
1334   1335   1336   1337
1357   1358   1359   1366

böhm karl

0193	0212	0221	0250
0253	0258	0261	0267
0268	0272	0273	0275
0277	0278	0279	0281
0282	0283	0284	0285
0286	0287	0288	0290
0296	0298	0299	0304
0305	0306	0312	0320
0335	0337	0372	0400
0411	0412	0413	0432
0433	0477	0480	0483
0489	0519	0521	0523
0529	0530	0537	0538
0543	0544	0545	0546
0551	0552	0554	0565
0567	0588	0593	0603
0616	0618	0649	0650
0671	0680	0682	0738
0739	0756	0791	0806
0807	0813	0825	0826
0832	0837	0853	0856
0857	0862	0867	0884
0885	0893	0900	0901
0902	0904	0906	0906a
0912	0919	0921	0928
0930	0931	0932	0938
0944	0948	0963	0967
0968	0972	0973	0974
0975	0983	0984	0992
0994	0999	1000	1001
1004	1013	1015	1019
1020	1021	1027	1028
1031	1036	1039	1040
1041	1042	1043	1044
1046	1047	1053	1056
1057	1059	1061	1067
1071	1075	1080	1087
1088	1089	1101	1107
1108	1109	1111	1122
1123	1124	1128	1129
1138	1143	1149	1151
1153	1161	1167	1173
1175	1179	1180	1183
1184	1189	1196	1199

boschetti kapellmeister
0003	0004	0008	0009

boskovsky willi
0579	0601	0620	0641
0674	0699	0705	0725
0742	0800	0815	0827
0851a	0854	0871	0890
0894	0898	0916	0918
0945	0959	0981	0985
0987	1007	1008	1009
1033	1058	1066	1085
1112	1141	1142	

boult sir adrian
0584

campo giuseppe del
0094

chailly riccardo
1163	1191	1354

cleva fausto
0716

cluytens andré
0605	0631	0775	0838

conz bernhard
0647

dobrowen issay
0079

dohnanyi christoph von
0991	1065	1074	1078
1079	1084	1110	1117
1125	1139	1158	1159
1191	1205	1320	1363

domingo placido
1155

dorati antal
1081

duhan hans
0143

egk werner
0241

ehrling sixten
1237

erede alberto
0459   0656   1010

fischer adam
1224   1304

fischer edwin
0258   0261   0316   0347
0436

foch dirk
0006

fricsay ferenc
0323   0348   0377   0708
0713   0740

furtwängler wilhelm

0104	0105	0106	0108
0110	0165	0178	0200
0226	0228	0266	0271
0280	0289	0300	0310
0314	0325	0332	0333
0336	0345	0346	0349
0359	0369	0370	0373
0374	0375	0376	0381
0390	0391	0392	0393
0402	0403	0405	0406
0408	0415	0416	0421
0422	0423	0424	0425
0427	0437	0438	0439
0440	0443	0444	0445
0449	0450	0451	0455
0470	0471	0472	0474
0478	0485	0488	0491
0492	0494	0495	0496
0503	0504	0505	0510
0511	0517	0520	0522
0525	0526	0527	0528

gavazzeni gianandrea
0710

giulini carlo maria
1156   1265   1266   1306
1307   1330   1332a   1350
1351   1374

gomez-martinez miguel
1155

guadagno anton
1258   1301

gui vittorio
0207

haitink bernard
1144   1168   1228   1285
1348   1364

harnoncourt nikolaus
1245   1280   1324   1346
1365

heger robert
0014   0018   0023   0026
0052   0054   0062   0063
0066   0067   0799

hollreiser heinrich
0513   0562   0659   0660
1073   1099

jerger wilhelm
0231   0259   0307

jochum eugen
0186   1032   1035   1212
1213   1229

kabasta oswald
0184   0215

kaiser doktor
0005

karajan herbert von

0317	0318	0319	0331
0338	0339	0340	0341
0342	0344	0350	0351
0352	0353	0354	0355
0357	0358	0363	0364
0379	0383	0384	0385
0386	0397	0418	0581
0587	0590	0592	0613
0614	0617	0635	0636
0637	0638	0648	0651
0652	0654	0657	0658
0662	0668	0676	0677
0679	0683	0686	0688
0691	0698	0703	0706
0707	0712	0714	0715
0723	0733	0737	0745
0745a	0749	0753	0754
0761	0763	0764	0765
0771	0772	0780	0786
0787	0788	0790	0792
0794	0795	0803	0804
0810	0814	0843	0845
0846	0861	0864	0883
0887	0905	0908	0925
0927	0929	0935	0949
0965	0966	0995	0996
1011	1016	1017	1018
1030	1038	1048	1050
1068	1069	1093	1094
1095	1096	1100	1102
1119	1120	1121	1127
1130	1131	1146	1148
1150	1152	1171	1177
1178	1200	1201	1204
1206	1218	1220	1230
1238	1252	1254	1259
1268	1270	1271	1272
1275	1284	1287	1292
1293	1295	1305	1309
1311	1323	1327a	1331
1332	1333	1355	1356
1360	1370	1372	1373

keilberth joseph
0615 0684 0755 0789

kempe rudolf
0442 0542 0604 0606
0632 0697 0724 0744

kertesz istvan
0702 0741 0768 0769
0770 0784 0816 0920
0952 0980 0989

khachaturian aram
0728

kitaenko dimitri
1231

kleiber carlos
1003 1014 1133 1140
1162 1166 1211 1232
1347 1367

kleiber erich
0016 0463 0516 0535
0540

klein josef
0007

klemperer otto
0612a 0760 0876 0877
0878 0879 0880

kletzki paul
0720

klobucar berislav
0669 0859 0899

knappertsbusch hans

0113	0115	0124	0125
0126	0128	0132	0133
0134	0137	0141	0147
0148	0149	0150	0151
0162	0164	0177	0179
0180	0185	0189	0190
0194	0195	0208	0209
0210	0211	0213	0217
0222	0223	0225	0232
0263	0274	0279	0292
0293	0312	0380	0399
0409	0410	0441	0476
0498	0509	0534	0541
0550	0557	0558	0586
0597	0598	0599	0611
0630	0655	0666	0719
0734	0747	0748	0757
0781			

kondrashin kyril
1157

kosler zdenek
0821

krauss clemens

0020	0021	0025	0027
0028	0030	0032	0035
0036	0037	0038	0043
0044	0045	0046	0047
0048	0049	0050	0051
0053	0059	0061	0064
0065	0070	0074	0078
0086	0087	0188	0198
0201	0203	0204	0214
0216	0219	0220	0227
0243	0246	0247	0248
0270	0301	0302	0303
0308	0311	0312	0313
0315	0328	0330	0396
0398	0414	0429	0435
0446	0448	0452	0453
0454	0456	0460	0462
0464	0465	0466	0467
0468	0469	0473	0475
0479	0481	0484	0486
0497	0499	0500	0501
0506	0507	0508	0515

krips josef

0056	0057	0058	0072
0109	0129	0133	0134
0135	0136	0139	0320
0322	0329	0362	0389
0394	0395	0404	0539
0560	0575	0595	0622
0809	0817	0828	0841
0842	0850	0860	0866
0872	0889	0895	0896
0911	0924	0936	0951
0955	0956	0977	1006

krombholc jaroslaw
0778

kubelik rafael

0518	0532	0547	0556
0570	0574	0580	0596
0608	0663	0694	0700
1022	1034		

kulka janos
0978

lehar franz
0075 0077 0093 0103
0196

leinsdorf erich
0612 0643 0644

levine james
1070 1126 1170 1176
1181 1216 1267 1290
1300 1308 1310 1313
1315 1321 1322 1341
1352 1375

loibner wilhelm
0171 0172 0174 0176
0181 0187 0387 0419
0447 0696

ludwig leopold
0202 0233 0237 0251
0262 0264 0729

lutze walter
0192

maazel lorin
0752 0762 0766 0777
0782 0783 0797 0808
0829 0835 0848 0873
0875 0946 0982 1012
1098 1164 1186 1187
1193 1198 1203 1210
1217 1225 1226 1234
1235 1236 1241 1242
1244 1246 1247 1251
1253 1262 1264 1269
1276 1282 1286 1299

mackerras sir charles
1082	1134	1160	1165
1197	1215	1243	

martinon jean
0607

matacic lovro von
0678	0701	0735	0758

mehta zubin
0805	0811	0839	0840
0844	0863	0882	0950
1037	1060	1063	1064
1083	1174	1195	1248
1368			

mengelberg willem
0247a   0247b

mitropoulos dimitri
0563	0568	0569	0573
0589	0594	0619	0653
0687	0690		

monteux pierre
0600	0626	0628	0640
0670			

moralt rudolf
0182	0197	0205	0206
0218	0229	0230	0238
0240	0242	0245	0252
0255	0257	0265	0276
0295	0312	0321	0334
0401	0413	0426	0428
0434	0459	0502	0536
0576	0602	0629	

münchinger karl
0531	0533	0582	0609
0639	0693	0704	0743
0802	0852	0858	1029

muti riccardo
0969 0988 1025 1072
1090 1103 1192 1219
1301a 1317 1324a 1353
1361

neumann vaclaw
1326

oistrakh david
0971

ormandy eugene
0759

paulik anton
0269 0388

pfitzner hans
0236 0309

pollini maurizio
1188

pretre georges
0750 0776 0779

previn andré
1169 1209 1261 1302
1316

pritchard sir john
1240

prohaska felix
0356 0361 0365 0367

quadri argeo
0692 0801

reichenberger hugo
0055 0069 0071 0088
0089

reichwein leopold
0173   0183   0191   0235
0249   0254   0256   0260

reiner fritz
0549   0571   0672   0675

rosé arnold
0118

rosenek leo
0082

rossi mario
0431   0555

rostropovich mstislav
1118

rühlmann francois
0060

sabata victor de
0096   0114   0120   0487

santi nello
0681   1223

sargent sir malcolm
0664   0721

sawallisch wolfgang
0709   0793   0926

schalk franz
0011   0029   0039

schmidt-isserstedt hans
0610   0627   0645   0820
0824   0849   0855   0888
0903

schneider peter
1283   1291

schneiderhan wolfgang
0997

schönherr max
0312   0420

schüler johannes
0244

schuricht carl
0461   0482   0512   0514
0553   0562   0577   0578
0685   0722   0736   0751
0774   0823

schwarz reinhard
1135

silvestri constantin
0633   0665   0667   0695

sinopoli giuseppe
1239   1250

solti sir georg
0566   0583   0585   0623
0624   0625   0642   0689
0717   0718   0730   0767
0785   0818   0819   0847
0851   0865   0868   0891
0909   0910   0933   1054
1086   1091   1105   1116
1136   1172   1202   1227
1274   1279   1298   1371

stein horst
0913   0922   0935   0937
0947   0957   0979   0993
1005   1106   1155   1233
1294

stolz robert
0670a

strauss richard
0224 0234 0239 0283
0291

swarowsky hans
0634

szell george
0080 0081 0378 0524
0591 0646 0798 0886
0907 0915

tennstedt klaus
1221

tietjen heinz
0175

toscanini arturo
0083 0121 0122 0153
0155 0157

varviso silvio
0796 0881

wacek leopold
0199

wagner robert
0621

wallberg heinz
0711 0964

walter bruno
0041 0085 0097 0098
0100 0116 0119 0127
0130 0131 0142 0144
0152 0154 0156 0158
0159 0160 0163 0166
0167 0168 0327 0343
0382 0407 0457 0490
0493 0548 0561 0564
0673

wand günter
0661

weingartner felix
0002	0084	0090	0091
0092	0099	0102	0107
0111	0112	0117	0123
0161			

weisbach hans
0244

zallinger meinhard von
0360   0417

unnamed conductors
| 0001 | 0010 | 0371 | 0773 |

Wiener Philharmoniker as opera orchestra
Index of complete opera recordings made in the Wiener
Staatsoper and elsewhere: numbers are session numbers,
not page numbers

die ägyptische helena strauss
0936

aida verdi
0547	0654	0758	0988
1146	1150	1177	1264

andrea chénier giordano
0536   0678

antigonae orff
0377

arabella strauss
0247	0324	0585	0615
0789	0899	1073	1086

ariadne auf naxos strauss
0290	0523	0643	0867
1080	1108	1151	1300

assassino nelle cattedrale pizetti
0668

baal cerha
1205

un ballo in maschera verdi
1370

il barbiere di siviglia rossini
0837

das bergwerk zu falun wagner-regeny
0711

der besuch der alten dame von einem
0947

la bohème puccini
0771

boris godunov mussorgsky
0810   0845   0935

capriccio strauss
0671   0779   1294

carmen bizet
0723   0772   0835   0843
0861   0864   1140   1253
1293   1309

la cenerentola rossini
0656   1208   1354

la clemenza di tito mozart
1070   1170   1353

les contes d'hoffmann offenbach
0850   1176

cosi fan tutte mozart
0521   0537   0618   0650
0680   0739   0832   0889
0901   0967   1021   1219
1352   1365

the cunning little vixen janacek
1197

dantons tod von einem
0323   0866

daphne strauss
0288   0806

don carlo verdi
0614   0681   0716   0859
0881   0934   1048   1069
1127

don giovanni mozart

0154	0213	0329	0402
0485	0522	0525	0526
0539	0546	0563	0644
0683	0761	0860	0883
0905	0925	0977	1101
1129	1331	1332	1355

der fliegende holländer wagner
0498

elektra strauss

0589	0603	0794	0825
0847	1053	1199	1376

l'elisir d'amore donizetti
1263

die entführung aus dem serail mozart

0295	0811	0828	0844
1279			

erwartung schoenberg
1158

evgeny onegin tchaikovsky
0701

falstaff verdi

0157	0590	0830	1136
1171	1204	1218	

faust gounod
0750

die feen wagner
1237

fidelio beethoven

0282	0328	0346	0375
0403	0494	0495	0544
0587	0731	0777	0884
0923	1113	1114	1217
1241			

die fledermaus j.strauss

0414	0676	0698	0938

la forza del destino verdi
0690   1025

die frau ohne schatten strauss
0480   0546   0552   0786
0787   1019   1107   1371

der freischütz weber
0430   0520   0963

friedenstag strauss
0188

from the house of the dead janacek
1165

la gioconda ponchielli
1304

giuditta lehar
0602

götterdämmerung wagner
0785

hänsel und gretel humperdinck
0775   1116   1172

idomeneo mozart
0565   0708   1071   1240

l'incoronazione di poppea monteverdi
0753

intermezzo strauss
0502   0755

iphigenie in aulis gluck
0738

l'italiana in algeri rossini
1338   1339

jenufa janacek
0778   0978   1215

kabale und liebe von einem
1084

katya kabanova janacek
1082

khovantschina mussorgsky
1369

die liebe der danae strauss
0465

lohengrin wagner
0746   0807   1283   1298

luisa miller verdi
1010

lulu berg
0893   1078   1246

macbeth verdi
0272   0793   0919

madama butterfly puccini
0669   1011   1030

manon massenet
0953

the makropoulos case janacek
1134

medea cherubini
0957

die meistersinger von nürnberg wagner
0155   0306   0409/0441   0529
0549   1054

il mondo della luna haydn
0647

norma bellini
1090

le nozze di figaro mozart

0156	0246	0397	0488
0540	0588	0612	0616
0762	0842	0856	0862
0965	0995	1017	1057
1095	1119	1183	1196
1310	1317		

orfeo ed euridice gluck
0648   0809

otello verdi
0438	0298	0706	0927
1105	1224		

palestrina pfitzner
0799

parsifal wagner
0703   0954

pelléas et mélisande debussy
0726

penelope liebermann
0524

pique dame tchaikovsky
1231

prince igor borodin
0735

der prozess von einem
0489

un re in ascolto berio
1269

das rheingold wagner
0624

rigoletto verdi
1156   1163

der rosenkavalier strauss
0066	0378	0486	0516
0550	0679	0688	0763
0792	0874	0891	0904
0911	0943	0951	0964
1125	1135	1230	1233
1268			

rusalka dvorak
1326

salome strauss
0330	0506	0634	0718
0821	0983	1013	1094
1100	1131		

die schule der frauen liebermann
0591

die schweigsame frau strauss
0649

la serva padrona pergolesi
0255

siegfried wagner
0730

simon boccanegra verdi
0710	0896	1260

der sturm martin
0559

tannhäuser wagner
0576	0749	0933

tosca puccini
0727	0745	0801	1301

la traviata verdi
0956	1223	1258

tristan und isolde wagner
0266	0689	0937	1003

il trovatore verdi
0737 0764 1093 1096
1120 1243

les troyens berlioz
1076

turandot puccini
0555 1201 1242

il viaggio a reims rossini
1345

die walküre wagner
0528 0819 1291

wozzeck berg
0551 0968 1159 1329

die zauberflöte mozart
0153 0212 0304 0374
0406 0418 0437 0538
0566 0646 0684 0733
0910 0926 0955 1016
1126 1181 1346

der zigeunerbaron j.strauss
0429 0659

Credits

Valued assistance with information for these discographies came from

Richard Chlupaty
Siam Chowkwanyun
Sigrit Fleiss
Johann Gratz
Michael Gray
Syd Gray
Clemens Hellsberg
Bill Holland
Gottfried Kraus
David Lampon
Douglas McIntosh
Bruce Morrison
Alan Newcombe
Richard Osborne
James Pearson
Brian Pinder
Christopher Raeburn
Jürgen Schmidt
Robin Scott
Angelo Scottini
Roger Smithson
Yoshihiko Suzuki
Malcolm Walker
Jerome Weber

Wilhelm FURTWÄNGLER

VIENNA PHILHARMONIC ORCHESTRA

BEETHOVEN
SYMPHONY N° 6
"PASTORAL"

"HIS MASTER'S VOICE"
LONG-PLAY 33⅓ R.P.M. RECORD

MOZART

'HAFFNER' Symphony No. 35 in D, K385
'JUPITER' Symphony No. 41 in C, K551
VIENNA PHILHARMONIC ORCHESTRA
Rafael Kubelik

BEETHOVEN
PIANO CONCERTO Nº 4 in G., Opus 58

WILHELM BACKHAUS
PIANO
with CLEMENS KRAUSS
CONDUCTING
THE VIENNA PHILHARMONIC ORCHESTRA

THE VIENNA OF JOHANN STRAUSS   KARAJAN/VPO   MONO RS-16216

The Vienna of Johann Strauss

Waltz/TALES FROM THE VIENNA WOODS
Overtures/FLEDERMAUS · GYPSY BARON   Polkas/ANNEN · AUF DER JAGD
JOSEF STRAUSS: DELIRIUM WALTZ

KARAJAN/VIENNA PHILHARMONIC

Discographies by Travis & Emery:
Discographies by John Hunt.

1987: 978-1-906857-14-1: From Adam to Webern: the Recordings of von Karajan.

1991: 978-0-951026-83-0: 3 Italian Conductors and 7 Viennese Sopranos: 10 Discographies: Arturo Toscanini, Guido Cantelli, Carlo Maria Giulini, Elisabeth Schwarzkopf, Irmgard Seefried, Elisabeth Gruemmer, Sena Jurinac, Hilde Gueden, Lisa Della Casa, Rita Streich.

1992: 978-0-951026-85-4: Mid-Century Conductors and More Viennese Singers: 10 Discographies: Karl Boehm, Victor De Sabata, Hans Knappertsbusch, Tullio Serafin, Clemens Krauss, Anton Dermota, Leonie Rysanek, Eberhard Waechter, Maria Reining, Erich Kunz.

1993: 978-0-951026-87-8: More 20th Century Conductors: 7 Discographies: Eugen Jochum, Ferenc Fricsay, Carl Schuricht, Felix Weingartner, Josef Krips, Otto Klemperer, Erich Kleiber.

1994: 978-0-951026-88-5: Giants of the Keyboard: 6 Discographies: Wilhelm Kempff, Walter Gieseking, Edwin Fischer, Clara Haskil, Wilhelm Backhaus, Artur Schnabel.

1994: 978-0-951026-89-2: Six Wagnerian Sopranos: 6 Discographies: Frieda Leider, Kirsten Flagstad, Astrid Varnay, Martha Moedl, Birgit Nilsson, Gwyneth Jones.

1995: 978-0-952582-70-0: Musical Knights: 6 Discographies: Henry Wood, Thomas Beecham, Adrian Boult, John Barbirolli, Reginald Goodall, Malcolm Sargent.

1995: 978-0-952582-71-7: A Notable Quartet: 4 Discographies: Gundula Janowitz, Christa Ludwig, Nicolai Gedda, Dietrich Fischer-Dieskau.

1996: 978-0-952582-72-4: The Post-War German Tradition: 5 Discographies: Rudolf Kempe, Joseph Keilberth, Wolfgang Sawallisch, Rafael Kubelik, Andre Cluytens.

1996: 978-0-952582-73-1: Teachers and Pupils: 7 Discographies: Elisabeth Schwarzkopf, Maria Ivoguen, Maria Cebotari, Meta Seinemeyer, Ljuba Welitsch, Rita Streich, Erna Berger.

1996: 978-0-952582-77-9: Tenors in a Lyric Tradition: 3 Discographies: Peter Anders, Walther Ludwig, Fritz Wunderlich.

1997: 978-0-952582-78-6: The Lyric Baritone: 5 Discographies: Hans Reinmar, Gerhard Huesch, Josef Metternich, Hermann Uhde, Eberhard Waechter.

1997: 978-0-952582-79-3: Hungarians in Exile: 3 Discographies: Fritz Reiner, Antal Dorati, George Szell.

1997: 978-1-901395-00-6: The Art of the Diva: 3 Discographies: Claudia Muzio, Maria Callas, Magda Olivero.

1997: 978-1-901395-01-3: Metropolitan Sopranos: 4 Discographies: Rosa Ponselle, Eleanor Steber, Zinka Milanov, Leontyne Price.

1997: 978-1-901395-02-0: Back From The Shadows: 4 Discographies: Willem Mengelberg, Dimitri Mitropoulos, Hermann Abendroth, Eduard Van Beinum.

1997: 978-1-901395-03-7: More Musical Knights: 4 Discographies: Hamilton Harty, Charles Mackerras, Simon Rattle, John Pritchard.

1998: 978-1-901395-94-5: Conductors On The Yellow Label: 8 Discographies: Fritz Lehmann, Ferdinand Leitner, Ferenc Fricsay, Eugen Jochum, Leopold Ludwig, Artur Rother, Franz Konwitschny, Igor Markevitch.

1998: 978-1-901395-95-2: More Giants of the Keyboard: 5 Discographies: Claudio Arrau, Gyorgy Cziffra, Vladimir Horowitz, Dinu Lipatti, Artur Rubinstein.

1998: 978-1-901395-96-9: Mezzo and Contraltos: 5 Discographies: Janet Baker, Margarete Klose, Kathleen Ferrier, Giulietta Simionato, Elisabeth Hoengen.

1999: 978-1-901395-97-6: The Furtwaengler Sound Sixth Edition: Discography and Concert Listing.
1999: 978-1-901395-98-3: The Great Dictators: 3 Discographies: Evgeny Mravinsky, Artur Rodzinski, Sergiu Celibidache.
1999: 978-1-901395-99-0: Sviatoslav Richter: Pianist of the Century: Discography.
2000: 978-1-901395-04-4: Philharmonic Autocrat 1: Discography of: Herbert Von Karajan [Third Edition].
2000: 978-1-901395-05-1: Wiener Philharmoniker 1 - Vienna Philharmonic and Vienna State Opera Orchestras: Discography Part 1 1905-1954.
2000: 978-1-901395-06-8: Wiener Philharmoniker 2 - Vienna Philharmonic and Vienna State Opera Orchestras: Discography Part 2 1954-1989.
2001: 978-1-901395-07-5: Gramophone Stalwarts: 3 Separate Discographies: Bruno Walter, Erich Leinsdorf, Georg Solti.
2001: 978-1-901395-08-2: Singers of the Third Reich: 5 Discographies: Helge Roswaenge, Tiana Lemnitz, Franz Voelker, Maria Mueller, Max Lorenz.
2001: 978-1-901395-09-9: Philharmonic Autocrat 2: Concert Register of Herbert Von Karajan Second Edition.
2002: 978-1-901395-10-5: Sächsische Staatskapelle Dresden: Complete Discography.
2002: 978-1-901395-11-2: Carlo Maria Giulini: Discography and Concert Register.
2002: 978-1-901395-12-9: Pianists For The Connoisseur: 6 Discographies: Arturo Benedetti Michelangeli, Alfred Cortot, Alexis Weissenberg, Clifford Curzon, Solomon, Elly Ney.
2003: 978-1-901395-14-3: Singers on the Yellow Label: 7 Discographies: Maria Stader, Elfriede Troetschel, Annelies Kupper, Wolfgang Windgassen, Ernst Haefliger, Josef Greindl, Kim Borg.
2003: 978-1-901395-15-0: A Gallic Trio: 3 Discographies: Charles Muench, Paul Paray, Pierre Monteux.
2004: 978-1-901395-16-7: Antal Dorati 1906-1988: Discography and Concert Register.
2004: 978-1-901395-17-4: Columbia 33CX Label Discography.
2004: 978-1-901395-18-1: Great Violinists: 3 Discographies: David Oistrakh, Wolfgang Schneiderhan, Arthur Grumiaux.
2006: 978-1-901395-19-8: Leopold Stokowski: Second Edition of the Discography.
2006: 978-1-901395-20-4: Wagner Im Festspielhaus: Discography of the Bayreuth Festival.
2006: 978-1-901395-21-1: Her Master's Voice: Concert Register and Discography of Dame Elisabeth Schwarzkopf [Third Edition].
2007: 978-1-901395-22-8: Hans Knappertsbusch: Kna: Concert Register and Discography of Hans Knappertsbusch, 1888-1965. Second Edition.
2008: 978-1-901395-23-5: Philips Minigroove: Second Extended Version of the European Discography.
2009: 978-1-901395--24-2: American Classics: The Discographies of Leonard Bernstein and Eugene Ormandy.

Discography by Stephen J. Pettitt, edited by John Hunt:
1987: 978-1-906857-16-5: Philharmonia Orchestra: Complete Discography 1945-1987

Available from: Travis & Emery at 17 Cecil Court, London, UK. (+44) 20 7 240 2129. email on sales@travis-and-emery.com .

© Travis & Emery 2009

Music and Books published by Travis & Emery Music Bookshop:
Anon.: Hymnarium Sarisburiense, cum Rubricis et Notis Musicis.
Agricola, Johann Friedrich from Tosi: Anleitung zur Singkunst.
Bach, C.P.E.: edited W. Emery: Nekrolog or Obituary Notice of J.S. Bach.
Bateson, Naomi Judith: Alcock of Salisbury
Bathe, William: A Briefe Introduction to the Skill of Song
Bax, Arnold: Symphony #5, Arranged for Piano Four Hands by Walter Emery
Burney, Charles: The Present State of Music in France and Italy
Burney, Charles: The Present State of Music in Germany, The Netherlands …
Burney, Charles: An Account of the Musical Performances … Handel
Burney, Karl: Nachricht von Georg Friedrich Handel's Lebensumstanden.
Cobbett, W.W.: Cobbett's Cyclopedic Survey of Chamber Music. (2 vols.)
Corrette, Michel: Le Maitre de Clavecin
Crimp, Bryan: Dear Mr. Rosenthal … Dear Mr. Gaisberg …
Crimp, Bryan: Solo: The Biography of Solomon
d'Indy, Vincent: Beethoven: Biographie Critique
d'Indy, Vincent: Beethoven: A Critical Biography
d'Indy, Vincent: César Franck (in French)
Frescobaldi, Girolamo: D'Arie Musicali per Cantarsi. Primo & Secondo Libro.
Geminiani, Francesco: The Art of Playing the Violin.
Handel; Purcell; Boyce; Geene et al: Calliope or English Harmony: Volume First.
Häuser: Musikalisches Lexikon. 2 vols in one.
Hawkins, John: A General History of the Science and Practice of Music (5 vols.)
Herbert-Caesari, Edgar: The Science and Sensations of Vocal Tone
Herbert-Caesari, Edgar: Vocal Truth
Hopkins and Rimboult: The Organ. Its History and Construction.
Hunt, John: Adam to Webern: the recordings of von Karajan
Isaacs, Lewis: Hänsel and Gretel. A Guide to Humperdinck's Opera.
Isaacs, Lewis: Königskinder (Royal Children) A Guide to Humperdinck's Opera.
Kastner: Manuel Général de Musique Militaire
Lacassagne, M. l'Abbé Joseph : Traité Général des élémens du Chant.
Lascelles (née Catley), Anne: The Life of Miss Anne Catley.
Mainwaring, John: Memoirs of the Life of the Late George Frederic Handel
Malcolm, Alexander: A Treaty of Music: Speculative, Practical and Historical
Marx, Adolph Bernhard: Die Kunst des Gesanges, Theoretisch-Practisch
May, Florence: The Life of Brahms
May, Florence: The Girlhood Of Clara Schumann: Clara Wieck And Her Time.
Mellers, Wilfrid: Angels of the Night: Popular Female Singers of Our Time
Mellers, Wilfrid: Bach and the Dance of God
Mellers, Wilfrid: Beethoven and the Voice of God
Mellers, Wilfrid: Caliban Reborn - Renewal in Twentieth Century Music

Music and Books published by Travis & Emery Music Bookshop:
Mellers, Wilfrid: François Couperin and the French Classical Tradition
Mellers, Wilfrid: Harmonious Meeting
Mellers, Wilfrid: Le Jardin Retrouvé, The Music of Frederic Mompou
Mellers, Wilfrid: Music and Society, England and the European Tradition
Mellers, Wilfrid: Music in a New Found Land: ... ... American Music
Mellers, Wilfrid: Romanticism and the Twentieth Century (from 1800)
Mellers, Wilfrid: The Masks of Orpheus: ...... the Story of European Music.
Mellers, Wilfrid: The Sonata Principle (from c. 1750)
Mellers, Wilfrid: Vaughan Williams and the Vision of Albion
Panchianio, Cattuffio: Rutzvanscad Il Giovine
Pearce, Charles: Sims Reeves, Fifty Years of Music in England.
Playford, John: An Introduction to the Skill of Musick.
Purcell, Henry et al: Harmonia Sacra ... The First Book, (1726)
Purcell, Henry et al: Harmonia Sacra ... Book II (1726)
Quantz, Johann: Versuch einer Anweisung die Flöte traversiere zu spielen.
Rameau, Jean-Philippe: Code de Musique Pratique, ou Methodes.
Rastall, Richard: The Notation of Western Music.
Rimbault, Edward: The Pianoforte, Its Origins, Progress, and Construction.
Rousseau, Jean Jacques: Dictionnaire de Musique
Rubinstein, Anton : Guide to the proper use of the Pianoforte Pedals.
Sainsbury, John S.: Dictionary of Musicians. Vol. 1. (1825). 2 vols.
Serré de Rieux, Jean de : Les dons des Enfans de Latone
Simpson, Christopher: A Compendium of Practical Musick in Five Parts
Spohr, Louis: Autobiography
Spohr, Louis: Grand Violin School
Tans'ur, William: A New Musical Grammar; or The Harmonical Spectator
Terry, Charles Sanford: J.S. Bach's Original Hymn-Tunes for Congregational Use.
Terry, Charles Sanford: Four-Part Chorals of J.S. Bach. (German & English)
Terry, Charles Sanford: Joh. Seb. Bach, Cantata Texts, Sacred and Secular.
Terry, Charles Sanford: The Origins of the Family of Bach Musicians.
Tosi, Pierfrancesco: Opinioni de' Cantori Antichi, e Moderni
Van der Straeten, Edmund: History of the Violoncello, The Viol da Gamba ...
Van der Straeten, Edmund: History of the Violin, Its Ancestors... (2 vols.)
Waltern: Musikalisches Lexicon
Walther, J. G.: Musicalisches Lexikon ober Musicalische Bibliothec

Travis & Emery Music Bookshop
17 Cecil Court, London, WC2N 4EZ, United Kingdom.
Tel. (+44) 20 7240 2129
© Travis & Emery 2009

www.ingramcontent.com/pod-product-compliance
Lightning Source LLC
Chambersburg PA
CBHW052103230426
43671CB00011B/1920